Interactive Practice Book

Hampton-Brown

EDGE

Reading, Writing & Language

NATIONAL GEOGRAPHIC LEARNING | CENGAGE Learning

Acknowledgments

Grateful acknowledgment is given to the authors, artists, photographers, museums, publishers, and agents for permission to reprint copyrighted material. Every effort has been made to secure the appropriate permission. If any omissions have been made or if corrections are required, please contact the Publisher.

Photographic Credits

Cover: Avian Island, the Pantanal, Mato Grosso, Brazil, Mike Bueno. Photograph © Mike Bueno/National Geographic Stock.

Acknowledgments continue on page Ack 1.

For product information and technology assistance, contact us at
Customer & Sales Support, 888-915-3276

For permission to use material from this text or product, submit all requests online at **www.cengage.com/permissions**
Further permissions questions can be emailed to
permissionrequest@cengage.com

National Geographic Learning | Cengage Learning
1 Lower Ragsdale Drive
Building 1, Suite 200
Monterey, CA 93940

Cengage Learning is a leading provider of customized learning solutions with office locations around the globe, including Singapore, the United Kingdom, Australia, Mexico, Brazil, and Japan. Locate your local office at **www.cengage.com/global**.

Visit National Geographic Learning online at **ngl.cengage.com**
Visit our corporate website at **www.cengage.com**

Printed in the USA.
Quad, Versailles, KY

ISBN: 978-12854-43423 (Practice Book)
ISBN: 978-12854-43485 (Practice Book Teacher's Annotated Edition)

Printed in the United States of America

20 21 22 23 24

Unit 2

Unit 4

Unit 6

Prepare to Read

▷ **The Good Samaritan**
▷ **The World Is in Their Hands**

Key Vocabulary

A. How well do you know these words? Circle a rating for each word. Check your understanding of each word by circling *yes* or *no*. Then, complete the sentences. If you are unsure of a word's meaning, refer to the Vocabulary Glossary, page 878, in your student text.

Rating Scale	
1	I have never seen this word before.
2	I am not sure of the word's meaning.
3	I know this word and can teach the word's meaning to someone else.

Key Word	Check Your Understanding	Deepen Your Understanding
❶ affect (u-**fekt**) *verb* **Rating:** **1 2 3**	What you choose to eat can **affect** your health. Yes No	One way I affect the environment positively is _____ _____ _____ _____ .
❷ conflict (**kon**-flikt) *noun* **Rating:** **1 2 3**	A **conflict** in a friendship is a good thing. Yes No	One conflict I recently had with another person was _____ _____ _____ _____ .
❸ contribute (kun-**tri**-byūt) *verb* **Rating:** **1 2 3**	You can **contribute** to a family meal by making a salad. Yes No	People can contribute to their community by _____ _____ _____ _____ .
❹ disrespect (dis-ri-**spekt**) *noun* **Rating:** **1 2 3**	When you give your seat on the bus to an elderly person, you are showing **disrespect**. Yes No	Teenagers in my school sometimes show disrespect by _____ _____ _____ .

Key Word	Check Your Understanding	Deepen Your Understanding
5 **generation** (je-nu-**rā**-shun) *noun* **Rating:** **1 2 3**	My grandparents and parents are part of my **generation**. **Yes** **No**	People in my parents' generation think _____ _____ _____ _____ .
6 **motivation** (mō-tu-**vā**-shun) *noun* **Rating:** **1 2 3**	One **motivation** for getting a job is to earn money. **Yes** **No**	A teenager's motivation for getting a part-time job might be _____ _____ _____ _____ .
7 **privilege** (**pri**-vu-lij) *noun* **Rating:** **1 2 3**	Driving the family car is an example of a **privilege**. **Yes** **No**	Something I consider to be a privilege is _____ _____ _____ _____ .
8 **responsible** (ri-**spon**-su-bul) *adjective* **Rating:** **1 2 3**	If you check out a book from the library, you are **responsible** for returning it. **Yes** **No**	My parents say I am responsible for _____ _____ _____ _____ .

B. Use one of the Key Vocabulary words to write about a difficult choice you, or someone you know, recently had to make.

_____

_____

Before Reading The Good Samaritan

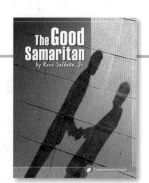

LITERARY ANALYSIS: Analyze Plot

The **plot** is the sequence of events in a story. A plot usually contains the following parts: exposition, conflict, complications, climax, and resolution.

A. Read the passage below. Write the complication, or the event that may contribute to a conflict, in the right column of the chart.

> **Look Into the Text**
>
> Mr. Sánchez told us, "If you help clean up the yard, you boys can use the pool any time you want so long as one of us is here." . . . After a hard day's work cleaning his yard, I so looked forward to taking a dip. I'd even worn my trunks under my work clothes. Then Mr. Sánchez said, "Come by tomorrow. I don't want you fellas to track all this dirt into the pool."

Characters	Setting	Complication
Narrator	modern day, somewhere warm	
Mr. Sánchez		
The Boys		

B. What do you think the conflict of the story will be? Why do you think so?

1. The conflict of the story will probably be _____
_____
_____.

2. What could happen that would bring about a resolution?
_____
_____

FOCUS STRATEGY: Make and Confirm Predictions

HOW TO MAKE AND CONFIRM PREDICTIONS

Focus Strategy

1. **Read the Story's Title** You may find a clue about the plot.

2. **Look at Art and Quotations** They may give clues about story events.

3. **Make Predictions** Put the clues together to predict events.

4. **Confirm or Change Predictions** Notice story details; then change your prediction, or confirm that your prediction is correct.

A. Read the passage. Use the strategies above to make a prediction. Answer the questions below.

Look Into the Text

The **Good** Samaritan
by René Saldaña, Jr.

No way was
I going to help
him out again!

1. What do you predict the story is about?

_____

_____

2. Which of the four strategies did you use to answer question 1?

_____

_____

B. As you read "The Good Samaritan," look for details that will help you confirm or change your prediction.

Selection Review The Good Samaritan

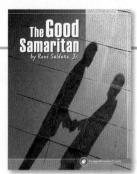

What Influences a Person's Choices?
Explore the effect of family and friends on choices.

A. In "The Good Samaritan," you learn how Rey makes a choice despite the conflict he has with Mr. Sánchez. Briefly describe each part of the plot in the chart below.

Parts of the Plot	The Good Samaritan
Characters and Setting	main characters: Rey, Mr. Sánchez
Conflict	
Complications	
Climax	
Resolution	

B. Use the information in the chart to answer the questions.

1. Why is it difficult for Rey to make the choice to help Mr. Sánchez?

_____

_____

2. What affects Rey's final choice to help Mr. Sánchez? Use **affects** in your answer.

_____

_____

3. How might the resolution have been different if Mr. Sánchez had apologized for his behavior?

_____

_____

The World Is in Their Hands

Interactive

by Eric Feil

Connect Across Texts

In "The Good Samaritan," Rey must decide whether to help a neighbor. What makes people choose to help others?

Changing the World

With sincere apologies to that old song, the children are not the future.

They are the present.

They are not going to lead the way one day.

They are leading it right now.

Youth activism levels are at all-time highs. Nearly three-quarters of young adults say they have **donated** money, clothes, or food to a community or church organization over the past few years. They **get involved** at national and local levels, and their numbers are growing. Doing good, not **gaining recognition**, is their **motivation**.

"We've seen a huge demand from young people who want their voices

A volunteer helps out at an event for youth with special needs.

Interact with the Text

1. Preview
Underline the title, heading, and caption. What is this article about? List three possible topics.

2. Set a Purpose
Who are the volunteers? Circle words that tell you who is volunteering. Then, think of a question you want answered, and write it below.

Key Vocabulary
● **motivation** *n.*, reason for doing something or thinking a certain way

In Other Words
Youth activism levels The numbers of young people who help others
donated given
get involved join, offer to help
gaining recognition getting attention

heard and who feel they've got something to **contribute** to society," says **Youth Service America** president and CEO Steve Culbertson. "And they're not going to wait until they grow up to do it."

Clearly. Millions of youth volunteers will be out in force again this year, from five-year-olds visiting and decorating senior citizen homes to high school kids tutoring **peers**. Distributing HIV/AIDS educational materials, cleaning up the environment, **registering voters**—the list of projects is almost as limitless as the **enthusiasm** and energy of the people engaged in them. Young people are making a difference in their

4. Text Features
Read the pie chart. Mark an X next to each of the largest portions. What do these reasons for volunteering have in common?

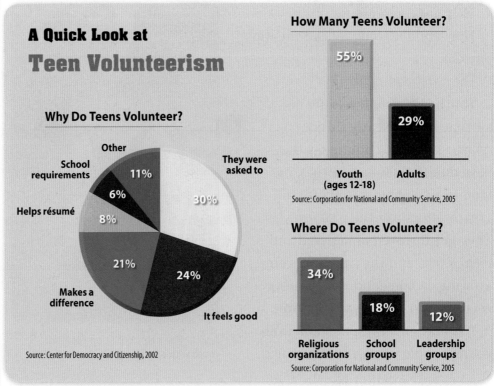

A Quick Look at
Teen Volunteerism

Why Do Teens Volunteer?

- Other 11%
- School requirements 6%
- Helps résumé 8%
- Makes a difference 21%
- It feels good 24%
- They were asked to 30%

Source: Center for Democracy and Citizenship, 2002

How Many Teens Volunteer?

- Youth (ages 12-18) 55%
- Adults 29%

Source: Corporation for National and Community Service, 2005

Where Do Teens Volunteer?

- Religious organizations 34%
- School groups 18%
- Leadership groups 12%

Source: Corporation for National and Community Service, 2005

Interpret the Data The pie graph says 30% of teens volunteer because they were asked to. Who might have asked them?

5. Interpret
According to the bar graphs, more teens than adults do volunteer work. Why?

Key Vocabulary
• **contribute** v., to give with others

In Other Words
Youth Service America youth volunteer organization
peers people who are the same age
registering voters signing people up to vote
enthusiasm excitement, eagerness
Data Facts, Information

△ Text Features A volunteer paints a mural to celebrate Youth Service Day.

communities. These volunteers also learn such life skills as planning events, raising funds, and holding leadership roles and responsibilities.

"Young people **have gotten sort of a negative rap**, when the majority of young people really are involved in their communities in very positive ways," says Carl Nelson. His company, State Farm, was the **Presenting Sponsor of** National Youth Service Day (NYSD) 2005, "a celebration of community service and service learning that goes on year-round."

Today's youth are building a unique background in **altruism**. And they are not going to leave their service history behind them when they enter the workforce. "We know that the one key predictor to lifetime service is whether you did it as a child," Culbertson states. "There's a whole **generation** of young people that have grown up giving back and

Key Vocabulary
• **generation** *n.*, people who are about the same age

In Other Words
have gotten sort of a negative rap are talked about in a bad way
Presenting Sponsor of company that paid for
altruism caring about the well-being of others

8. Interpret

Circle words that describe this young generation. What is so special about this generation of young people? Use one of the Key Vocabulary words in your explanation.

making that a **fundamental** part of their lives and it's not something you give up."

Not when they are so **engaged**, so passionate. Not where events like NYSD show them that there is a **diverse** group of peers striving for a common goal: a better world for everyone. "They're the most **tolerant** generation we've ever seen in history," Culbertson says. "They can't imagine that somebody should be left out of society simply because they're black or they're gay or they have a disability or they come from an ethnic background that's unusual. They just don't look at those differences as anything more than just part of what it means to be a

9. Text Features

Circle the sentence that states information about college freshmen. Why is this information important?

Volunteer Work:
By the Numbers

Teenagers volunteer 2.4 billion hours annually — worth $34.3 billion to the U.S. economy.
Source: Independent Sector/Gallup, 1996, and 1999 hourly value

82.6% of incoming college freshmen did volunteer work, compared to 66% in 1989.
Source: UCLA/Higher Education Research Institute Annual Freshmen Survey, 2001

The number of high school students involved in service learning increased 3,663% in the past decade from 81,000 to 2,967,000.
Source: U.S. Department of Education, 1999

A library volunteer keeps his audience's attention.

▲ **Interpret the Data** How do the numbers in this boxed feature support the main ideas of this article?

In Other Words

fundamental basic and important
engaged interested
diverse mixed
tolerant accepting, open-minded

human. They don't let those differences get in the way of progress. That's what makes this the greatest generation I think we've ever seen in this country, and nobody knows it."

They do now. ❖

Interact with the Text

10. Interpret
Reread the last sentence. What does this last sentence tell you about what the author's purpose for writing the article might be?

Selection Review The World Is in Their Hands

A. The text features in this selection, graphs, photos, and captions provide useful information about teen volunteerism. Answer the questions below.

1. Reread the information in the graphics on pages 12 and 14. What do these facts suggest about the future of teen volunteerism?

_____

_____

_____

_____

2. Which text feature in the article gave you the most information? Why?

_____

_____

_____

_____

Selection Review continued

B. Answer the questions.

1. How did using the text features in the article help you understand the rise of teen volunteerism in this country? Cite specific examples from the text to support your ideas.

_____

_____

_____

_____

2. The article suggests that the current generation of teens is more altruistic than previous generations. List the details that support this main idea in the diagram below.

Main-Idea Diagram

Main Idea: Teens today are more altruistic than previous generations.
Detail:
Detail:

Do you agree with the main idea of this article? Why or why not?

_____

_____

_____

_____

_____

_____

_____

_____

WRITING: Write About Literature

A. Plan your writing. List examples from both texts of reasons that teens choose to help others. Then list your reasons.

The Good Samaritan	The World Is in Their Hands	My Reasons
Rey wants to use Mr. Sánchez's pool.	Teens want their voices to be heard.	

Rank your reasons in order of importance.

1. Most Important: _____

2. Second: _____

3. Third: _____

4. Fourth: _____

B. Write a paragraph presenting your reasons in order of importance, ending with the reason you think is most important. Use examples from both selections to support your ideas.

_____

_____

_____

_____

_____

_____

LITERARY ANALYSIS: Analyze Theme

The **theme** of a selection is the central idea or message. It can be stated directly or implied. Clues about the theme can be found in the story events, characters, dialogue, and title.

A. List examples from "The Good Samaritan" of events, characters, and dialogue that can be used as clues to figure out the theme.

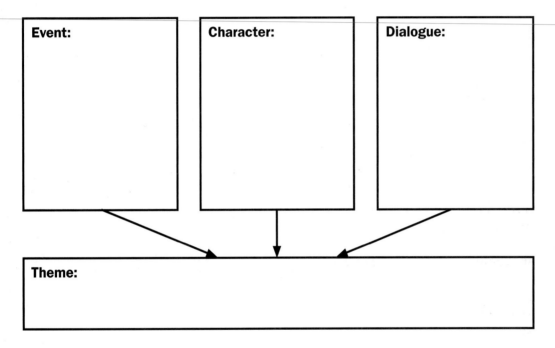

B. Answer the questions.

1. What do you think is the theme of "The Good Samaritan"?

_____

_____

2. How does the title give a clue to the theme?

_____

_____

C. Write about a time you or someone you know was a "Good Samaritan."

_____

_____

_____

_____

_____

_____

VOCABULARY STUDY: Prefixes

A **prefix** is a word part that comes at the beginning of a word and changes the meaning of that word.

A. *Mis-* is a common prefix that means "wrong" or "badly." Add *mis* to each word. Write what the new word means. Use a dictionary to confirm the meaning of the word.

Word	New Word	Meaning
behave		
count		
fortune		
inform		
understand		

B. Use each word from the list below and make a new word by adding it to one of the prefixes in the chart. Then write the definition of the new word.

believable   build   cycle   order

Prefix	Meaning	New Word	Definition
bi-	two		
dis-	reverse, opposite		
re-	again, repeatedly		
un-	not		

C. Use the chart above to write a definition for each of these words.

bilingual _____

disengage _____

react _____

unlock _____

Prepare to Read

▸ Thank You, M'am
▸ Juvenile Justice from Both Sides of the Bench

Key Vocabulary

A. How well do you know these words? Circle a rating for each word. Check your understanding of each word by circling *yes* or *no.* Then complete the sentences. If you are unsure of a word's meaning, refer to the Vocabulary Glossary, page 878, in your student text.

Rating Scale

1	I have never seen this word before.
2	I am not sure of the word's meaning.
3	I know this word and can teach the word's meaning to someone else.

Key Word	Check Your Understanding	Deepen Your Understanding
1 circumstances (**sur**-kum-stans-uz) *noun* **Rating:** 1 2 3	Choosing your friends and what you wear are **circumstances** within your control. **Yes** **No**	Some of the positive circumstances in my life are _____ _____ _____ _____ _____.
2 commit (ku-**mit**) *verb* **Rating:** 1 2 3	It is irresponsible to **commit** yourself to a job you can't finish. **Yes** **No**	Many people commit acts of heroism, such as _____ _____ _____ _____ _____.
3 consequence (**kon**-su-kwens) *noun* **Rating:** 1 2 3	The **consequence** of failing a class is always positive. **Yes** **No**	The consequence of breaking rules at school is _____ _____ _____ _____ _____.
4 contact (**kon**-takt) *noun* **Rating:** 1 2 3	Sending a letter through the mail is the fastest way to get in **contact** with a person. **Yes** **No**	When I want to get in contact with my friends, I use a ___ _____ _____ _____ _____.

Key Word	Check Your Understanding	Deepen Your Understanding
5 empathy (**em**-pu-thē) *noun* **Rating:** 1 2 3	Being sensitive to a person's feelings is an example of how a person shows **empathy**. **Yes** **No**	A friend of mine showed empathy by _____ _____ _____ _____.
6 juvenile (**joo**-vu-nīl) *adjective; noun* **Rating:** 1 2 3	**Juvenile** people are considered mature and responsible. **Yes** **No**	Teenagers are juvenile when they _____ _____ _____ _____.
7 maturity (mu-**choor**-u-tē) *noun* **Rating:** 1 2 3	Expecting someone else to fix your mistakes is an example of **maturity**. **Yes** **No**	I showed maturity when I _____ _____ _____ _____.
8 salvage (**sal**-vuj) *verb* **Rating:** 1 2 3	Spreading rumors about a friend is a good way to **salvage** a bad friendship. **Yes** **No**	If I am doing poorly in class, I can salvage my grade by _____ _____ _____.

B. Write a sentence about yourself using one of the Key Vocabulary words.

_____

_____

Before Reading Thank You, M'am

LITERARY ANALYSIS: Analyze Characterization

Authors use **characterization** to show what a character is like.

A. Read the passage below. Find the character clues that tell you what Mrs. Jones is like. Write the clues in the chart.

Look Into the Text

> She was a large woman with a large purse that had everything in it but a hammer and nails. It had a long strap, and she carried it slung across her shoulder. It was about eleven o'clock at night, dark, and she was walking alone, when a boy ran up behind her and tried to snatch her purse. The strap broke with the sudden single tug the boy gave it from behind. But the boy's weight and the weight of the purse combined caused him to lose his balance. Instead of taking off full blast as he had hoped, the boy fell on his back on the sidewalk and his legs flew up. The large woman simply turned around and kicked him right square in his blue-jeaned sitter. Then she reached down, picked the boy up by his shirt front, and shook him until his teeth rattled.

Type of Clue	Mrs. Jones
Physical traits	
Words or thoughts	
Actions	
Reactions of others	

B. Complete the sentence about Mrs. Jones's character.

Mrs. Jones seems like a character who _____

_____

_____.

FOCUS STRATEGY: Clarify Ideas

HOW TO CLARIFY IDEAS

1. **Reread** Go back to see if you missed something important.

2. **Read On** Keep reading. The author may answer your question later.

A. Read the passage. Use the strategies above to clarify the ideas as you read. Answer the questions below.

Look Into the Text

> After that, the woman said, "Pick up my pocketbook, boy, and give it here."
>
> She still held him tightly. But she bent down enough to permit him to stoop and pick up her purse. Then she said, "Now ain't you ashamed of yourself?"
>
> Firmly gripped by his shirt front, the boy said, "Yes'm."
>
> The woman said, "What did you want to do it for?"
>
> The boy said, "I didn't aim to."
>
> She said, "You a lie!"
>
> By that time two or three people passed, stopped, turned to look, and some stood watching.
>
> "If I turn you loose, will you run?" asked the woman.
>
> "Yes'm," said the boy.
>
> "Then I won't turn you loose," said the woman. She did not release him.
>
> "Lady, I'm sorry," whispered the boy.

1. Why didn't the boy run?

_____

_____

2. Which of the two strategies did you use to answer question 1?

_____

_____

B. Return to the passage above and circle the words or sentences that gave you the answer to the first question.

Selection Review Thank You, M'am

 What Influences a Person's Choices?
Find out how circumstances affect choices.

A. In "Thank You, M'am," you found out how circumstances can affect the choices people make. Complete the charts below.

Mrs. Jones	
Her circumstances:	Her choices:

Roger	
His circumstances:	His choices:

B. Use the information in the charts to answer the questions.

1. Why does Mrs. Jones make the choice to help Roger?

_____

_____

2. How could Roger's circumstances change because of Mrs. Jones? Use **circumstances** in your answer.

_____

_____

_____

3. How might Roger's choices be different in the future? Why?

_____

_____

Juvenile Justice
from Both Sides of the Bench
by Janet Tobias and Michael Martin

Connect Across Texts

In "Thank You, M'am," Mrs. Jones shows **empathy** *for Roger despite what he does. In these interviews, read how real-life judges and attorneys deal with teens who* **commit** *crimes.*

Recent legislation in many U.S. states makes it easier to try, or judge, **juvenile** offenders in adult criminal court and not in juvenile court. As a result, more and more teen offenders are **doing time** alongside adults in prison.

Teens who are tried as adults can also receive longer sentences, or periods of punishment. Many people believe such punishment is a better fit for more serious crimes. They see this as more important than how old the person is.

Public opinion has changed over the last hundred years. In 1899, the first juvenile court was set up in Illinois. Then, most people believed juveniles were not as responsible for their actions as adults. Illinois wanted to protect each young person, even while it protected the public from crime. The goal of juvenile court was to help offenders make better choices about the future.

Today, however, many people believe that harsh punishment is the better way to stop teens from committing crimes in the future. To explore this topic, the Public Broadcasting System's *Frontline* TV news team interviewed **people from both sides of "the bench."**

Key Vocabulary
empathy *n.*, the understanding of someone else's problems, feelings, or behavior
- **commit** *v.*, to perform, do, or carry out something, often a crime
juvenile *adj.*, young; *n.*, young person

In Other Words
Recent legislation New laws
doing time being punished
people from both sides of "the bench" judges, who sit on one side of the bench, or desk, and lawyers, who stand on the other side

Interact with the Text

1. Clarify Ideas/Paraphrase
Circle a sentence that supports the idea that juvenile offenders should be tried in juvenile court. Write the sentence in your own words.

2. Clarify Ideas/Paraphrase
Underline a sentence that supports the idea that juvenile offenders should be tried in adult court. Write the sentence in your own words.

3. Clarify Ideas/Paraphrase
Underline the main points in Judge Edwards's answer to the second question. Write a paraphrase of his answer.

_____
_____
_____
_____
_____
_____
_____
_____

4. Interpret
What is the Judge's strongest or most powerful idea? Use one of the Key Vocabulary words in your response.

_____
_____
_____
_____
_____
_____
_____
_____
_____
_____
_____
_____

Judge Thomas Edwards
Until recently he was the presiding judge of the Juvenile Court of Santa Clara County, a division of the California Superior Court. He heard between 300 and 350 cases a month.

Q. Why should we treat a 14-year-old offender differently than a 24-year-old offender?

A. It depends on many, many **circumstances**. But very generally, the 14-year-old does not have the level of **maturity**, thought process, decision-making, experience, or wisdom that a 24-year-old presumably has.

Secondly, a 14-year-old is still growing, may not appreciate the **consequences** of that type of behavior, and **is susceptible to** change, at least to a higher degree than a 24-year-old is. . . . I think we have a real shot at trying to straighten out the 14-year-old, and even the people who are a little bit hard-nosed in the system, such as your average **prosecutor**, will sometimes grudgingly admit that, with a 14-year-old, given the proper level of accountability and the proper types of programs to change their behavior, we have a chance at **salvaging** these kids.

Q. Are there kids who don't belong in juvenile court?

A. Oh, sure. Yes. I've had **sociopaths** in court here. I've had only a few of them, and I've been doing this for a long time. I can only really count maybe a half a dozen, and only two in particular that I would be very frightened to see on the street. But I see them from time to time.

Key Vocabulary
- **circumstances** _n._, situation
  maturity _n._, the time when a person has all the abilities of an adult
- **consequence** _n._, result
  salvage _v._, to save or rescue

In Other Words
is susceptible to probably will
prosecutor lawyer whose job is to get punishment for criminals
sociopaths people who do not know right from wrong

Judge LaDoris Cordell
A state court trial judge since 1982, until recently she served on the Superior Court of Santa Clara County, where she heard both juvenile and adult cases.

Q. Why should we treat a 14-year-old offender differently than a 24-year-old offender?

A. The problem is that we're taking 14-year-olds, 15-year-olds, 16-year-olds, and we're giving up on them. We're saying, "You've committed a crime, and we're just going to give up on you. You're out of here; society has no use for you." We're throwing away these kids. And I have found, in my own experience, that there are salvageable young people. They have committed some very horrible kinds of crimes, but they are able to get their lives together and **be productive members of society**. I think it is a mistake to just . . . give up on these young people. There is so much more that goes into why that person got there at that point in time so young in their lives.

Q. Do you think any kid ever belongs in adult court?

A. Yes. . . . I have come across some young people who are so **sophisticated** and who have committed such **heinous** crimes that the adult system is the place for them to be. I haven't come across a lot, but there have been some. . . . It can happen, and it does [happen].

In Other Words

be productive members of society work and be responsible like other people
sophisticated clever in a grown-up way
heinous horrible, evil

5. Text Features
Captions provide additional information. In this article, the writer states that judges "hear" cases. Reread the caption and describe what you think hearing a case means, in your own words.

6. Text Features
Remember that brackets and ellipses are important text features. Circle the text features in Judge Cordell's answer. Write what each text feature means.

Bridgett Jones
Former supervisor of the Juvenile Division of the Santa Clara County Public Defender's Office

8. Interpret
Do you agree that a young person needs the support of his or her community? Why or why not?

Q. Why should we treat a 14-year-old offender differently than a 24-year-old offender?

A. I think the community understands, or should understand, that the younger a person is, the more likely it is that they can change. And the best way I've heard it put is from a **victim** in a very serious case.

This person had been **maimed** for life. He had **indicated to** the young person who shot him, or was **alleged** to have shot him, that he would rather meet up with this person ten years down the road as a graduate from a college versus a graduate from [prison].

He [understood] that this person was eventually going to get back out and be in our community. They don't go away. They come back. And the younger they are, the more likely it is that they are going to come back into our community. So I guess as a community we have to decide what is it we're willing to get back in the long run.

Children are not little adults. They think differently. They respond and react to things differently than adults do. . . . So why should the consequences be the same as for an adult?

The only thing that's going to work with kids like [these] is a willingness of the community to **redeem** them and saying, "Look, your life's not over, there's still hope for you."

In Other Words
victim person hurt by a crime
maimed physically hurt, wounded
indicated to told or shown
alleged suspected
redeem help and forgive

Social Studies Background
A district attorney prosecutes, or seeks punishment for, someone charged with a crime. If the person cannot afford a lawyer, a public defender has the job of advising and representing the person.

Kurt Kumli
The supervising deputy district attorney for the Juvenile Division of the Santa Clara County District Attorney's Office, he has practiced exclusively in juvenile court.

Interact with the Text

9. Text Features
Draw a circle around the information that is in italics. Write a sentence about why this background information is important.

Q. Why should we treat a 14-year-old offender differently than a 24-year-old offender?

A. If we could take every kid and surround the kid with full-time staffs of psychologists and drug and alcohol counselors, then perhaps no kid should be in adult court. But the fact is, there are only a limited number of **resources** in the juvenile justice system. . . . You have to make **the hard call**, sometimes, as to whether or not the high-end offenders really are the **just recipients of** the [limited] resources that the juvenile justice system has available to it.

Q. What does it take to rehabilitate young offenders?

A. What works is different for every kid, but the one rule that I think is applicable, after years of seeing this, is "the sooner, the better." We need to reach these kids with **alternatives**, with opportunities, before they start to feel [like nobody cares]. If we took half of the money that we spend on **incarceration** and put it in **front-end programs** to give these kids alternatives, then we wouldn't have as many **back-end kids** that we needed to incarcerate. And I think that is the immediate answer.

In Other Words

resources staff people and services
the hard call a difficult decision
just recipients of people who should receive
rehabilitate help, fix the problems of
alternatives other choices
incarceration keeping people in jail

front-end programs programs that help kids before they get into trouble
back-end kids kids who have already committed crimes

10. Interpret
Which person's opinion in this article surprised you the most? Why?

Judge Nancy Hoffman
Judge Hoffman served on the Superior Court of Santa Clara County, where she handled both juvenile and adult cases. She is currently retired.

Q. **What does it take to rehabilitate young offenders?**

A. I would like to see groups . . . working with troubled families and youth, before they get to middle school and . . . high school. Something is causing the **minor** to do things like not go to school, stay out till three o'clock in the morning . . . We **intervene** with a minor, but there's very little done with the family, and we're sending the minor right back in that situation. ❖

In Other Words
minor person under the age of 18
intervene get involved to prevent or solve problems

Selection Review Juvenile Justice from Both Sides of the Bench

A. Choose a topic and write three details from the interview that relate to it. Identify the speaker of each viewpoint.

> **Topic 1:** Differences between young and adult offenders
> **Topic 2:** Ideas about rehabilitating young offenders

Details for Topic _____:

1. _____

2. _____

3. _____

B. Answer the questions.

1. How did the text features help you to find the information?

_____

_____

2. Which speaker's views are closest to your own? Which speaker do you disagree with? Why?

_____

WRITING: Write About Literature

A. Plan your writing. Read the opposing opinions. Put an *X* next to the opinion you agree with. Then list examples from each text to support the opinion.

☐ **Opinion 1:** Juvenile offenders should be treated differently than adult offenders.

☐ **Opinion 2:** Most juvenile offenders should be treated the same as adult offenders.

Thank You, M'am	Juvenile Justice

B. What is your opinion? Write an opinion statement. Remember to use the text evidence you listed in the chart to support your statement.

_____

_____

_____

_____

_____

_____

_____

_____

LITERARY ANALYSIS: Analyze Dialogue

What a character says, or **dialogue**, is an important part of characterization. Writers use speaker words and quotation marks to show what characters say and how they say it.

Example: "Lady, I'm sorry," <u>whispered</u> the boy.

A. Brainstorm words that show how characters speak. List them in the chart.

Speaker Words	
1. shouted	5.
2. mumbled	6.
3.	7.
4.	8.

B. Rewrite these sentences as dialogue. Use quotation marks and the speaker words from the chart, above.

1. Mrs. Jones told Roger to pick up her pocketbook.

_____

2. Roger apologized to Mrs. Jones.

_____

3. Mrs. Jones asked Roger if he would run.

_____

4. Mrs. Jones told Roger she would not let him go.

_____

C. Write a conversation you have had with a friend recently using dialogue. The dialogue is started for you.

" _____," I shouted to my friend in the hallway. _____

_____

_____

_____

_____

_____

VOCABULARY STUDY: Greek Roots

Greek roots are word parts in many English words. If you know the meaning of a word part, you can figure out the meaning of the word.

A. *Tele* is a common Greek root that means "far off." Write what you think each word means. Confirm the definition for each word in the dictionary.

Word	What I Think It Means	Definition
telecom		
telecommute		
telegram		
telephoto		
telescope		

B. The chart below shows some common Greek roots and their meanings. Complete the chart by listing words you've heard that contain each root.

Greek Root	Meaning	Words I've Used
auto	self	automobile
bio	life	
graph	write, draw	
phone, phono	sound	
log	word, thought, speech	

C. Use the chart above to write a definition of each of these words.

autobiography _____

biology _____

telegraph _____

phonograph _____

logic _____

Prepare to Read
▶ The Necklace
▶ The Fashion Show

Key Vocabulary

A. How well do you know these words? Circle a rating for each word. Check your understanding of each word by circling the synonym. Then write a definition of the word in your own words. If you are unsure of a word's meaning, refer to the Vocabulary Glossary, page 854, in your student text.

Rating Scale	
1	I have never seen this word before.
2	I am not sure of the word's meaning.
3	I know this word and can teach the word's meaning to someone else.

Key Word	Check Your Understanding	Deepen Your Understanding
1 humiliating (hyū-**mi**-lē-ā-ting) *adjective* **Rating:** 1 2 3	A **humiliating** experience is _____. secretive embarrassing	My definition: _____ _____ _____ _____ _____
2 imitation (im-u-**tā**-shun) *noun* **Rating:** 1 2 3	An **imitation** of something is _____. an original a copy	My definition: _____ _____ _____ _____ _____
3 inspire (in-**spīr**) *verb* **Rating:** 1 2 3	To **inspire** people is to _____ them. motivate criticize	My definition: _____ _____ _____ _____ _____
4 luxury (**luk**-shu-rē) *noun* **Rating:** 1 2 3	If something is a **luxury**, it is _____. a necessity an extravagance	My definition: _____ _____ _____ _____ _____

Key Word	Check Your Understanding	Deepen Your Understanding
5 **perceive** (per-**sēv**) *verb* **Rating:** 1 2 3	To **perceive** is to _____ something in a particular way. **see** **ignore**	My definition: _____ _____ _____ _____
6 **poverty** (**pov**-er-tē) *noun* **Rating:** 1 2 3	To live in a state of **poverty** is to live in a state of _____. **need** **rest**	My definition: _____ _____ _____ _____
7 **symbol** (**sim**-bul) *noun* **Rating:** 1 2 3	A **symbol** is a _____ of something else. **representation recommendation**	My definition: _____ _____ _____ _____
8 **value** (**val**-ū) *verb* **Rating:** 1 2 3	To **value** something is to _____ it. **summarize** **appreciate**	My definition: _____ _____ _____ _____

B. Use one of the Key Vocabulary words to write about a person who has had a positive influence on you.

_____

_____

Before Reading The Necklace

LITERARY ANALYSIS: Analyze Setting

The **setting** tells when and where a story takes place. It also includes details about the characters' circumstances.

A. Read the passage below. Pay attention to clues in the text that tell you about the setting. Write the clues in the chart.

> ### Look Into the Text
>
> Then one evening, her husband came home and proudly handed her a large envelope . . .
>
> She . . . threw the invitation onto the table and murmured, "What do you want me to do with that?"
>
> "But, my dear, I thought you would be so pleased. This is a big event! I had a lot of trouble getting this invitation. All the clerks at the Ministry want to go, but there are only a few invitations reserved for workers. You will meet all the most important people there."
>
> She gave him an irritated look and said, impatiently, "I do not have anything I could wear. How could I go?"

Setting Chart
What is happening?   A couple disagrees about going to a fancy party for rich people.
Who are the characters?
Where does this scene occur?
When does this scene take place?
Why does the husband think his wife will be pleased?

B. Complete this sentence about the setting.

The couple's social status and disagreement is an important part of the setting because_____.

FOCUS STRATEGY: Clarify Vocabulary

HOW TO CLARIFY VOCABULARY

Focus Strategy

1. **Look for Context Clues** When you read an unfamiliar word, other words or phrases near it can give you hints to its meaning.

2. **Figure Out Word Meaning** What *doesn't* the word mean? This will give you a clue about the word's meaning.

3. **Test Your Meaning** Does your meaning make sense in the sentence?

A. Read the passage below. Use the strategies above to clarify the vocabulary as you read. Then answer the questions.

> **Look Into the Text**
>
> He was stunned and said, "Mathilde, how much would it cost for a suitable dress that you could wear again?"
>
> She thought for several seconds, wondering how much she could ask for without a shocked refusal from her thrifty husband.
>
> Finally, she answered, "I am not sure exactly, but I think I could manage with four hundred *francs*."
>
> His face turned pale because that was exactly the amount of money he had saved to buy a new rifle. He wanted to go hunting in Nanterre the next summer with some of his friends.
>
> However, he said, "All right. I'll give you four hundred *francs*, but try to find a beautiful dress."

1. Read the sentences around the word *thrifty*. What does the word *thrifty* not mean? Explain.

   _____

   _____

2. What does the word *thrifty* mean? What strategy did you use to find out the meaning?

   _____

   _____

B. Reread the passage above and circle the clues that told you what *thrifty* means.

What Influences a Person's Choices?
Discover how society influences choices.

A. In "The Necklace," you found out how circumstances can influence the choices people make. Complete the chart below with the consequences of the Loisels' circumstances.

Cause-and-Effect Chart

Circumstances	Consequences
Madame Loisel lives in a society that values wealth. Monsieur Loisel is a thrifty man with a modest income. The Loisels don't have enough money to replace the lost necklace.	She is not satisfied with what her husband provides and asks her friend for a jeweled necklace.

B. Use the information in the chart to answer the questions.

1. What circumstances cause Madame Loisel to want to live a different life?

_____

_____

2. Why does Madame Loisel choose to borrow a luxury item? Use the word **luxury** in your response.

_____

_____

3. How might their final situation have been different if the Loisels had told the truth to Madame Forestier? Why?

_____

_____

_____

Connect Across Texts
In "The Necklace," Madame Loisel makes a choice because she worries about what others think. Now read this memoir. How do the opinions of others affect Farah's decision?

THE FASHION SHOW

by Farah Ahmedi
with Tamim Ansary

At just 17, Farah Ahmedi entered an essay contest. Since then, her memoir, *The Other Side of the Sky*, has inspired people everywhere with her life story as a proud Afghan American.

▲ Farah Ahmedi was a junior in high school when she published *The Other Side of the Sky: A Memoir.*

Interact with the Text

1. Interpret
Circle the words and phrases that are clues to what this selection is about. What do you think the author's reason for writing might be?

Farah Ahmedi didn't have much of a childhood. She was still recovering from losing her leg in **a land mine accident** when a rocket attack destroyed her home in Kabul, Afghanistan. Four years and many challenges later, Farah and her mother found their way to a **suburb of** Chicago. Farah learned English, started high school, and began to make choices that would change her life. Despite her disability, she wanted to fit in. She wanted to "wear high-heeled shoes." Here, Farah remembers one of those choices.

During our second summer in America, I switched schools. The **ESL department** at my new high school had an international club. Kids from other countries met every Wednesday after school to play games, talk, and have fun. Ms. Ascadam, the teacher who sponsored this group, decided that the international kids should throw a party at the end of the year and present a show. She told us each to bring food from our country to the party, and she encouraged us to think about participating in the show as well.

The first part of the show would be a dance performance by the kids from Mexico. The next part would be a **fashion show**. Kids from any country could be in the fashion show, and they would model clothes from their own culture, but no one had to do it.

From Kabul to Chicago

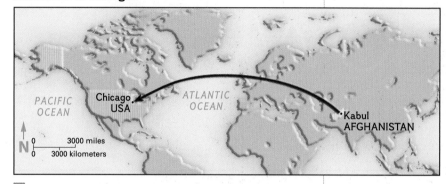

⚠ Interpret the Map Use the scale to calculate how far Farah and her mother traveled to their new home.

In Other Words

a land mine accident an explosion caused by a bomb buried in the ground
suburb of town outside of
ESL department English classes for students who spoke other languages
fashion show display of special clothes

Historical Background

Afghanistan has been at war for more than forty years. In 2001, the U.S. and other countries invaded the country to force the Taliban, the ruling group, to leave.

I felt **torn and confused**. I could not take part in the dance, of course, but should I be in the fashion show? I really wanted to do it. I had two beautiful **Afghan outfits** I could model. But I was also thinking, *My leg is damaged. What if I fall down?*

Finally, I said to myself, *Okay, next Wednesday I'll sit in on the practice session and see what it's like, and then I'll decide.*

That day the girl who always picked on me came to the practice session, because she was planning to be in the fashion show. The moment she saw me sitting there, she could tell I was thinking of entering the show, too. She didn't tell me to my face that I could not

WHAT IF I FALL DOWN?

do it, but she immediately called out to the teacher. "Ms. Ascadam," she said, "when you model clothes at a fashion show, isn't this how you have to walk?   Isn't this how models walk on a **runway**?"

Then she began to walk the way she thought a model should walk—with long strides, placing one foot in front of the other in a straight line that made her back end swing from side to side. "Is this the way you should walk?" she said. "If someone can't walk like this, should she be in the fashion show? She would just spoil the whole thing, wouldn't she?" And she kept walking back and forth, swinging from side to side.

It made me so angry, because I knew that she was really saying, *Farah can't do this. She has a problem with her legs. She shouldn't be in the fashion show.* She didn't say my name, but she was talking about me and only me, and everyone knew it.

That girl broke my heart. I felt as if somebody had punched me or slapped me. I felt as if someone had gotten into my throat and started pushing me and pressing me and choking me. I could not stay in that room. I turned and **fled**, my eyes stinging with tears. At home I

In Other Words
torn and confused mixed up, upset
Afghan outfits sets of clothes from Afghanistan
runway stage
fled ran away

2. Viewpoint
Circle the words and phrases in the first paragraph that tell you about Ahmedi feelings. Explain why she felt confused about participating in the fashion show.

_____

_____

_____

_____

_____

_____

_____

3. Viewpoint
Underline the action words and phrases that describe how Ahmedi felt about what the girl said. Explain her response.

_____

_____

_____

_____

_____

_____

_____

_____

_____

_____

threw myself on my bed and just lay there, weeping and feeling sorry for myself—sorry about being only half a woman. I felt like everyone knew that I was not whole and that's what they thought about every time they looked at me. That girl had finally succeeded in getting through my defenses and poking me right where it hurt the most and where I would always hurt.

Farah Ahmedi shares her memoir with First Lady Laura Bush.

And what happened just then?

My friend Alyce called.

"Hey," she said. "How are you, sweetie? Are you well?"

I started to **bawl**.

She said, "What is it? What are you crying about?"

I spilled the whole story.

Alyce said, "Now don't **get all hung up on** what other people say. You just go ahead and do it. You tell your teacher you want to be in the fashion show."

But I just went on crying. "You don't understand. It's not *just* what 'other people say.' The terrible thing is, that girl is right! I *can't* be in a fashion show! It's true. How can someone like me be in a fashion show? With my limp? I can't walk like a model." That girl's cruelty **wounded** me, to be sure, but what really hurt was the truth she was telling. "Why are you trying to **inspire** me to do something I should never even try?" I **ranted** at Alyce.

It was one of those moments, you see. And Alyce just let me rage.

Key Vocabulary
inspire *v.*, to encourage someone to take action

In Other Words
bawl cry hard
I spilled the whole story. I told her everything.
get all hung up on worry about, feel upset about
wounded hurt
ranted yelled angrily

But then she said, "No, people aren't looking at you that way. Here, we **value** who you are as a person. You go right ahead and enter the fashion show fearlessly."

Well, I thought about it. I thought I should do it just to **spite** the girl who tried to keep me out of the show. I decided I had to do it, even if it meant falling down in the middle of the runway—because if I let that girl get away with talking about me as if I were half human, she would never stop. She would make me **her scapegoat**, and others would take up her view as well. I had to stand up for myself, because this was not just about a fashion show. It was about claiming my humanity. I had to do it.

I went to my teacher the next day and told her I wanted to enter the fashion show. She hugged me. "Farah," she said, "this makes me so, so happy!"

After that I started to practice walking. No, I started to practice *strutting* down a runway.

On the day of the fashion show, I hurried to the dressing room to get ready. I had two dresses to wear, an orange one and a purple one. Backstage the makeup people put cosmetics on my face and curled my hair, so that I looked really different than usual. The teacher saw me and said, "Oh my gosh, you look so pretty!"

The fashion show began. Each model was supposed to go out and walk around the stage in a diamond-shaped pattern. At each point of the diamond we were supposed to pause, face the audience, and **strike a pose**.

When my turn came, I went strutting out. I threw my shoulders back and held my head up high so that my neck stretched long. I didn't fall, and I didn't shake. I didn't even feel nervous.

Key Vocabulary
value *v.*, to think something is important or useful

4. Interpret
Ahmedi decided to participate in the fashion show. What can you conclude about Ahmedi's values? Explain.

_____

_____

_____

_____

_____

_____

5. Viewpoint
Underline the words and phrases in the last paragraph that give you an idea about how the author felt when she walked down the runway. How are her feelings different from her earlier feelings? Why did they change?

_____

_____

_____

_____

_____

_____

_____

_____

_____

_____

6. Clarify Vocabulary

Circle the words and phrases that tell you what *beamed* means. Explain how you found your answer.

_____

_____

_____

_____

_____

_____

Alyce told me later that no one could tell about my legs. I moved in time to the music, showed the clothes off well, and smiled—I did just fine! My mother **beamed**. She didn't say much at the time, but later on, at home, she told me she felt proud of me. Imagine that! Proud that her daughter stood up before an audience of strangers and modeled our beautiful Afghan clothes: She, too, has come a long way since we arrived in America.

After the show the party began. We had all brought special foods from our various cultures. My mother had cooked a fancy Afghan rice dish. We ate and chatted and felt happy. That night, though it wasn't **literally** true, I felt that I was wearing high-heeled shoes at last. ❖

In Other Words
beamed smiled with joy
literally actually

Selection Review The Fashion Show

A. Answer the questions.

1. The author of "The Fashion Show" chose to write her story as a memoir. How did writing from her own viewpoint make the story more powerful?

_____

_____

_____

2. Who do you think inspired Ahmedi? Why?

_____

_____

B. List the words that were difficult for you to understand. Circle one of the words and explain how the reading strategy helped you.

1. Words that were difficult: _____

_____

2. Reading strategy I used: _____

_____

Reflect and Assess

WRITING: Write About Literature

A. Plan your writing. Think about how Madame Loisel in "The Necklace" and Farah Ahmedi in "The Fashion Show" make choices that have surprising consequences. List examples from both texts in the chart below.

	Choice	Consequence
Madame Loisel	borrows a friend's necklace	loses the necklace
Farah Ahmedi		

B. Write a response log, describing a time when a choice you made had surprising consequences. Compare your experience to Madame Loisel's and Farah's. Use examples from the chart to support your writing.

_____

_____

_____

_____

_____

_____

LITERARY ANALYSIS: Analyze Setting and Theme

Setting is the time and place in which a story unfolds. A story's setting affects the characters and the **theme**, or message, of the story.

A. Complete each chart below with details from each selection.

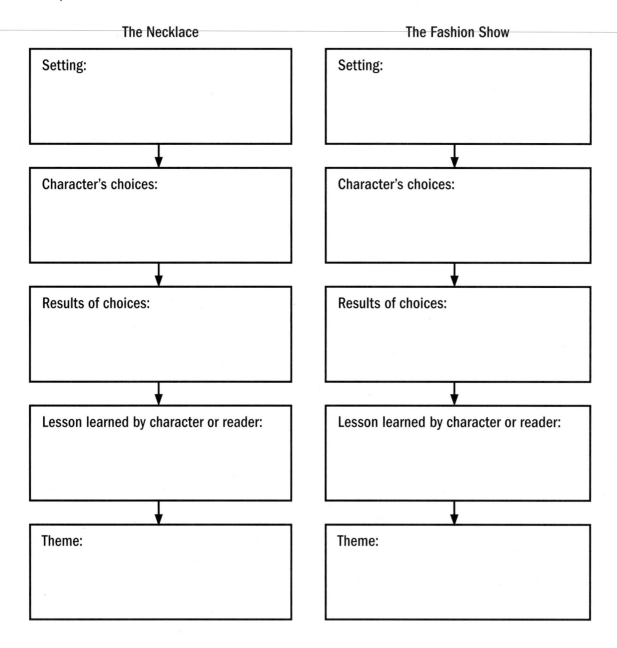

The Necklace

Setting:

Character's choices:

Results of choices:

Lesson learned by character or reader:

Theme:

The Fashion Show

Setting:

Character's choices:

Results of choices:

Lesson learned by character or reader:

Theme:

B. How does setting affect the actions of Madame Loisel and Farah Ahmedi? Compare the themes.

_____

_____

_____

VOCABULARY STUDY: Suffixes

A **suffix** is a word part added to the end of a word. Suffixes can change verbs or adjectives into nouns.

A. Change each verb or adjective in the chart into a noun by adding the suffix. Then write the meanings of each noun. Use a dictionary to check the meanings.

Verb or Adjective	Suffix	Noun	Meaning
work	-er		
enjoy	-ment		
kind	-ness		
aggravate	-tion		

B. List two more nouns for each suffix in the chart above.

1. _____
2. _____
3. _____
4. _____

C. Write sentences using one of the words you wrote containing each suffix.

1. _____
   _____
2. _____
   _____
3. _____
   _____
4. _____
   _____

Read for Understanding

1. Genre What kind of text is this passage? How do you know?

2. Topic Write a topic sentence to tell what the text is mostly about.

Reread and Summarize

3. Word Choice In each section, circle three words or phrases that express the big ideas in that section. Note next to each word or phrase why you chose it.

· Section 1: paragraphs 1–18
· Section 2: paragraphs 19–42

4. Summary Use your topic sentence and notes from item 3 to write a summary of the selection.

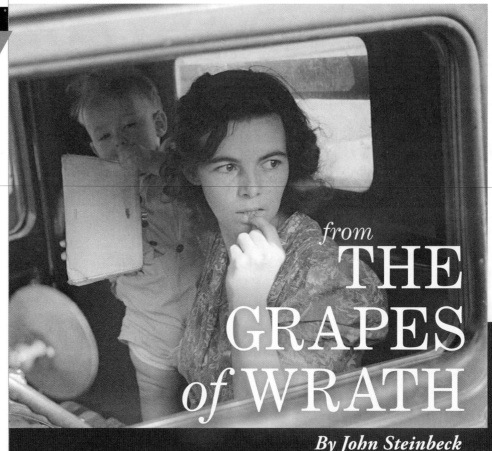

Farm wife waiting in the car while her husband attends the auction, Oskaloosa, Kansas, 1938, John Vachon. Photographic negative, Library of Congress

from
THE GRAPES *of* WRATH

By John Steinbeck

1 "...the road is full a them families goin' west. Never seen so many. Gets worse all a time. Wonder where the hell they all come from?"

2 "Wonder where they all go to," said Mae. "Come here for gas sometimes, but they don't hardly never buy nothin' else. People says they steal. We **ain't got nothin' layin'** around. They never stole nothin' from us."

3 Big Bill, munching his pie, looked up the road through the screened window. "Better tie your stuff down. I think you got some of 'em comin' now."

4 A 1926 Nash **sedan** pulled wearily off the highway. The back seat was piled nearly to the ceiling with sacks, with pots and pans, and on the very top, right up against the ceiling, two boys rode. On the top of the car, a mattress and a folded tent; tent poles tied along the running board. The car pulled up to the gas pumps. A dark-haired, hatchet-faced man got slowly out. And the two boys slid down from the load and hit the ground.

In Other Words

a them families goin' of those families going
ain't got nothin' layin' don't have anything lying
sedan medium-sized car

Historical Background

In the early 1930s, a drought hit the midwestern U.S. and farmers in the area lost all their crops. This area became known as the **Dust Bowl** because of the wind storms that swept dust over everything. Many families packed what little they had left and drove west to work in the fields of California.

5   Mae walked around the counter and stood in the door. The man was dressed in gray wool trousers and a blue shirt, dark blue with sweat on the back and under the arms. The boys in overalls and nothing else, ragged patched overalls. Their hair was light, and it stood up evenly all over their heads, for it had been **roached**. Their faces were streaked with dust. They went directly to the mud puddle under the hose and dug their toes into the mud.

6   The man asked, "Can we **git** some water, ma'am?"

7   A look of annoyance crossed Mae's face. "Sure, go ahead." She said softly over her shoulder, "I'll keep my eye on the hose." She watched while the man slowly unscrewed the radiator cap and ran the hose in.

8   A woman in the car, a flaxen-haired woman, said, "See if you can't git it here."

9   The man turned off the hose and screwed on the cap again. The little boys took the hose from him and they upended it and drank thirstily. The man took off his dark, stained hat and stood with a curious **humility** in front of the screen. "**Could you see your way to** sell us a loaf of bread, ma'am?"

> *The man...stood with a curious humility in front of the screen.*

10   Mae said, "This ain't a grocery store. We got bread to make **san'widges**."

11   "I know, ma'am." His humility was **insistent**. "We need bread and there **ain't nothin' for quite a piece**, they say."

12   " 'F we sell bread we gonna run out." Mae's tone was **faltering**.

13   "We're hungry," the man said.

14   "**Whyn't** you buy a san'widge? We got nice san'widges, hamburgs."

15   "We'd sure **admire** to do that, ma'am. But we can't. We got to make a dime do all of us." And he said embarrassedly, "We **ain't got but** a little."

16   Mae said, "You can't get no loaf a bread for a dime. We only got fifteen-cent loafs."

17   From behind her Al growled, "God Almighty, Mae, give 'em bread."

18   "We'll run out 'fore the bread truck comes."

In Other Words
roached brushed to stand upright
git get
humility modesty, lack of pride
Could you see your way to Would you
san'widges sandwiches
insistent demanding, persistent

ain't nothin' for quite a piece isn't anything for quite a while
faltering uncertain, hesitating
Whyn't Why don't
admire like
ain't got but only have

Reread and Analyze

5. Characterization
Reread paragraph 5. What technique does the author use to describe the man and his sons?

_____
_____
_____
_____
_____

6. Details Underline a description from paragraph 5 and tell what this says about the family.

_____
_____
_____
_____

7. Dialogue Reread paragraph 7. Underline dialogue that shows Mae's feelings about the family. What do Mae's remarks show about her character?

_____
_____
_____
_____
_____

8. Dialogue Examine what Mae says in paragraphs 10–18. Highlight 3 examples of dialogue that suggests Mae does not want to be generous.

9. Characterization Reread paragraph 21. Highlight an action that shows how the boys feel about the candy. What does this detail tell you about the boys?

_____

_____

_____

_____

_____

10. Characterization Reread paragraph 29. Underline something the father does that is unexpected. Explain what this shows about the father.

_____

_____

_____

_____

_____

_____

_____

_____

_____

_____

_____

_____

_____

19   "Run out, then, goddamn it," said Al. And he looked sullenly down at the potato salad he was mixing.

20   Mae shrugged her plump shoulders and looked to the truck drivers to show them what she was up against.

21   She held the screen door open and the man came in, bringing a smell of sweat with him. The boys edged in behind him and they went immediately to the candy case and stared in—not with **craving** or with hope or even with desire, but just with a kind of wonder that such things could be. They were alike in size and their faces were alike. One scratched his dusty ankle with the toe nails of his other foot. The other whispered some soft message and then they straightened their arms so that their clenched fists in the overall pockets showed through the thin blue cloth.

> ### *The boys...went immediately to the candy case and stared in...*

22   Mae opened a drawer and took out a long waxpaper-wrapped loaf. "This here is a fifteen-cent loaf."

23   The man put his hat back on his head. He answered with **inflexible** humility, "Won't you—can't you see your way to cut off ten cents' worth?"

24   Al said snarlingly, "Goddamn it, Mae. Give 'em the loaf."

25   The man turned toward Al. "No, we want ta buy ten cents' worth of it. We got it **figgered awful** close, mister, to get to California."

26   Mae said **resignedly**, "You can have this for ten cents."

27   "That'd be robbin' you, ma'am."

28   "Go ahead—Al says to take it." She pushed the waxpapered loaf across the counter. The man took a deep leather pouch from his rear pocket, untied the strings, and spread it open. It was heavy with silver and with greasy bills.

29   "May soun' funny to be so **tight**," he apologized. "We got a thousan' miles to go, an' we don' know if we'll make it." He dug in the pouch with a forefinger, located a dime, and pinched in for it. When he put it down on the counter he had a penny with it. He was about to drop the penny back into the pouch when **his eye fell on** the boys frozen before the candy counter. He moved slowly down to them. He pointed in the case at big long sticks of striped peppermint. "Is them penny candy, ma'am?"

In Other Words
craving want, hunger
inflexible unchanging
figgered awful counted very
resignedly giving up, yielding
tight worried about spending money
his eye fell on he saw

30   Mae moved down and looked in. "Which ones?"

31   "There, them stripy ones."

32   The little boys raised their eyes to her face and they stopped breathing; their mouths were partly opened, their half-naked bodies were **rigid**.

33   "Oh—them. Well, no—them's two for a penny."

34   "Well, gimme two then, ma'am." He placed the copper cent carefully on the counter. The boys **expelled** their held breath softly. Mae held the big sticks out.

35   "Take 'em," said the man.

36   They reached **timidly**, each took a stick, and they held them down at their sides and did not look at them. But they looked at each other, and their mouth corners smiled rigidly with embarrassment.

37   "Thank you, ma'am." The man picked up the bread and went out the door, and the little boys marched stiffly behind him, the red-striped sticks held tightly against their legs. They leaped like chipmunks over the front seat and onto the top of the load, and they burrowed back out of sight like chipmunks.

38   The man got in and started his car, and with a roaring motor and a cloud of blue oily smoke the ancient Nash climbed up on the highway and went on its way to the west.

39   From inside the restaurant the truck drivers and Mae and Al stared after them.

40   Big Bill **wheeled** back. "Them wasn't two-for-a-cent candy," he said.

41   "What's that to you?" Mae said fiercely.

42   "Them was nickel apiece candy," said Bill. ❖

Critical Viewing: Setting ▷
This photo was taken during the Dust Bowl. How do the setting details in the photo compare with the details in the story?

In Other Words
rigid stiff, not moving
expelled let out
timidly shyly, without confidence
wheeled turned the conversation

Reread and Analyze

11. Characterization
Highlight details that show Bill's reaction to Mae's selling of the candy. What does his reaction reveal about the price of the candy?

12. Characterization
What does Mae's action in selling the candy show about her character?

Discuss

13. Synthesize With the class, list some of the details that the author uses to show what Mae is like. Discuss what the author shows about Mae with these details.

_____   _____
_____   _____
_____   _____
_____   _____
_____   _____
_____   _____

Then, with the class, discuss the change that takes place in Mae.

_____
_____
_____
_____
_____
_____

14. Write Use your notes from question 13 to write about the techniques that authors use to portray characters. Include specific examples from the story to support your ideas.

_____
_____
_____
_____
_____
_____
_____
_____
_____
_____

Connect with the **EQ** What Influences a Person's Choices?
Consider what causes people to change their minds.

15. **Viewpoint** What circumstances influence Mae's choice in the selection? Does it seem like the right choice? Explain.

_____

_____

_____

_____

_____

_____

_____

_____

_____

_____

16. **Theme** In this selection, what is the writer's message about the choices we should make about how to treat others?

_____

_____

_____

_____

_____

_____

_____

_____

_____

_____

Key Vocabulary Review

A. Use the words to complete the paragraph.

affect	consequence	disrespect	salvage
conflict	contribute	juvenile	value

Shawn and Jacob argued about the direction of our project. Their continued _____
(1)

began to _____ the group. They showed _____ to each other, and
(2)   (3)

they refused to _____ any new ideas. The _____ of their actions were
(4)   (5)

getting serious, and we were afraid we wouldn't finish on time. The rest of us worked hard to

_____ the project and create something we could _____. Their immature and
(6)   (7)

_____ behavior almost cost us a good grade.
(8)

B. Use your own words to write what each Key Vocabulary word means.
Then write a synonym for each word.

Key Word	My Definition	Synonym
1. empathy		
2. generation		
3. humiliating		
4. imitation		
5. inspire		
6. luxury		
7. perceive		
8. poverty		

Unit 1 Key Vocabulary

• affect	• consequence	empathy	• inspire	• motivation	responsible
• circumstances	contact	• generation	juvenile	• perceive	salvage
• commit	• contribute	humiliating	luxury	poverty	• symbol
• conflict	disrespect	imitation	maturity	privilege	value

• **Academic Vocabulary**

C. Answer the questions using complete sentences.

1. What **circumstances** might cause a person to make a bad decision?

   _____

   _____

2. Describe how you show **maturity**.

   _____

   _____

3. Why might two people lose **contact** with each other?

   _____

   _____

4. What **privilege** do you enjoy the most?

   _____

   _____

5. What **symbol** do you see every day?

   _____

   _____

6. What is your **motivation** to succeed?

   _____

   _____

7. Why might someone **commit** a crime?

   _____

   _____

8. Why are you **responsible**?

   _____

   _____

Prepare to Read

▷ **Creativity at Work**
▷ **The Hidden Secrets of the Creative Mind**

Key Vocabulary

A. How well do you know these words? Circle a rating for each word. Check your understanding of each word by circling *yes* or *no*. Then complete the sentences. If you are unsure of a word's meaning, refer to the Vocabulary Glossary, page 878, in your student text.

Rating Scale

1	I have never seen this word before.
2	I am not sure of the word's meaning.
3	I know this word and can teach the word's meaning to someone else.

Key Word	Check Your Understanding	Deepen Your Understanding
❶ career (ku-**rear**) *noun* **Rating:** **1 2 3**	Doctors, artists, and teachers are examples of people who have a specific **career**. **Yes**　　　　**No**	A career I might be interested in pursuing some day is _____ _____ _____ _____ .
❷ collaborate (ku-**lab**-u-rāt) *verb* **Rating:** **1 2 3**	World leaders sometimes **collaborate** to find peaceful solutions. **Yes**　　　　**No**	I collaborate with other people to _____ _____ _____ _____ _____ .
❸ commitment (ku-**mit**-munt) *noun* **Rating:** **1 2 3**	Employees show their **commitment** to their jobs by doing as little work as possible. **Yes**　　　　**No**	I show commitment when I _____ _____ _____ _____ _____ .
❹ evaluate (i-**val**-ū-āt) *verb* **Rating:** **1 2 3**	Judges **evaluate** contestants in talent shows. **Yes**　　　　**No**	I can evaluate a video game by _____ _____ _____ _____ _____ .

Key Word	Check Your Understanding	Deepen Your Understanding
5 **expectation** (ek-spek-**tā**-shun) *noun* **Rating:** **1 2 3**	An **expectation** is something you do not think will happen. **Yes** **No**	One expectation I have for myself is _____ _____ _____ _____ _____ .
6 **insight** (**in**-sīt) *noun* **Rating:** **1 2 3**	Reading several books about a subject can provide **insight** into the topic. **Yes** **No**	I have always wanted insight into _____ _____ _____ _____ _____ .
7 **talent** (**tal**-unt) *noun* **Rating:** **1 2 3**	Someone who can sing, dance, and play many musical instruments has very little **talent**. **Yes** **No**	One talent I have is _____ _____ _____ _____ _____ .
8 **transform** (trans-**form**) *verb* **Rating:** **1 2 3**	A painter can **transform** a blank canvas into a beautiful image. **Yes** **No**	Two things in my life that I wish I could transform are _____ _____ _____ _____ .

B. Use one of the Key Vocabulary words to explain how you think using your creativity helps you in your everyday life.

_____

_____

LITERARY ANALYSIS: Analyze Author's Purpose

An **author's purpose** for writing a news article is to share factual information with readers in a clear and interesting way. The author includes specific examples and reliable facts to support this purpose.

A. Read the passage below. Write the details in the passage in the 5Ws Chart. Then answer the question about the article.

Look Into the Text

Pushing the Limits

   The program began in 1991 as a collaboration between Susan Rodgerson—a white, middle-class artist—and five African American teen friends who started painting in her studio. The friends needed to sell their artwork in order to buy supplies and make more art. Sheer economics inspired an entrepreneurial zeal, and they approached Boston colleges, nonprofits, and corporations as potential customers. An audience was found and a program bloomed—with youth at the helm.

5Ws Chart

Who?	What?	Where?	When?	Why?
Susan Rodgerson and five African American teen friends				

B. Why do you think the author wrote the article?

_____

_____

_____

FOCUS STRATEGY: Identify Main Ideas and Details

> ## HOW TO IDENTIFY MAIN IDEAS AND DETAILS
>
> Focus Strategy
>
> **1. Find the Important Details** Find information that tells *who, what, where, when,* and *why.*
>
> **2. State the Main Idea** What is the most important idea of the paragraph? Restate it in your own words.

A. Read the passage. Highlight the most important words, phrases, or sentences. Then answer the 5W questions.

> **Look Into the Text**
>
> Last year, a large Boston bank commissioned a large-scale painting of modern Boston. It was based on Paul Gauguin's signature masterpiece, *Where Do We Come From? What Are We? Where Are We Going?* After hanging alongside the colorful Gauguin original in the Museum of Fine Arts, this painting now greets travelers at Logan Airport, where it is on permanent display.

1. Who? _a large Boston bank_

2. What? _____

3. Where? _____

4. When? _____

5. Why? _____

B. Write the main idea of the paragraph in your own words.

Main Idea: _____

_____

_____

_____

 Does Creativity Matter?
Consider ways to express your creativity.

A. In "Creativity at Work," you learned how students express their creativity. Write four important benefits of Artists for Humanity, using the web below.

Details Web

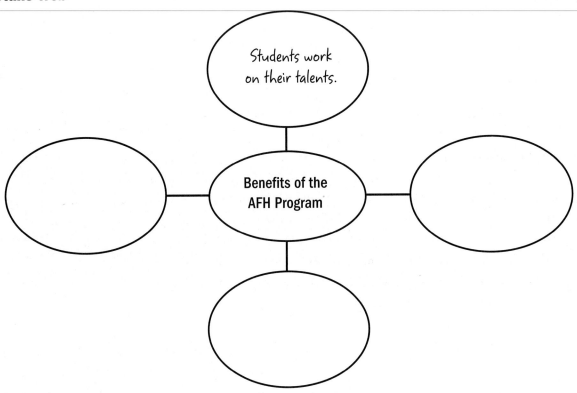

Students work on their talents.

Benefits of the AFH Program

B. Use the information in the web to answer the questions.

1. Why is AFH so important to people in Boston?

_____

_____

2. How do the students in this program collaborate to enhance their creativity? Use **collaborate** in your answer.

_____

_____

3. How might a program like this benefit your community?

_____

_____

_____

The Hidden SECRETS of the Creative Mind

by Francine Russo

Connect Across Texts

"Creativity at Work" describes teens who use their creativity to begin careers in art. In this interview, a psychologist tells artists, inventors—and all of us—how to make the most of our creativity.

What is creativity? Where does it come from? The workings of the creative mind have been studied over the past twenty-five years by an army of researchers. But no one has a better **overview** of this mysterious mental process than Washington University psychologist R. Keith Sawyer. In an interview with journalist Francine Russo, he suggests ways in which we can **enhance** our creativity, not just in art and science, but in everyday life.

Q: Has new research changed any of our popular ideas about creativity?

A: **Virtually** all of them. Many people believe creativity comes in a sudden moment of **insight** and that this "magical" burst of an idea is different from our everyday thinking. But research has shown that when you're creative, your brain is using the same **mental building blocks** you use every day—like when you figure out a way around a traffic jam.

Q: Then how do you explain the "aha!" moment we've all had in the shower or the gym—or anywhere but at work?

A: In creativity research, we refer to the three Bs—for the bathtub, the bed, and the bus. They are places where ideas have famously and suddenly emerged. When we take time off from working on a problem, we change what we're doing and **our context**. That can

Interact with the Text

1. Main Ideas and Details
Underline the sentence that tells what this article will be mostly about. Write the main idea of the article in your own words.

2. Interpret
Why do you think the writer chose Sawyer to interview? Does he seem credible?

Key Vocabulary
● **insight** *n.*, understanding

In Other Words
overview understanding
enhance improve
Virtually Almost
mental building blocks ways of thinking
our context where and how we are doing it

3. Development of Ideas

How does the author respond to Sawyer's explanation about the "aha" moment? Is this effective? Explain.

4. Main Idea and Details

What idea does the author want the reader to learn from this graphic? Circle the sentence that answers this question. Then explain how you can apply this concept to your own life.

---

activate different areas of our brain. If the answer wasn't in the part of the brain we were using, it might be in another. If we're lucky, in the next context we may hear or see something that relates to the problem that we had temporarily put aside.

Q: Can you give us an example of that?

A: In 1990 a team of NASA scientists was trying to fix the lenses in the Hubble telescope, while it was already in orbit. An expert suggested that tiny mirrors could correct the images, but nobody could figure out how to fit them into the hard-to-reach space inside. Then

THE BRAIN: Use It or Lose It

There are two hemispheres, or sides, in the human brain. Both sides work together, although certain **mind functions** are only controlled by one hemisphere.

Take note: What we do during our teenage years may affect how our brains develop. If a skill is not used, the part of the brain needed for that skill dies.

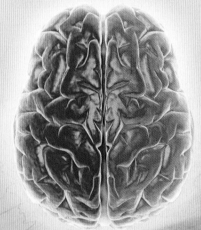

Left Brain Functions

Language and Reading

Math and Science

Reasoning

Right-Hand Control

Right Brain Functions

Insight

Art and Music

Imagination

Left-Hand Control

⚠ **Interpret the Diagram** How does the diagram help you understand how the brain functions?

In Other Words
activate turn on
mind functions jobs done by the brain

engineer Jim Crocker, taking a shower in a German hotel, noticed the European-style showerhead on **adjustable rods**. He realized the Hubble's little mirrors could be **mounted onto** similar folding arms. And this **flash** was the key to fixing the problem.

Q: How have researchers studied this creative flash?

A: Some psychologists set up video cameras to watch creative people work, asking them to describe their thought processes out loud or interrupting them frequently to ask how close they were to a solution. In other experiments, subjects worked on problems that, when solved, tend to result in the sensation of sudden insight. In one experiment, they were asked to look at words that came up one at a time on a computer screen and to think of the one word that was associated with all of them. After each word they had to give their best guess. Although many swore they had no idea until a sudden burst of insight at about the twelfth word, their guesses got closer to the solution. Even when an idea seems sudden, our minds have actually been working on it all along.

Q: Are there other generalizations you can make about creative people?

A: Yes. They have tons of ideas, many of them bad. The trick is to **evaluate** them and **purge** the bad ones. But even bad ideas can be useful. Sometimes you don't know which sparks are important until later. But the more ideas you have, the better.

Q: So how can the average person get more ideas?

A: Ideas don't magically appear from nowhere. They always build on what came before. And collaboration is key. Look at what others are doing. Brainstorm with different people. Research and evidence suggest that this leads to new ideas.

Interact with the Text

5. Main Idea and Details
Highlight the most important idea in the answer to the first question on this page. Underline the detail that supports it. In your own words, write a sentence that tells how scientists explain the creative flash.

6. Development of Ideas
Why does the interviewer ask how the average person could get more ideas? Circle Sawyer's advice. Is the writer's question effective?

Key Vocabulary
● **evaluate** *v.*, to decide how good or valuable something is

In Other Words
adjustable rods metal bars that can move back and forth
mounted onto placed on
flash idea, understanding
purge get rid of

7. Main Idea and Details
Summarize Sawyer's advice about how to encourage your own creativity. Do you agree? Why or why not?

Q: What advice can you give us nongeniuses to help us be more creative?

A: Take risks, and expect to make lots of mistakes. Work hard, and take frequent breaks, but stay with it over time. Do what you love, because creative breakthroughs take years of hard work. Develop a **network of colleagues**, and schedule time for free, unstructured discussions. Most of all, forget those romantic myths that creativity is all about being artsy and gifted and not about hard work. They **discourage** us because we're waiting for that one full-blown moment of inspiration. And while we're waiting, we may never start working on what we might someday create. ❖

In Other Words
network of colleagues group of people who are interested in working on the same things
discourage take hope away from

Selection Review The Hidden Secrets of the Creative Mind

A. Write three details from the article that best support how people develop creative thinking skills.

Detail 1: _____

Detail 2: _____

Detail 3: _____

B. Answer the questions.

1. How did the author help you understand the interview?

_____

2. Which main idea from the article did you find difficult to understand? Which detail made it clearer for you?

_____

WRITING: Write About Literature

A. Plan your writing. Read what you wrote in the Anticipation Guide on page 118 of your student text. Choose one of the statements. List ideas from each text that confirm or change the opinions you made in the chart below.

Creativity at Work	Hidden Secrets

B. What are your thoughts and feelings about creativity now that you have read both selections? Write an opinion paragraph responding to one of the statements from the chart. Support your opinion with information from both texts and your own experiences.

_____

_____

_____

_____

_____

_____

LITERARY ANALYSIS: Analyze Description

Description is the way writers use words to help readers create pictures in their minds. Description is used in both fiction and nonfiction.

A. Choose descriptions from "Creativity at Work" and write them below. Then write what the description helped you picture.

Description	What You Picture
"high-contrast, hyper-realistic paintings"	the colors and types of paintings

B. Rewrite these sentences using words that appeal to the five senses.

1. The spaghetti was good.

   The spaghetti had a delicious sauce made out of sweet, ripe tomatoes and spicy basil.

2. The flower was pretty.

   _____

3. The house is small.

   _____

4. The boy was tired.

   _____

C. Write a paragraph describing how cats and dogs are different. Be sure to use words that appeal to the reader's five senses.

   _____
   _____
   _____
   _____
   _____
   _____

VOCABULARY STUDY: Context Clues

Context clues are words and phrases in the text that can help you figure out the meaning of an unfamiliar word. Context clues include definitions or examples.

A. Read the sentences below, and underline the context clues that you can use to figure out the meaning of the underlined word.

1. Half of the profit, or money made on the project, is given back to the organization.

2. The student's dedication, or commitment, is very strong.

3. Many people believe creativity comes in a sudden moment of insight and that this "magical" burst of an idea is different from our everyday thinking.

4. We ask market value. We don't give it away or devalue the work. We charge a fair dollar.

B. Write what each word means by using the context clues you underlined above.

Word	What It Means
dedication	
insight	
market value	
profit	

C. Write a sentence for each of the words from the chart above.

1. _____

_____

2. _____

_____

3. _____

_____

4. _____

_____

Prepare to Read

▷ **Hip-Hop as Culture**
▷ **I Am Somebody**

Key Vocabulary

A. How well do you know these words? Circle a rating for each word. Check your understanding of each word by circling *yes* or *no*. Then, write a definition in your own words. If you are unsure of a word's meaning, refer to the Vocabulary Glossary, page 878, in your student text.

Rating Scale	
1	I have never seen this word before.
2	I am not sure of the word's meaning.
3	I know this word and can teach the word's meaning to someone else.

Key Word	Check Your Understanding	Deepen Your Understanding
❶ achieve (u-**chēv**) *verb* **Rating:** **1 2 3**	Athletes train to **achieve** physical excellence. **Yes No**	My definition: _____ _____ _____ _____ _____ .
❷ assert (u-**surt**) *verb* **Rating:** **1 2 3**	Many people who call in to radio talk shows do so to **assert** their opinions. **Yes No**	My definition: _____ _____ _____ _____ _____ .
❸ culture (**kul**-chur) *noun* **Rating:** **1 2 3**	People can share their **culture** with others by explaining their customs and beliefs. **Yes No**	My definition: _____ _____ _____ _____ _____ .
❹ evolve (ē-**valv**) *verb* **Rating:** **1 2 3**	Clothing styles and trends rarely **evolve** over time. **Yes No**	My definition: _____ _____ _____ _____ _____ .

Key Word	Check Your Understanding	Deepen Your Understanding
5 **heritage** (**her**-u-tij) *noun* **Rating:** 1 2 3	Your **heritage** never affects how others treat you. **Yes** **No**	My definition: _____ _____ _____ _____ _____.
6 **innovator** (in-nu-**vā**-tur) *noun* **Rating:** 1 2 3	A clothing designer strives to be an **innovator** of fashion. **Yes** **No**	My definition: _____ _____ _____ _____ _____.
7 **perspective** (pur-**spek**-tiv) *noun* **Rating:** 1 2 3	A writer can use charts and graphs to help explain his or her **perspective** on an issue. **Yes** **No**	My definition: _____ _____ _____ _____ _____.
8 **self-esteem** (**self** es-**tēm**) *noun* **Rating:** 1 2 3	Failure increases people's **self-esteem**. **Yes** **No**	My definition: _____ _____ _____ _____ _____.

B. Use one of the Key Vocabulary words to write about how music affects your life.

_____

_____

Before Reading Hip-Hop as Culture

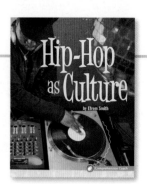

LITERARY ANALYSIS: Analyze Author's Purpose

In an essay, the **author's purpose** can be to entertain, inform, persuade, and/or share opinions and ideas about a subject.

A. Read the passage below. Find details that show the author's purpose. Write the details in the chart.

Look Into the Text

Hip-hop has taken over the music industry in the same way the Williams sisters have taken over tennis. Look at the way the National Basketball Association uses hip-hop players like Shaquille O'Neal and Allen Iverson—and hip-hop culture in general—to sell soda, candy, and clothes to young people. To see hip-hop as simply rap is to not understand the impact and influence of a greater movement.

Rap music is just one element of hip-hop. In fact, true hip-hop heads understand that hip-hop isn't just about music. It's a culture, a way of life, a language, a fashion, a set of values, and a unique perspective.

To Entertain	To Inform	To Share Opinions and Ideas
The author mentions celebrities like Shaquille O'Neal, Allen Iverson, and the Williams sisters.		

B. Complete the sentence about the author's purpose.

I think the author chose to write about hip-hop because _____

_____

_____

FOCUS STRATEGY: Summarize Nonfiction

HOW TO SUMMARIZE NONFICTION

Focus Strategy

1. **Identify the Topic** Repeated words and ideas often point to the main topic.

2. **Read Carefully** Picture what the author is describing.

3. **Summarize Each Section** Pause when you finish each section. List important details and main ideas.

4. **Think Beyond the Text** After reading, ask what you have learned and how your thinking has changed.

A. Read the passage. Use the strategies above to summarize the section. List three important details. Then, write the main idea.

Look Into the Text

Hip-hop tells the stories of the multiethnic urban youth and the communities they live in. Hip-hop is about inner-city and lower-class life. It's about trying to live out the American dream from the bottom up. It's about trying to make something out of nothing. Hip-hop is about the youth culture of New York City taking over the world. Hip-hop is about dance, art, expression, pain, love, racism, sexism, broken families, hard times, overcoming adversity, and even the search for God.

Detail 1: _____

_____

Detail 2: _____

_____

Detail 3: _____

_____

Main Idea: _____

_____

B. Return to the passage above. Underline which details changed your thinking or taught you something new about hip-hop.

Selection Review Hip-Hop as Culture

 Does Creativity Matter?
Explore the effect of music on our lives.

A. In "Hip-Hop as Culture," you found out that hip-hop is a way of life that influences many people in many ways. Complete the T Chart below.

T Chart

What Hip-Hop Is	What Hip-Hop Influences

B. Use the information in the chart to answer the questions.

1. Why is hip-hop important to youth culture?

_____

_____

2. How has hip-hop influenced American culture? Use **culture** in your answer.

_____

_____

3. What other types of "cultures" have led to changes in our society? Explain.

_____

_____

_____

_____

I AM SOMEBODY

BY GRANDMASTER FLASH

Connect Across Texts

In "Hip-Hop as Culture," Efrem Smith says that hip-hop tells the stories of "youth and the communities they live in." The following song lyrics describe how a legendary hip-hop artist feels about his own community.

Hey people
We got a little something that we wanna tell you all,
   so listen, understand
Yo, God made one no better than the other
Every girl becomes a woman, every boy a man

5   While you're livin' in your mansion, drivin' big cars
There's another on the street, cold sleepin' on the ground
And when you walk by, yo, don't act cold-blooded
'Cause it just ain't fair to kick a man when he's down

    'Cause he is somebody (Say it loud)
10   **Like I am somebody**
    You are somebody
    Like I am someone (Say it loud)

In Other Words

mansion big, expensive house
cold-blooded in a rude, heartless way
kick a man when he's down treat a man badly
   when he is already hurting

Interact with the Text

1. Structure
Describe how the lyrics are like a poem.

_____

_____

_____

_____

_____

2. Summarize Lyrics
Circle the words and phrases that are repeated in the chorus. What is the main idea these words suggest?

_____

_____

_____

_____

_____

_____

_____

3. Summarize Lyrics
Write the main idea of
lines 17–20 in your own
words. Circle the words and
phrases that helped you
determine the main idea.

Whether you're here or you're gone, you're right or you're wrong
You were meant to be somebody from the second you were born
15 Don't criticize and knock one another
It ain't really that hard to just be a brother

So be good, speak up, don't wait for it to happen
Life is passing you by, and homeboy, you're cold nappin'
Don't be gettin' hung up on what you're not
20 Be proud of what you are and whatever you got

'Cause it's a cold, cruel world causing kids to cry
If you're hangin' your head, cold kiss it goodbye
Stand up for your heritage, rejoice in the fact
Whether you're red, white, tan, yellow, brown, or black

25 **'Cause you are somebody (Say it loud)**
Like I am somebody
He is somebody
Like I am someone (Say it loud)

There are firemen, bankers, messengers, preachers
30 Brokers, policemen, executives, teachers,
Journalists, janitors, architects, doctors,
Restaurant workers, nurses, chief rockers

Key Vocabulary
  heritage *n.*, background, race, or
    ethnic group you belong to

In Other Words
criticize talk badly about
cold nappin' wasting your time
Don't be gettin' hung up on Don't worry about
rejoice in be happy about
Brokers People who trade stocks
Journalists News writers and reporters

If you feel you're somebody, be proud, and show it

'Cause everybody's somebody, (ugh) and ya know it

35 It doesn't matter if you're black, white, or Chinese

Livin' in the States or reside overseas

'Cause you and I are special, same as everyone else

If you don't believe me, you're only cheating yourself

We all got a purpose in life to achieve

40 That's a fact, and here's another that you better believe

That I am somebody (Say it loud)

Like you are somebody

He is somebody

Like I am someone (Say it loud)

45 You got wealth, good health, and you're stuck on yourself

Well let me tell you that you're better than nobody else

'Cause you got no self-esteem, so I'm richer

And when you leave this earth, you can't take money witcha

So play your dumb game, call me out my name,

50 But nothing you can do could make me feel shame

We're all created equal, we live and we die

So when you try to bring me down, I keep my head up high

4. Summarize Lyrics

Circle the words in lines 33–36 that also appear in the chorus. What does this repetition suggest?

_____

_____

_____

_____

_____

5. Structure

Underline the rhyming words in lines 49–52. Write a 5th line for this verse that rhymes with the last line.

_____

_____

_____

_____

_____

_____

6. Summarize Lyrics

Write the main idea of lines 49–52 in your own words.

_____

_____

_____

_____

_____

Key Vocabulary

• **achieve** *v.*, to succeed or do well

self-esteem *n.*, feeling that you are valuable, confidence in yourself

In Other Words

reside overseas living in another country

stuck on yourself too proud of yourself

call me out my name speak rudely about me

7. Interpret

Highlight the advice the songwriter gives in the first verse on this page. Write in your own words what these song lyrics mean to you.

_____

_____

_____

_____

_____

_____

_____

Don't judge a book by its cover

'Cause it's never what it seems

55   Now I know what I'm sayin',

And I feel I gotta scream

That I am somebody (Say it loud)

Like you are somebody

He is somebody

60   Like I am someone

So be yourself, HUH! ❖

Selection Review I Am Somebody

A. Return to the text, and reread the main ideas you wrote in your answers to questions 2, 3, and 6. Based on these three main ideas, how would you summarize the message of this song?

_____

_____

B. Answer the questions.

1. How did knowing that song lyrics are like poems help you as you read?

_____

_____

2. Imagine you are the songwriter and want to write an additional verse. Who would you write it to? What message would it have?

_____

_____

_____

_____

Reflect and Assess

WRITING: Write About Literature

A. Plan your writing. In the Venn Diagram, list the important ideas from each selection. Then write one important idea that fits both selections in the center.

Venn Diagram

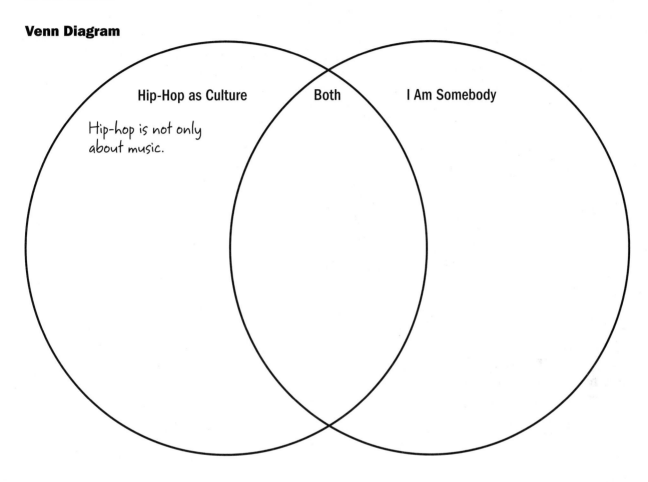

Hip-Hop as Culture

Hip-hop is not only about music.

Both

I Am Somebody

B. Write your own song lyrics. Create a four-line verse that expresses the main idea found in both selections.

_____

_____

_____

_____

_____

_____

_____

_____

_____

LITERARY ANALYSIS: Analyze Style and Word Choice

Word choice is the kind of language a writer uses. It is an important part of a writer's **style**, or particular way of writing. Word choice often changes based on a writer's audience.

A. List examples of word choice and style from each selection

Hip-Hop as Culture	I Am Somebody

B. Explain why the author of each selection may have chosen the style that was used.

1. "Hip-Hop as Culture"

_____

_____

_____

2. "I Am Somebody"

_____

_____

_____

C. The author of "Hip-Hop as Culture" uses a formal style with several examples of slang. How effective was his style in getting his message across?

_____

_____

_____

_____

VOCABULARY STUDY: Context Clues for Idioms

Idioms are expressions that mean something different from the literal, or exact, meaning of their words. **Context clues** can help you figure out the meaning of an idiom.

A. Read the song lyric below. Underline the common idioms in the passage. (Hint: There are five.)

> So be good, speak up, don't wait for it to happen
> Life is passing you by, and homeboy, you're cold nappin'
> Don't be gettin' hung up on what you're not
> Be proud of what you are and whatever you got

B. Write the meaning of three of the idioms below. Use a resource to help you figure out the meaning, if needed.

1. _____

2. _____

3. _____

C. Read the sentences that contain common idioms. Use the context of each sentence to figure out the meaning. Rewrite the sentence to show the idiom's real meaning.

1. The man's son is a chip off the old block.

_____

_____

2. I'm very tired, so I think I will hit the hay.

_____

_____

3. I'm undecided about going out tonight, so let's play it by ear.

_____

_____

4. I wanted to throw a surprise party for my friend, but my sister let the cat out of the bag.

_____

_____

5. The teacher wanted the children to sit down, so she told them to take their seats.

_____

_____

Prepare to Read

▶ **Slam: Performance Poetry Lives On**
▶ **Euphoria**

Key Vocabulary

A. How well do you know these words? Circle a rating for each word. Check your understanding of each word by marking an *X* next to the correct definition. Then, complete the sentences. If you are unsure of a word's meaning, refer to the Vocabulary Glossary, page 878, in your student text.

Rating Scale	
1	I have never seen this word before.
2	I am not sure of the word's meaning.
3	I know this word and can teach the word's meaning to someone else.

Key Word	Check Your Understanding	Deepen Your Understanding
❶ compose (kum-**pōz**) *verb* **Rating:** **1 2 3**	☐ to create something ☐ to read something thoroughly	I like to compose _____ _____ _____ _____ .
❷ euphoria (ū-**for**-ē-u) *noun* **Rating:** **1 2 3**	☐ extreme happiness ☐ a very loud noise	I was filled with euphoria when I _____ _____ _____ _____ .
❸ expression (eks-**pre**-shun) *noun* **Rating:** **1 2 3**	☐ the act of compromising ☐ the act of communicating	One type of creative expression that is important to me is _____ _____ _____ .
❹ improvisation (im-prah-vu-**zā**-shun) *noun* **Rating:** **1 2 3**	☐ acting without a plan ☐ speaking with notes	I used improvisation when I _____ _____ _____ _____ .

Key Word	Check Your Understanding	Deepen Your Understanding
5 phenomenon (fi-**nahm**-u-nahn) *noun* **Rating:** **1 2 3**	☐ a unique situation or occurrence ☐ an ordinary situation or occurrence	A current phenomenon in technology is _____ _____ _____ _____ _____ .
6 recitation (re-su-**tā**-shun) *noun* **Rating:** **1 2 3**	☐ a private thought ☐ a public reading	I would like to hear a recitation of _____ _____ _____ _____ _____ .
7 structure (**struk**-chur) *noun* **Rating:** **1 2 3**	☐ the way something is organized ☐ the way something looks	I like structure when I _____ _____ _____ _____ .
8 transcend (tran-**send**) *verb* **Rating:** **1 2 3**	☐ to rise above something ☐ to sink below something	In my dreams, I transcend my limits when I _____ _____ _____ _____ .

B. Use one of the Key Vocabulary words to write about a time when you were proud of something you created.

_____

_____

Before Reading Slam: Performance Poetry Lives On

LITERARY ANALYSIS: Analyze Author's Purpose

An **essay** is a short nonfiction piece on a single topic that informs, persuades, or entertains. When you read an essay, think about the author's purpose for writing.

A. Read the passage below. Look for clues in the passage that tell you what the author thinks about poetry and poetry slams. Then list the clues in the Idea Web.

Look Into the Text

Poetry doesn't have to be the twelve lines on a page in a book that is sitting in the dustiest corner of the library. Poetry doesn't have to be something you don't understand. Poetry is moving, breathing, ever changing.

Want proof? Take a trip to the Urban Word Annual Teen Poetry Slam at the Nuyorican Poets Cafe in New York City.

Gathered in this tight space are hundreds of teens from every corner of the city. They've come together to compete for one of five top spots in Brave New Voices, the Eighth Annual National Youth Poetry Slam Festival.

Idea Web

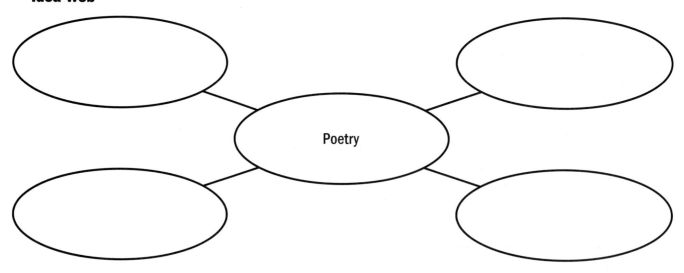

B. Use the information in the web to complete the sentence about the author's purpose.

The author wrote this essay about poetry slams because _____

_____.

FOCUS STRATEGY: Determine Importance

HOW TO DETERMINE IMPORTANCE

1. **Read Carefully** Identify the main idea of the section and how each detail supports that main idea.

2. **Record Your Ideas** In a Response Journal, record details from the text and tell how they support the main idea.

3. **Summarize the Important Ideas** Retell the most important ideas in your own words.

Read the passage. Record important ideas and details in the Response Journal below. Use the strategies above to determine what's important and why.

Look Into the Text

"A poetry slam is like a lyrical boxing match that pits poets against other poets in a bout," according to journalist Shilanda L. Woolridge. In simpler words, a slam is a competition in which poets perform original works alone or in teams. They recite their poems for an audience that boos and cheers as it votes on the best performers. Each poet's work is judged as much on the manner of its performance as on its content or style.

Details	Importance
A slam is like a lyrical boxing match.	The author includes this to show that poetry slams are exciting.

B. Summarize the most important idea of the passage in your own words.

_____

_____

Selection Review Slam: Performance Poetry Lives On

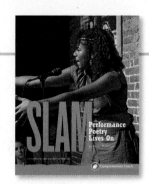

 Does Creativity Matter?
Discover one way to find your voice.

A. In "Slam: Performance Poetry Lives On," you found out how slam poetry encourages creativity and self-expression. Complete the Main-Idea Diagram.

Main-Idea Diagram

> **Main Idea:**
>
> Slam poetry helps teens and young adults express their creativity.

> **Detail:**

> **Detail:**

> **Detail:**

B. Use the information in the Main-Idea Diagram to answer the questions.

1. How does slam poetry encourage people to be creative?

   _____

   _____

2. Why is slam poetry such a popular form of expression with teens and young adults? Use **expression** in your answer.

   _____

   _____

3. Why is it important for teens to have a way to express their creativity?

   _____

   _____

Connect Across Texts

The article "Slam: Performance Poetry Lives On" describes how performance poetry has become a modern creative art. How does the author of the following slam poem show the ways that creativity matters to her?

Euphoria
by Lauren Brown

today I'm filled with such a feeling of greatness and immortality
I must sit on my hands to control them from dancing
I find blinking a hazard
it takes too much time and leaves me in the darkness
5   when I could be seeing and living the manic colors
everything in me is magnified and exposed
but no one seems to notice
the air caresses my flesh
and my heart beats faster
10   and my pulse pulses with the concrete rhythm of the song
permanently playing

in my mind
I want to write everything I have ever felt before in my whole existence and

15   paste them on
the walls
I want to dance with such balance and magnificence
that the whole world will want to dance too

Interact with the Text

1. Structure
Free verse poems have a loose structure. Give three examples of the loose structure in this poem.

2. Determine Importance
What is the main idea of the poem? Underline an important phrase and explain how it supports the main idea.

Key Vocabulary
euphoria *n.*, great joy and happiness
● **structure** *n.*, the way something is set up, organization

In Other Words
immortality the ability to live forever
hazard danger
manic wild, excited
magnified and exposed made bigger and visible for everyone to see
caresses softly touches

3. Interpret

A simile uses the words *like* or *as* to compare two things. Highlight the simile in lines 25–27. What is the simile comparing? What do you think the poet means?

I want to sing like the angels
20 to part my lips and have the loveliness of my song drip out of the corners of

my mouth
and to echo into everyone's ears and have a piece of my song glued into their minds
25 I want to be able to use my hands in ways I never have before
and to feel other people's emotions like sandpaper on my tongue . . .
. . . maybe I will

Key Vocabulary
expression *n.*, creative communication

In Other Words
sandpaper rough paper used to make wood smooth

Selection Review Euphoria

A. Reread the poem, and choose an important detail or image. Complete the sentences.

The speaker says _____

This detail is important because _____

B. Answer the questions.

1. How does the free form of this poem help you understand the poet's feelings?

_____

_____

2. How does the poet want to express her feelings and ideas? List one example from the poem.

_____

_____

Reflect and Assess

WRITING: Write About Literature

A. Plan your writing. List words and phrases from each text that would make people interested in attending or participating in a poetry slam.

Slam: Performance Poetry Lives On	Euphoria

B. Imagine you are holding a poetry slam at your school. Create a flyer to advertise the event. Use phrases from both texts for ideas.

Integrate the Language Arts

LITERARY ANALYSIS: Literary Movements: Poetry Across Cultures

Poetry, like many other forms of literature, changes across different times and cultures. A category of poetry, such as slam poetry, has many different roots.

A. There are many roots of slam poetry. Reread "Slam: Performance Poetry Lives On" to find the roots and list them in the Details Web.

Details Web

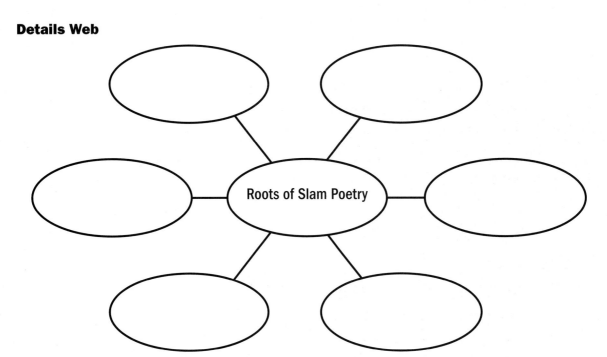

Roots of Slam Poetry

B. Which forms of poetry that you listed above seem similar? Write a description of how you think slam came to be.

_____

_____

_____

_____

C. What form of poetry do you find the most interesting? Write a short paragraph explaining why.

_____

_____

_____

_____

_____

_____

VOCABULARY STUDY: Context Clues for Idioms

The context in which an **idiomatic expression**, or idiom, appears can help you figure out what it means.

A. Read the idiomatic expressions. Find the context, and then write what you think each idiom means.

Idiomatic Expression	What I Think It Means
His eyes are bigger than his stomach when he is hungry.	
You should count your blessings because other people have much less than you.	
Cut it out, or I will make you stop.	

B. Read the sentences that include idiomatic expressions. Underline each idiom, then circle the context clues that give you the idiom's meaning.

1. My mom wanted us to stop, so she told us to hold our horses.

2. I wanted to wish the actor good luck, so I told him he should break a leg.

3. My identical twin looks so much like me that he's a dead ringer.

C. Write a paragraph describing a recent event you have attended. Use at least two idiomatic expressions in your writing.

_____

_____

_____

_____

_____

_____

_____

_____

Read for Understanding

1. Genre What kind of text is this passage? How do you know?

2. Topic Write a topic sentence to tell what the text is mostly about.

Reread and Summarize

3. Word Choice In each section, circle three words or phrases that express the big ideas in that section. Note next to each word or phrase why you chose it.

· Section 1: paragraphs 1–6
· Section 2: paragraphs 7–13

4. Summary Use your topic sentence and notes from item 3 to write a summary of the selection.

from
THE CREATIVITY CRISIS

BY
PO BRONSON
AND ASHLEY
MERRYMAN

1 Back in 1958, Ted Schwarzrock was an 8-year-old third grader when he became one of the "Torrance kids," a group of nearly 400 Minneapolis children who completed a series of creativity tasks newly designed by professor E. Paul Torrance. Schwarzrock still vividly remembers the moment when a **psychologist** handed him a fire truck and asked, "How could you improve this toy to make it better and more fun to play with?" He recalls the psychologist being excited by his answers. In fact, the psychologist's session notes indicate Schwarzrock rattled off 25 improvements, such as adding a removable ladder and springs to the wheels. That wasn't the only time he impressed the scholars, who judged Schwarzrock to have "unusual visual perspective" and "an ability to synthesize diverse elements into meaningful products."

2 The accepted definition of creativity is production of something original and useful, and that's what's reflected in the tests. There is never one right answer. To be creative requires divergent thinking (generating many unique ideas) and then convergent thinking (combining those ideas into the best result).

In Other Words
psychologist doctor who studies the mind

3   Nobody would argue that Torrance's tasks, which have become **the gold standard** in creativity assessment, measure creativity perfectly. What's shocking is how incredibly well Torrance's creativity index predicted those kids' creative accomplishments as adults. Those who came up with more good ideas on Torrance's tasks grew up to be **entrepreneurs**, inventors, college presidents, authors, doctors, diplomats, and software developers. The **correlation** to lifetime creative accomplishment was more than three times stronger for childhood creativity than childhood **IQ**.

4   Like intelligence tests, Torrance's test—a 90-minute series of discrete tasks, administered by a psychologist—has been taken by millions worldwide in 50 languages. Yet there is one crucial difference between IQ and CQ scores. With intelligence, there is a **phenomenon** called the Flynn effect—each generation, scores go up about 10 points. Enriched environments are making kids smarter. With creativity, a reverse trend has just been identified and is being reported for the first time here: American creativity scores are falling.

5   The potential consequences are sweeping. The necessity of human ingenuity is undisputed. A recent IBM poll of 1,500 CEOs identified creativity as the No. 1 "leadership competency" of the future. Yet it's not just about sustaining our nation's economic growth. All around us are matters of national and international importance that are crying out for creative solutions. Such solutions emerge from a healthy marketplace of ideas, sustained by a populace constantly contributing original ideas and receptive to the ideas of others.

American creativity scores are falling.

6   To understand exactly what should be done requires first understanding the new story emerging from **neuroscience**. The lore of pop psychology is that creativity occurs on the right side of the brain. But we now know that if you tried to be creative using only the right side of your brain, it'd be like living with ideas perpetually at the tip of your tongue, just beyond reach.

7   When you try to solve a problem, you begin by concentrating on obvious facts and familiar solutions, to see if the answer lies there. This is a mostly left-brain stage of attack. If the answer doesn't come, the right and left hemispheres of the brain activate together. **Neural networks** on the right side scan remote memories that could be vaguely relevant. A wide range of

Key Vocabulary
• **phenomenon** *n.*, something different that people get really excited about

In Other Words
the gold standard in known as the best
entrepreneurs creative business people
correlation connection
IQ intelligence
neuroscience the science of the brain
Neural networks Nerve connections

5. Authors' Purpose
Why did the authors write this text?

What clues in the text support your answer?

6. Author's Purpose
Highlight a fact in paragraph 4. Explain how it supports the authors' purpose.

7. Authors' Purpose
Reread paragraph 5. Underline another fact and explain how it supports the authors' purpose.

8. Details Reread paragraph 7 and think about the process of solving a problem. Underline the first two steps that the authors describe.

9. Details Reread paragraph 8 and underline the next two steps of the process.

10. Author's Purpose How does the information in paragraphs 7 and 8 support the authors' purpose?

_____

_____

_____

_____

_____

_____

_____

_____

_____

_____

_____

_____

_____

distant information that is normally **tuned out** becomes available to the left hemisphere, which searches for unseen patterns, alternative meanings, and **high-level abstractions**.

8   Having glimpsed such a connection, the left brain must quickly lock in on it before it escapes. The attention system must radically reverse gears, going from defocused attention to extremely focused attention. In a flash, the brain pulls together these **disparate shreds of thought** and binds them into a new single idea that enters consciousness. This is the "aha!" moment of **insight**, often followed by a spark of pleasure as the brain recognizes the **novelty** of what it's come up with.

9   Is this learnable? Well, think of it like basketball. Being tall does help to be a pro basketball player, but the rest of us can still get quite good at the sport through practice. In the same way, there are certain innate features of the brain that make some people naturally prone to divergent thinking. But convergent thinking and focused attention are necessary, too, and those require different neural gifts. Crucially, rapidly shifting between these modes is a top-down

> This is the "aha!" moment of insight...

function under your mental control. University of New Mexico neuroscientist Rex Jung has concluded that those who diligently practice creative activities learn to recruit their brains' creative networks quicker and better. A lifetime of consistent habits gradually changes the neurological pattern.

10   In early childhood, distinct types of free play are associated with high creativity. Preschoolers who spend more time in role-play (acting out characters) have higher measures of creativity: voicing someone else's point of view helps develop their ability to analyze situations from different **perspectives**. When playing alone, highly creative first graders may act out strong negative emotions: they'll be angry, hostile, anguished. **The hypothesis is** that play is a safe harbor to work through forbidden thoughts and emotions.

11   In middle childhood, kids sometimes create paracosms—fantasies of entire alternative worlds.

▶ **Critical Viewing: Theme** What comparison does the artist make here? What message does that send?

Iker Ayestaran.

Key Vocabulary
● **insight** *n.*, understanding
● **perspective** *n.*, point of view

In Other Words
tuned out ignored
high-level abstractions complicated ideas
disparate shreds of thoughts separate ideas
novelty creative newness
The hypothesis is This may mean

Left and right brain functions. Vector illustration, Doggygraph(alias)/Shutterstock.com.

Kids revisit their paracosms repeatedly, sometimes for months, and even create languages spoken there. This type of play peaks at age 9 or 10, and it's a very strong sign of future creativity. A Michigan State University study of MacArthur "genius award" winners found a remarkably high rate of paracosm creation in their childhoods.

12   From fourth grade on, creativity no longer occurs **in a vacuum**; researching and studying become an integral part of coming up with useful solutions. But this transition isn't easy. As school stuffs more complex information into their heads, kids get overloaded, and creativity suffers. When creative children have a supportive teacher—someone **tolerant of unconventional** answers, occasional disruptions, or detours of curiosity— they tend to **excel**. When they don't, they tend to underperform and drop out of high school or don't finish college at high rates.

13   Creativity has always been prized in American society, but it's never really been understood. While our creativity scores **decline unchecked**, the current national strategy for creativity consists of little more than praying for a Greek muse to drop by our houses. The problems we face now, and in the future, simply demand that we do more than just hope for inspiration to strike. Fortunately, the science can help: we know the steps to lead that **elusive muse** right to our doors. ❖

In Other Words

in a vacuum only when playing
tolerant of unconventional who likes unusual
excel succeed, do very well
decline unchecked keep going down
elusive muse difficult to find source of
  creativity

11. Word Choice
Reread paragraph 10 and highlight a definition that the authors set off with punctuation. How does this definition support the authors' purpose?

_____

_____

_____

_____

_____

_____

_____

_____

_____

_____

12. Word Choice Highlight another definition in paragraph 11. Explain why the authors include this definition.

_____

_____

_____

_____

_____

_____

_____

_____

_____

_____

_____

Discuss

13. **Synthesize** With the class, list three important facts from "The Creativity Crisis." Discuss how this information incudes details like who, what, where, why, and when. Take notes.

_____

_____

_____

_____

_____

_____

14. **Write** Use your notes from question 13 to write a paragraph about the authors' purpose for writing "The Creativity Crisis." Use the questions below to organize your thoughts.

   A. What is the authors' main purpose for writing "The Creativity Crisis"?

   B. What do the authors include in the selection to meet this purpose?

   C. How do the authors use definitions in the selection?

   D. Do the authors successfully meet their purpose for writing? Explain.

   _____

   _____

   _____

   _____

   _____

   _____

   _____

Does Creativity Matter?
Investigate where creativity comes from.

15. **Viewpoint** What evidence from the text supports the idea that creativity is important? Cite specific examples to support your answer.

_____

_____

_____

_____

_____

_____

16. **Theme** What do the authors think must be done about creativity? Cite details from the selection to support your analysis.

_____

_____

_____

_____

_____

_____

Key Vocabulary Review

A. Use these words to complete the paragraph.

achieve   compose   innovator   talent

career   expression   recitation   transform

What is your special skill or _____(1)? Maybe you might _____(2) songs or can perform a _____(3) of a famous poem. You might even be an _____(4) of your style and begin new clothing trends. The possibilities are endless. Creative _____(5) has the power to _____(6) your life. Who knows, you may even _____(7) success and make a _____(8) out of it!

B. Use your own words to write what each Key Vocabulary word means. Then write a synonym for each word.

Key Word	My Definition	Synonym
1. collaborate		
2. commitment		
3. euphoria		
4. evaluate		
5. evolve		
6. improvisation		
7. insight		
8. phenomenon		

• achieve	• commitment	• evaluate	heritage	• perspective	• structure
assert	compose	evolve	improvisation	• phenomenon	talent
career	• culture	expectation	innovator	recitation	transcend
collaborate	euphoria	expression	• insight	self-esteem	• transform

• **Academic Vocabulary**

C. Complete the sentences.

1. My **perspective** on books and movies might change when _____

_____.

2. Some holidays my **culture** celebrates are _____

_____.

3. One way I **assert** my beliefs is by _____

_____.

4. I admire people who **transcend** _____

_____.

5. I learn about my **heritage** from _____

_____.

6. My **expectation** for the future is _____

_____.

7. One way I can improve my **self-esteem** is to _____

_____.

8. **Structure** is important when you write because _____

_____.

Prepare to Read

▶ The Sword in the Stone
▶ Was There a Real King Arthur?

Key Vocabulary

A. How well do you know these words? Circle a rating for each word. Check your understanding of each word by circling the correct synonym. Then write a definition. If you are unsure of a word's meaning, refer to the Vocabulary Glossary, page 878, in your student text.

Rating Scale	
1	I have never seen this word before.
2	I am not sure of the word's meaning.
3	I know this word and can teach the word's meaning to someone else.

Key Word	Check Your Understanding	Deepen Your Understanding
1 conscientiously (kon-shē-**en**-shus-lē) *adverb* **Rating:** 1 2 3	If you do something **conscientiously,** you do it _____. carelessly carefully	My definition: _____ _____ _____ _____ _____
2 endure (in-**dyur**) *verb* **Rating:** 1 2 3	To **endure** is to _____. continue end	My definition: _____ _____ _____ _____
3 evidence (**e**-vu-duns) *noun* **Rating:** 1 2 3	**Evidence** is _____. theory proof	My definition: _____ _____ _____ _____
4 genuine (**jen**-yū-win) *adjective* **Rating:** 1 2 3	If something is **genuine**, it is _____. real false	My definition: _____ _____ _____ _____

Key Word	Check Your Understanding	Deepen Your Understanding
5 historian (hi-**stor**-ē-un) *noun* **Rating:** 1 2 3	A **historian** is an _____. amateur expert	My definition: _____ _____ _____ _____ _____
6 investigation (in-ves-ti-**gā**-shun) *noun* **Rating:** 1 2 3	An **investigation** is a _____. search class	My definition: _____ _____ _____ _____ _____
7 just (**just**) *adjective* **Rating:** 1 2 3	A **just** person is _____. unfair fair	My definition: _____ _____ _____ _____ _____
8 skeptic (**skep**-tik) *noun* **Rating:** 1 2 3	A **skeptic** is a _____. believer doubter	My definition: _____ _____ _____ _____ _____

B. Use one of the Key Vocabulary words to write about one of your heroes.

_____

_____

Before Reading The Sword in the Stone

LITERARY ANALYSIS: Analyze Cultural Perspective

Most stories are told from a **cultural perspective** that reflects the customs, beliefs, and attitudes of a particular society or era. The cultural perspective can affect many elements of the story, including its plot, characters, settings, and themes.

A. Read the passage below. As you read, look for details that reflect the cultural perspective. Then write the details in the chart.

> **Look Into the Text**
>
> Tossing the hay onto the wagon was men's work. Arthur was not yet strong enough to lift a sheaf, but Kay had grown several inches in the last few months and was almost a man. In a few weeks' time he would leave the schoolroom for good to take up his duties as a squire. Kay could toss the heavy sheaves as well as any of the farmhands. At the end of the day he would climb up on top, pulling Arthur after him, and together they would ride back to the hay barn for supper—a splendid feast of rabbit stew and apple pies which the women had been preparing for most of the day, washed down with jugs of frothing cider.

Selection Detail	What It Shows About the Culture

B. Use the information in the chart to answer the question about the cultural perspective in "The Sword in the Stone."

What does Arthur's society see as signs of adulthood in males? _____

_____

FOCUS STRATEGY: Make Inferences

Focus Strategy

How to Make Inferences

1. **Read and Record** Write the author's important ideas.

2. **Think About What You Know** Add your knowledge about the topic.

3. **Consider All the Information** Infer new ideas about the topic from the information you have.

4. **Read On** Find out if the text proves or changes your inferences.

A. Read the passage. Think about the author's important ideas as you read. Then use your knowledge about the ideas to make inferences.

Look Into the Text

> Tossing the hay onto the wagon was men's work. Arthur was not yet strong enough to lift a sheaf, but Kay had grown several inches in the last few months and was almost a man. In a few weeks' time he would leave the schoolroom for good to take up his duties as a squire. Kay could toss the heavy sheaves as well as any of the farmhands. At the end of the day he would climb up on top, pulling Arthur after him, and together they would ride back to the hay barn for supper—a splendid feast of rabbit stew and apple pies which the women had been preparing for most of the day, washed down with jugs of frothing cider.

Author's Ideas	My Knowledge	My Inference
"Tossing the hay onto the wagon was men's work."		
"Kay would leave the schoolroom for good and take up his duties as a squire."		

B. Highlight key words and phrases in the passage that helped you make inferences.

Selection Review The Sword in the Stone

 What Makes a Hero?
Discover how legends begin.

A. In "The Sword in the Stone," you learn how an ordinary boy becomes a
king. Complete the Cluster with examples of Arthur's heroism and the
qualities that a hero possesses.

Cluster

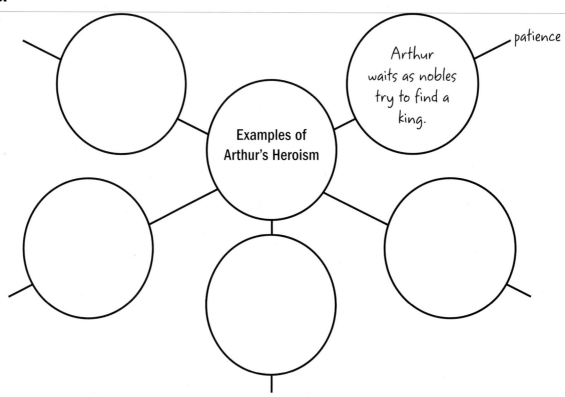

Examples of
Arthur's Heroism

Arthur
waits as nobles
try to find a
king.

patience

B. Use the information in the Cluster to answer the questions.

1. How might Arthur have been different if he had known that he would
   eventually be king?

   _____

   _____

2. What events in the story show that Arthur will be a just king? Use **just**
   in your answer.

   _____

   _____

3. Does Arthur have the qualities of a hero? Why or why not?

   _____

   _____

   _____

Was There a Real King Arthur?

Interactive

by Robert Stewart

Connect Across Texts
The short story "The Sword in the Stone" retells a heroic legend that has been told for centuries. The following article about history examines its lasting appeal. What makes this hero's legend **endure**?

King Arthur is a mysterious figure, and his tale has a long and complex history. Writers from every age have constructed their own version of Arthur, tailored to suit the spirit of their times. But was there a real King Arthur? If so, exactly who was the **historical figure** behind the folk tale? How did the world-famous legend **emerge**? It is one of history's greatest unsolved riddles.

Almost everyone has heard of King Arthur. He was the ancient British king who pulled the sword from the stone. He consulted the magician Merlin, led the knights of the Round Table, married the beautiful Guinevere, and set an example of bravery and chivalry. According to British legend, though he is long dead, he lies somewhere in the hills, waiting for the moment when his countrymen need him most. Then he will awake and save them.

Is this history? Much of it certainly is not. The magical Merlin sounds **suspect**, and how could a sword possibly be embedded in a stone in the first place? That all sounds like **folklore**. But just because the story is folklore now does not necessarily mean that it did not have a historical seed. It is for that seed that **historians** and **archaeologists** have long been looking.

Interact with the Text

1. Text Structures
Remember that nonfiction authors often organize their ideas into text structures. Circle a word that signals sequence in the second column. How does this word help you follow the author's thinking?

2. Interpret
Look at visuals in the time line on pages 104–105. How do the maps help you understand the events?

Key Vocabulary
endure v., to continue or go on
historian n., person who studies the past and interprets it

In Other Words
historical figure real person from the past
emerge come about
suspect hard to believe
folklore tales or beliefs shared by many people
archaeologists scientists who study past cultures

British and World History Before 1100

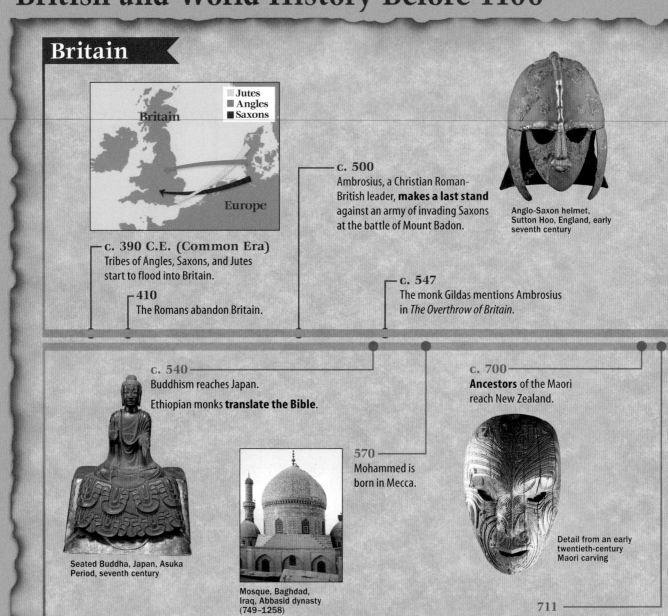

Britain

Britain

Jutes
Angles
Saxons

Britain

Europe

c. 390 C.E. (Common Era)
Tribes of Angles, Saxons, and Jutes start to flood into Britain.

410
The Romans abandon Britain.

c. 500
Ambrosius, a Christian Roman-British leader, **makes a last stand** against an army of invading Saxons at the battle of Mount Badon.

Anglo-Saxon helmet, Sutton Hoo, England, early seventh century

c. 547
The monk Gildas mentions Ambrosius in *The Overthrow of Britain*.

c. 540
Buddhism reaches Japan.

Ethiopian monks **translate the Bible**.

570
Mohammed is born in Mecca.

c. 700
Ancestors of the Maori reach New Zealand.

Seated Buddha, Japan, Asuka Period, seventh century

Mosque, Baghdad, Iraq, Abbasid dynasty (749–1258)

Detail from an early twentieth-century Maori carving

711
Muslim **forces** cross the Straits of Gibraltar and conquer Spain.

The World

In Other Words

c. about (abbreviation used for estimated dates)
makes a last stand fights to defend his land
translate the Bible change the Bible from one language to another

Ancestors Family members from past generations
forces armies, soldiers

Portrait of Alfred the Great, 849–899

Anglo-Saxons

Danes

Norman coat of arms, c. 1066

886

England is split between Danish **territory** to the east (the Danelaw), and Anglo-Saxon land to the west.

1066

Normans from early France conquer Britain. The Norman Conquest leads to many changes in English language, culture, and government.

c. 870

An army of Danes moving across England is defeated by Alfred the Great of Wessex.

Nennius names King Arthur as the hero of the Battle of Mt. Badon in his *History of the Britons*.

1013

King Swein of Denmark takes control of England. The Anglo-Saxon King Ethelred **flees** to Normandy.

800

Charlemagne, king of the Franks, is crowned Holy Roman Emperor. His lands cover much of Europe.

873

Arab mathematicians invent the **concept** of zero.

1031

Christians begin to reconquer Spain.

1045

Printing with movable type is invented in China.

Charlemagne is crowned by Pope Leo III, December 25, 800.

A doorway in the Alhambra Palace, Granada, Spain, c. 1300

⏶ **Interpret the Time Line** This time line shows major world events that occurred at the same time. What does this show about the legend of Arthur?

In Other Words

concept idea or notion
territory land
flees escapes

Where Is Arthur?

A historian usually starts by looking for written **evidence**. The first mention of someone who might be Arthur is in a book called *The Overthrow of Britain* **compiled** by the British monk Saint Gildas (c. 516–570 C.E.). In this book, a British leader named Ambrosius slows the **advance** of the invading Angles and Saxons, who are later defeated at the Battle of Mount Badon in about 500 C.E. Gildas does not mention Arthur, nor say that Ambrosius fought at Badon. However, some historians have wondered if Ambrosius and Arthur are **one and the same**. This is historical evidence, but was it Arthur?

At the same time, **bards** in Wales and Brittany, in France, were entertaining their hosts with stories of a hero named Arthur. This one had a personality much like that of

Europe in the Early Middle Ages (c. 500–800 C.E.)

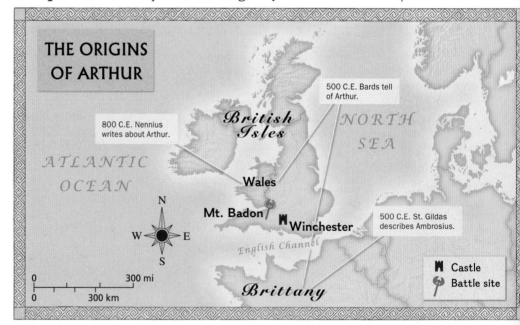

THE ORIGINS OF ARTHUR

800 C.E. Nennius writes about Arthur.

500 C.E. Bards tell of Arthur.

British Isles

NORTH SEA

ATLANTIC OCEAN

Wales

Mt. Badon

Winchester

500 C.E. St. Gildas describes Ambrosius.

English Channel

Brittany

N W E S

0   300 mi
0   300 km

⚑ Castle
⚑ Battle site

▲ Interpret the Map What do the captions on the map show?

Key Vocabulary
● **evidence** *n.*, information that helps prove something

In Other Words
compiled put together from different sources
advance forward movement
one and the same the same person
bards storytellers from ancient times

the Arthur we know, and he **slew** monsters and wicked giants. Folk heroes are sometimes based on history. But was this Arthur real?

The next piece of written evidence comes from the early ninth century, when Arthur was named by the Welsh monk Nennius in his *History of the Britons*. According to Nennius, Arthur was a British war leader who fought a series of twelve battles against the Angles and Saxons, of which Badon was the last. The similarities with Ambrosius are unmistakable.

And that, together with poems and a few other writings of the same time, is all of the written evidence we have for King Arthur. All of the details—Lancelot, Guinevere, the sword in the stone, Camelot and the Round Table, Merlin the magician—appear only in literature. Much of it was written long after the Norman Conquest of 1066.

For hundreds of years after that, people were **content** to leave Arthur as a legend. Then, in the early twentieth century, some historians began to wonder. Could Arthur possibly be real after all? One popular view held by many scholars was that Arthur was actually a late-Roman **cavalry commander** who had led British forces against the invading Anglo-Saxons.

Archaeologists have also been looking around Britain for evidence of the real Arthur. One such **investigation** took place in 1976 in the city of Winchester in southern England. Hanging there, in the Great Hall of Winchester Castle, is an enormous round table-top. It is made of solid oak, is eighteen feet (5.4 meters) in diameter, weighs one-and-a-quarter tons (1,138 kilograms), and has places for twenty-five people marked on it. Many argued that it was the actual Round Table of legend. Historically, Winchester had become the capital of the Saxon kings of Wessex in the seventh century. Could the Saxons possibly have turned Arthur's capital into their own?

Unfortunately, the belief did not stand up to modern scientific investigation. **Tree-ring and radiocarbon dating**, plus a study

Key Vocabulary
- **investigation** *n.*, careful search or study that looks for facts

In Other Words
slew killed
content happy, satisfied
cavalry commander leader of a group of soldiers riding on horses
Tree-ring and radiocarbon dating Scientific methods used to measure time

Interact with the Text

5. Text Structures
Look at the beginning of each paragraph in column one. Which text structure is the author using in this section? Why? Circle the signal words the author uses.

6. Interpret
Highlight at least three details about the table-top in the Great Hall of Winchester Castle. Explain why the author includes these details.

7. Interpret
Look back at the time line on pages 104–105. Use it to tell why the Winchester Castle round table (right) was not Arthur's.

of **medieval carpentry practices**, revealed that the table was actually constructed in the 1270s at the start of Edward I's **reign**. This was during a time when the king himself was taking a great interest in everything associated with Arthur. Experts now think that the table at Winchester was probably made to be used at the many knightly tournaments that Edward himself liked to hold.

Although no **genuine** Arthurian objects have ever been discovered, many possible Arthurian places have been investigated. Geoffrey of Monmouth, an author of the 1100s, said that Tintagel in Cornwall was Arthur's birthplace, and there is even a suitably ruined castle perched on a cliff there. But, unfortunately, the castle is no older than Geof-

frey himself. Writers choose places as settings for their books for many different reasons. Geoffrey may have added the reference to Tintagel simply to please a rich local nobleman.

In the 1960s, the search for Camelot heated up when archaeologists **excavated** an **Iron Age hill fort** at Cadbury Castle in southern England. Local legend held that Arthur and his knights lay sleeping under the hill. John Leland, a historian writing during King Henry VIII's reign, had stated that the local people often called the **fortified remains** "Camalat—King Arthur's palace."

Exhaustive excavations conducted by the archaeologist Leslie Alcock yielded evidence dating from about Arthur's time of a wall encircling an extensive hilltop

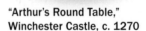

"Arthur's Round Table,"
Winchester Castle, c. 1270

Key Vocabulary
genuine *adj.*, real, true

In Other Words
medieval carpentry practices ways carpenters worked in the Middle Ages
reign rule, time as king
excavated dug up
Iron Age hill fort fort built c. 1000 B.C.E.
fortified remains ruins

Local legends held that Arthur and his knights lay sleeping under the hill at Cadbury Castle (left). Geoffrey of Monmouth claimed that Tintagel Castle (right) was Arthur's birthplace.

compound. At its center was a large aisled hall. Some see the remains of a stout defensive wall around a great feasting hall such as might befit a king named Arthur. But **skeptics** see only a moderately sized barn surrounded by walls barely able to contain horses and cattle, let alone keep determined enemies away.

So King Arthur remains a mystery. Though archaeologists can find no evidence for Arthur, this fact alone does not disprove his existence. Archaeologists are the first to explain that lack of proof is not a convincing argument against the existence of a person, place, or event. All it takes is one small piece of evidence—one small "voice"—to overcome the **accumulated** weight of silence. Such a discovery may well lie in the future.

Key Vocabulary
skeptic *n.*, person who doubts facts and beliefs that are generally accepted by others

In Other Words
compound group of buildings in an enclosed space
accumulated piled up

Interact with the Text

8. Interpret
Highlight the most important ideas in the second column. Summarize the author's argument.

_____
_____
_____
_____
_____
_____
_____
_____
_____
_____
_____
_____
_____

9. Text Structures
Underline signal words
and phrases in the last
two paragraphs. Explain
how one of the words or
phrases helps you follow
the author's thinking and
find the information you
need to know.

_____

_____

_____

_____

_____

_____

Why Do We Need Arthur?

But there is another Arthurian mystery. Why is it that we so much want King Arthur to be real? Why do historians and archaeologists continue this search? One of the great attractions of the Arthur story is that it contains something for everyone—action, mystery, romance, the struggle between good and evil. And the tales **have a ring of truth** because some have their roots in genuine ancient traditions.

And the idea of a once and future king, sleeping somewhere, awaiting his time to return, is not **unique to** the Arthur story. In Denmark, the knight Holger Danske sleeps. In Spain it is El Cid. In Germany it is Frederick Barbarossa. Arthur **embodies** real human needs and desires. We _want_ him to be real. ❖

In Other Words
have a ring of truth sound like they might
   be true
unique to found only in
embodies represents, stands for

Selection Review Was There a Real King Arthur?

A. Choose one of the text structures below. Explain how the text features help you understand the information about King Arthur.

| Text structure 1: | **Cause and Effect** |
| Text structure 2: | **Compare and Contrast** |

The author uses text structure ____ to

_____

_____

_____

B. Answer the questions.

1. Return to the inference you made in Question 4 on page 106. How does the evidence in the article support or change this inference as you read?

_____

_____

_____

Reflect and Assess

WRITING: Write About Literature

A. Why do many cultures tell legends about heroes like King Arthur? Plan your writing. List examples from both texts that might provide an answer.

The Sword in the Stone	Was There a Real King Arthur?
Arthur is an example of someone who is honest and hardworking.	The story of Arthur can be easily adapted for different people in different time periods.

B. What is your opinion? Write an opinion statement that answers the question. Use examples from both texts to support your opinion.

_____

_____

_____

_____

_____

_____

_____

_____

_____

_____

_____

Integrate the Language Arts

LITERARY ANALYSIS: Compare Characters' Motives and Traits

Readers get to know a character in a story through the character's **actions**, **dialogue**, **motives**, and **traits**.

A. List details that you find out about Arthur, using information from "The Sword in the Stone."

Clues	Arthur
Actions	
Dialogue	
Motives	
Traits	

B. Characters' motivations affect story events. Imagine Arthur is motivated by greed. How might each event have a different outcome than what you read in the story?

1. Kay forgets his sword.

_____

_____

2. The nobles refuse to believe that Arthur should be king.

_____

_____

3. Arthur becomes king.

_____

_____

C. How can actions, words, motives, and traits show what a character is like? Write a description of another character that includes each element.

_____

_____

_____

VOCABULARY STUDY: Word Families

Word families are groups of words that are related by meaning. Knowing the meaning of one part of an unfamiliar word can help you understand what the entire word means.

A. Read the Key Vocabulary words in the chart below, and write a new word that is from the same family.

Key Vocabulary	New Word
conscientiously	conscience
endure	
evidence	
historian	
investigation	
just	

B. Write what you think each word that you listed above means. Use a dictionary to confirm the meaning.

1. _____
2. _____
3. _____
4. _____
5. _____
6. _____

C. Write sentences containing the new words.

1. _____
2. _____
3. _____
4. _____
5. _____
6. _____

Prepare to Read
▶ A Job for Valentín
▶ In the Heart of a Hero

Key Vocabulary

A. How well do you know these words? Circle a rating for each word. Check your understanding of each word by circling *yes* or *no*. Then complete the sentences. If you are unsure of a word's meaning, refer to the Vocabulary Glossary, page 878, in your student text.

Rating Scale	
1	I have never seen this word before.
2	I am not sure of the word's meaning.
3	I know this word and can teach the word's meaning to someone else.

Key Word	Check Your Understanding	Deepen Your Understanding
❶ anxiety (ang-**zī**-ut-ē) *noun* **Rating:** 1 2 3	Someone with **anxiety** about flying would look forward to a ten-hour plane ride. **Yes** **No**	I feel anxiety about _____ _____ _____ _____ _____ .
❷ distracted (di-**strakt**-id) *adjective* **Rating:** 1 2 3	People who drive are often **distracted** by their cell phones. **Yes** **No**	I get distracted by _____ _____ _____ _____ .
❸ inherent (in-**hair**-unt) *adjective* **Rating:** 1 2 3	Good study skills must be learned; therefore, they are **inherent.** **Yes** **No**	I am someone with an inherent talent for _____ _____ _____ _____ .
❹ inhibit (in-**hib**-it) *verb* **Rating:** 1 2 3	Fear of driving could **inhibit** travel. **Yes** **No**	People can inhibit others when _____ _____ _____ _____ .

Key Word	Check Your Understanding	Deepen Your Understanding
5 prejudiced (**prej**-u-dist) *adjective* **Rating:** 1 2 3	People who accept others for their differences are **prejudiced.** **Yes** **No**	I don't like it when people are prejudiced toward _____ _____ _____ _____ .
6 protest (**prō**-test) *verb* **Rating:** 1 2 3	Laborers sometimes **protest** unfair pay and working conditions. **Yes** **No**	I would protest if _____ _____ _____ _____ .
7 survivor (sur-**vī**-vur) *noun* **Rating:** 1 2 3	A **survivor** of a natural disaster is a lucky person. **Yes** **No**	I know a survivor of _____ _____ _____ _____ .
8 tragedy (**tra**-ju-dē) *noun* **Rating:** 1 2 3	An event that causes thousands of people to lose their homes is a **tragedy.** **Yes** **No**	A tragedy that affected many people was _____ _____ _____ _____ .

B. Use one of the Key Vocabulary words to write about someone you admire.

_____

_____

Before Reading A Job for Valentín

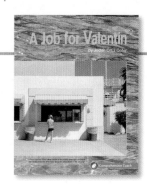

LITERARY ANALYSIS: Analyze Viewpoint

In **first-person point of view**, the narrator tells the story as he or she experiences it and uses the pronouns *I* and *me*. The information is limited to only his or her thoughts and experiences.

A. Read the passage below. Write the clues in the chart that reveal first-person point of view.

Look Into the Text

> Bob Dylan laughs and kisses my hand.
> "My Chiquita banana," he says, "stay true to me. Don't give my whereabouts out to the enemy. I shall return."
> "Bye," I say. I am such a great conversationalist, inside my own head.
> But he's already looking away. We have both heard familiar giggles. It's Clarissa and Anne. I see him waving to them, letting them get a view of his entire, glorious self. He looks over his shoulder at me and winks, covering all the bases.

Elements of First-Person Narrator Point of View	Text Clues
First-person pronouns	
What the narrator sees	
What the narrator hears	
What the narrator feels	

B. Answer the question.

What is the narrator's view of Bob Dylan? _____

_____

_____

FOCUS STRATEGY: Make Inferences

How to Make Inferences

1. **Record Information and Ideas** Note what the narrator thinks, says, and does. Think about your own experience.

2. **Connect the Inferences** Add up what you know to form big ideas about the narrator.

3. **Read On** Revise your inferences as you learn more information.

A. Read the passage. Use the strategies above to make inferences. Answer the questions below.

Look Into the Text

The only thing I don't really like is that Mrs. O'Brien expects to be told if I ever see Bob Dylan messing around on the job.

"People's lives, children's lives, are in that young man's hands," she says. "Keep an eye on him, Teresa, and use that phone to call me, if you need to."

I say, "Yes, ma'am," even though I feel funny about being asked to spy on Bob Dylan. He's a senior at my school and, yeah, a crazy man sometimes. But if they gave him the job as a lifeguard, they ought to trust him to do it right.

---

1. How does Teresa feel about Mrs. O'Brien? How do you know?

_____

_____

2. How does thinking about your own experiences help you infer how Teresa feels?

_____

_____

B. Return to the passage above. Circle words and phrases that helped you answer question 1.

Selection Review A Job for Valentín

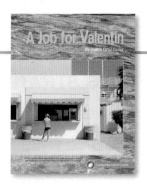

 What Makes a Hero?
Consider the everyday heroes in your community.

A. In "A Job for Valentín," you found out how Valentín became a hero in unexpected ways. Make inferences about Valentín and Teresa by completing the Inference Chart below.

Inference Chart

Event	What the Narrator Says, Feels, or Thinks	What You Know
Teresa is told she must work with Valentín for the summer.		
Teresa does not tell on Bob Dylan.		
Valentín laughs when Teresa yells at Marciela.		

B. Use the information in the chart to answer the question.

1. As you were reading, what inference did you make about Valentín and Teresa?

_____

_____

2. How may Teresa have been prejudiced toward Valentín before he helped save Pablito? Use **prejudiced** in your answer.

_____

_____

_____

3. How will Teresa treat Valentín from now on?

_____

_____

In the Heart of a Hero

Interactive

FEATURE ARTICLE

by Johnny Dwyer

Connect Across Texts

In "A Job for Valentín," the hero is not who we expect. This feature article explores why some people act as heroes when others cannot.

On a sunny Sunday last month, the glass-like surface of Lake George, in New York's Adirondack Mountains, was dotted with boats. Just before three, the afternoon's **tranquility shattered**. The *Ethan Allen*, a tour boat carrying almost fifty senior citizens, tipped crazily. Within thirty seconds, it had **capsized** and its passengers were struggling for their lives.

Brian Hart was on the lake that day, paddling a canoe with Brianna, his youngest daughter, and three of her cousins. When he saw the boat overturn, he didn't hesitate, immediately calling 911—"Get to the lake real quick"—even as he headed for the nearest dock. There, he dropped the girls and phoned his brother, Eric. Two minutes later, Eric, 42, and his son, E.J., scooped up Brian in the family fishing boat, and the three of them sped to the scene. Brian and Eric dove straight in and started **hauling survivors** onto life preservers, seat cushions— anything that would float. When other boats arrived, the Hart brothers **hoisted** victims into them for nearly half an hour.

Onlookers gasped in horror, watching the **tragedy unfold**; many

It was a calm, beautiful day before the *Ethan Allen* capsized on Oct. 2, 2005.

Interact with the Text

1. Make Inferences
Underline words that describe Brian's and Eric's actions. What can you infer about what the two men are like?

_____

_____

_____

_____

_____

Key Vocabulary
• **survivor** *n.*, person who lives through a hardship or disaster
tragedy *n.*, terrible disaster

In Other Words
tranquility shattered calmness was wrecked
capsized turned upside down
hauling pulling
hoisted lifted
unfold happen over time

called for help. Those who saw the brothers' actions surely wondered at their uncommon courage: *Do they know what they're doing? Will they be able to save anyone? Will they die trying?* Later—over dinner, perhaps, or just before they drifted off to sleep—these **bystanders** likely pondered another set of questions both simple and complex: *What makes a hero? Why do some of us dive in when others simply cannot?*

In Brian's case, the answer may lie in his **biological makeup**. "I guess my boys were always fearless," says Donald Hart, 71, Brian and Eric's father. "Not only that day, but in childhood, with the motorbikes, snowmobiles. I wasn't surprised they would do something like that."

Dr. Frank Farley, a psychologist who has studied heroic behavior, says that something literally in a hero's **DNA** may contribute to brave actions. Heroes, he says, often have what he calls "Big T"—or thrill-seeking, risk-taking personalities. "They're not satisfied with normal levels of **stimulation**, so they seek out more of it," says Farley.

Recovery divers prepare to search for the *Ethan Allen* after it sank in Lake George, New York, in October 2005.

⚠ **Interpret the Visuals** What additional information do the map and caption give you about the photo?

In Other Words
bystanders people who stood by and watched
biological makeup nature
DNA genetic code
stimulation excitement

When Brian plunged into the lake and swam into the crowd of struggling passengers, he remained calm and focused. "Situational heroes," as Farley refers to regular people who **rise to the occasion** in emergencies, simply aren't **inhibited** by "**uncertainty**, which is one of the biggest sources of human fear."

Brian had something else, too, that **complemented** his **inherent** fearlessness: his comfort in the water, particularly this water. As a boy, he'd learned to paddle and fish on Lake George, and later scuba dived and piloted his first motorboat there. "We always used to horse around, brothers grabbing you in the water. I'm sure a lot of people who came [to the scene] in boats didn't jump in because they didn't have the comfort level I had."

And beyond that? Perhaps empathy.

Is it **a coincidence** that this man who dove into the water had once been rescued on Lake George? In 1978, Brian was thrown from a motorboat. He floated dazed—but uninjured—for fifteen minutes until a boater fished him out.

Donald wonders about the circumstances of rescues—a man with the heart of a hero finding himself in the right place at the right time—and **speculates on** what his boys might have taken from hearing about his own experience: "Something like this, it's a series of events that happens, and if there's

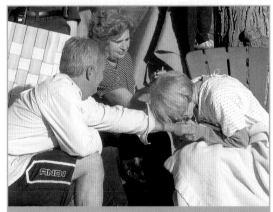

Ethan Allen survivor Carol Charlton holds Brian Hart's hand.

Interact with the Text

2. Interpret
Circle the most important information about the study of heroes on page 120. How might this explain Brian's actions?

3. Feature Article
Feature articles often include quotations. Circle Brian's quotation. How do his thoughts affect your understanding of the event?

4. Make Inferences
Underline what happened to Brian. How do you think this event affected Brian's behavior?

Key Vocabulary
- **inhibit** *v.*, to stop or hold a person back from doing something
- **inherent** *adj.*, natural, basic

In Other Words
rise to the occasion do more than they thought they could
uncertainty doubt
complemented added to
a coincidence just chance
speculates on guesses about

5. Feature Article
Mark an X next to each line of dialogue. Explain how this conversation is an effective way to end the article.

_____

_____

_____

_____

_____

_____

_____

_____

a lesson, maybe it's that there's an outside source, a God above."

Whether **Providence** or circumstance, when Hart, exhausted, finally returned to shore, Brianna asked, "Did you save everybody?"

"Yes," he lied. She's 8 years old; there's time yet for truth.

"Daddy, why did you go back?" she asked.

"The people needed my help."

For some—for heroes—it's as simple as that.   ❖

In Other Words
Providence God's plan

Selection Review In the Heart of a Hero

A. Newspaper articles mainly report the basic facts. Give two examples of things this feature article addressed that a news story might not have.

1. _____

_____

2. _____

_____

B. Answer the questions.

1. How do you think other people might feel toward Brian Hart?

_____

_____

2. In your opinion, which of the author's explanations for heroic behavior is most convincing? Give examples from the text to support your answer.

_____

_____

Reflect and Assess

WRITING: Write About Literature

A. Plan your writing. Think about your definition of a real hero. Then list the qualities that Valentín and Brian Hart have that make them real heroes.

Valentín	Brian Hart
considerate of others	

B. Imagine that you can nominate a Hero of the Year. Choose Valentín or Brian Hart. Write a letter to the prize committee describing why the person fits your definition of a real hero.

_____

_____

_____

_____

_____

_____

_____

_____

_____

_____

_____

LITERARY ANALYSIS: Identify Multiple Themes in a Text

A **theme** is a main idea or lesson in a story. The author uses characters, dialogue, and plot events to make a general statement about people or life.

A. Read each example from "A Job for Valentín." List possible themes.

Example	Possible Theme
"I got assigned a 'mentally challenged' assistant by the city. There's a new program to put retarded people to work at simple jobs so they can make some money, learn a skill, or something."	
"I feel scared that I may drown, but I have to reach Pablito."	
"I also expect to get fired for not reporting that Bob Dylan was not at his post."	

B. What do the plot events tell you about the story's theme? Read each plot event and write a possible theme.

Plot event: Valentín saves Pablito and Terry from drowning.

_____

Plot event: Terry learns to communicate in Valentín's language.

_____

Plot event: Mrs. O'Brien offers Valentín and Terry a year-round job.

_____

C. Think about someone you know, have read about, or have seen on TV who is an everyday hero. Write a brief paragraph explaining why.

_____

_____

_____

_____

VOCABULARY STUDY: Borrowed Words

Borrowed words come into one language from another language. Dictionaries tell you the language or languages a word has been borrowed from.

A. Read the list of some common abbreviations that you will see in the dictionary and that tell you the language a word has been borrowed from. Look up the words in the chart below and identify the language of origin. Then write the definition of each word.

Language of Origin Key

Fr: French	*Gk:* Greek
ME: Middle English	*MF:* Middle French
It./Ital: Italian	*L:* Latin
Sp./Span: Spanish	*Pg/Port:* Portuguese

Word	Origin	Definition
astronomy		
dictionary		
evacuate		
podiatrist		

B. Use a dictionary to look up the borrowed words below. Write the languages from which they originated.

flute   ME from Middle French origin

money

music

pizza

C. Find four more words in the dictionary that have been borrowed from the languages listed below.

French

Spanish

Italian

Portuguese

Prepare to Read

▶ **The Woman in the Snow**
▶ **Rosa Parks**

Key Vocabulary

A. How well do you know these words? Circle a rating for each word. Check your understanding of each word by circling *yes* or *no*. Then complete the sentences. If you are unsure of a word's meaning, refer to the Vocabulary Glossary, page 878, in your student text.

Rating Scale	
1	I have never seen this word before.
2	I am not sure of the word's meaning.
3	I know this word and can teach the word's meaning to someone else.

Key Word	Check Your Understanding	Deepen Your Understanding
❶ authority (u-**thor**-u-tē) *noun* **Rating:** **1 2 3**	A principal has **authority** in a school. **Yes**　　**No**	Parents have the authority to _____ _____ _____ _____ .
❷ boycott (**boi**-kot) *noun* **Rating:** **1 2 3**	If you plan a **boycott** of a restaurant, you plan to eat there every day. **Yes**　　**No**	People can start a boycott of a company _____ _____ _____ _____ .
❸ compassion (kum-**pash**-un) *noun* **Rating:** **1 2 3**	People who give money to charities show no **compassion** for those in need. **Yes**　　**No**	I show compassion for others when _____ _____ _____ _____ .
❹ desperately (**des**-pur-it-lē) *adverb* **Rating:** **1 2 3**	Some people act **desperately** when they are afraid. **Yes**　　**No**	I would act desperately if I had to _____ _____ _____ _____ .

Key Word	Check Your Understanding	Deepen Your Understanding
5 **discrimination** (di-skrim-u-**nā**-shun) *noun* **Rating:** 1 2 3	Allowing all citizens to vote is an example of **discrimination**. **Yes** **No**	I experienced discrimination when _____ _____ _____ _____ _____ .
6 **persistent** (pur-**sis**-tunt) *adjective* **Rating:** 1 2 3	A **persistent** person gives up easily. **Yes** **No**	I am persistent when _____ _____ _____ _____ _____ .
7 **provoke** (pru-**vōk**) *verb* **Rating:** 1 2 3	It is possible to **provoke** a person who dislikes you. **Yes** **No**	When people act meanly, they provoke _____ _____ _____ _____ .
8 **segregation** (seg-ri-**gā**-shun) *noun* **Rating:** 1 2 3	**Segregation** brings people together. **Yes** **No**	In the past, segregation in the United States _____ _____ _____ _____ _____ .

B. Use one of the Key Vocabulary words to tell how you could improve a situation in your community.

_____

_____

Before Reading The Woman in the Snow

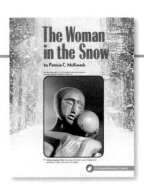

LITERARY ANALYSIS: Analyze Viewpoint

Third-person omniscient point of view is told by a narrator who is not a character in the story. The narrator is omniscient, or all-knowing. This kind of narrator can reveal the thoughts and feelings of all the characters.

A. Read the passage below. Look for clues that tell you the text is told by a third-person omniscient narrator. Paraphrase the text clues in the chart.

> ### Look Into the Text
>
> Grady Bishop had just been hired as a driver for Metro Bus Service. When he put on the gray uniform and boarded his bus, nothing mattered, not his obesity, not his poor education, not growing up the eleventh child of the town drunk. Driving gave him power. And power mattered.
>
> One cold November afternoon Grady clocked in for the three-to-eleven shift. "You've got Hall tonight," Billy, the route manager, said matter-of-factly.

Elements of Third-Person Omniscient	Text Clues
Events are told by narrator	Grady Bishop is hired by the bus service.
Narrator is all-knowing	
Narrator tells thoughts and feelings of characters	

B. Answer these questions.

1. What does the narrator know about Grady?

_____

_____

2. Which information would Billy, the route manager, most likely not know? Why?

_____

_____

FOCUS STRATEGY: Make Inferences

HOW TO MAKE INFERENCES

1. **Make an Initial Inference** Make an inference about a character or story event.

2. **Add New Information** Include information from the story that supports your inference.

3. **Make a New Inference** Revise your inference based on new ideas and information from the text.

A. Read the passage. Use the strategies above to make inferences as you read. Answer the questions below.

> **Look Into the Text**
>
> Most Metro drivers didn't like the Hall Street assignment in the best weather, because the road twisted and turned back on itself like a retreating snake. When slick with ice and snow, it was even more hazardous. But Grady had his own reason for hating the route. The Hall Street Express serviced black domestics who rode out to the fashionable west end in the mornings and back down to the lower east side in the evenings.
>
> "You know I can't stand being a chauffeur for a bunch of colored maids and cooks," he groused.

1. What inference can you make about Grady?

_____

_____

2. Which strategies did you use to answer question number 1?

_____

_____

B. Make a new inference. Underline the new information that helps you make the new inference.

_____

_____

Selection Review The Woman in the Snow

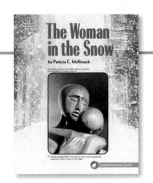

 What Makes a Hero?
Explore how heroes change the world around them.

A. In "The Woman in the Snow," you learn how people can change the world around them with their attitudes and choices. List the choices the characters make and how these choices affect other people in the Character Description Chart.

Character Description Chart

Character	Character's Attitudes and Choices	Effect the Character Has on Others
Grady	Grady is a racist. He likes the power he has over people.	He leaves Eula Mae and her baby to die in the snow.
Ray		
Eula Mae		

B. Use the information in the chart to answer the questions.

1. Why does Ray make the decision to help Eula Mae, even though he doesn't believe she's real?

_____

_____

2. Why does Grady lack compassion? Use **compassion** in your answer.

_____

_____

3. What heroic qualities does Ray have? Cite two examples from the text.

_____

_____

_____

Connect Across Texts

In "The Woman in the Snow," an ordinary person makes an extraordinary choice. Read this profile about another person's extraordinary choice.

Rosa Parks

by Rita Dove

"Our mistreatment was just not right, and I was tired of it."

—Rosa Parks

Interact with the Text

1. Interpret
Look at the photo and read the quote. What do you predict this magazine profile will be about?

_____

_____

_____

_____

_____

2. Interpret
Circle the people that Parks is compared to in the second paragraph. What do these people all have in common?

_____

_____

_____

_____

_____

_____

_____

3. Development of Ideas
Write two details that develop the idea about how African American bus passengers were treated in Montgomery. Highlight the text on page 133 where you found your answer.

_____

_____

_____

_____

_____

_____

_____

_____

_____

_____

_____

_____

We know the story. One December evening, a woman left

work and boarded a bus for home. She was tired; her feet ached. But this was Montgomery, Alabama, in 1955. As the bus became crowded, the woman, a black woman, was ordered to give up her seat to a white passenger. When she remained seated, that simple decision eventually led to the end of **segregation** in the South, **ushering in** a new era of the civil rights movement.

This, anyway, was the story I had heard from the time I was curious enough to **eavesdrop on** adult conversations. I was 3 years old when a white bus driver warned Rosa Parks, "Well, I'm going to have you arrested," and she replied, "You may go on and do so." As a child, I didn't understand how doing nothing had caused so much activity, but I recognized the **template**: David slaying the giant Goliath, or the boy who saved his village by sticking his finger in the **dike**.   And perhaps it is the **lure of fairy-tale retribution** that colors the lens we look back through. Parks was 42 years old when she refused to give up her seat. She has insisted that her feet were not aching; she was, by her own testimony, no more tired than usual. And she did not plan her fateful act: "I did not get on the bus to get arrested," she has said. "I got on the bus to go home."

In Alabama in the 1950s, by law, if the white sec of the bus was full, blacks had to give up their se to allow whites to sit down.

Montgomery's segregation laws were complex. Blacks were required to pay their fare to the driver, then get off and reboard through the back door. Sometimes the bus would drive off before the paid-up customers made it to the back entrance. If the white section was full and another white customer entered, blacks were

Key Vocabulary
segregation *n.*, the act of separating or keeping apart

In Other Words
ushering in introducing, beginning
eavesdrop on listen secretly to
template pattern, model
dike barrier to prevent flooding
lure of fairy-tale retribution appeal of evil people being punished

required to give up their seats and move farther to the back. A black person was not even allowed to sit across the aisle from whites. At the time, two-thirds of the bus riders in Montgomery were black.

Parks was not the first to be **detained for this offense**. Eight months earlier, Claudette Colvin, 15, refused to give up her seat and was arrested. And then in October, a young woman named Mary Louise Smith was arrested. Smith paid the fine and was released.

Six weeks later, the time was ripe. The facts, rubbed shiny for retelling, are these: On December 1, 1955, Mrs. Rosa Parks, **seamstress** for a department store, boarded the Cleveland Avenue bus. She took a seat in the fifth row—the first row of the "Colored Section." The driver was the same one who had put her off a bus twelve years earlier for refusing to get off and reboard through the back door. ("He was still mean-looking," she has said.) Did that make her stubborn? Or had her work in the N.A.A.C.P. sharpened her **sensibilities** so that she knew what to do—or more precisely, what not to do: Don't frown, don't struggle, don't shout, don't pay the fine?

After her first arrest in December, 1955, Rosa Parks was arrested again in February, 1956. This time the charge was helping organize a bus boycott.

She was arrested on a Thursday; **bail was posted** by Clifford Durr, the white lawyer whose wife had employed Parks as a seamstress.

In Other Words
detained for this offense held in jail for breaking this law
seamstress a woman who sewed clothes
sensibilities awareness and understanding
bail was posted money to release Rosa from jail was paid

Cultural Background
The **National Association for the Advancement of Colored People** (N.A.A.C.P.) was founded in 1909. Over the years, it has fought for the civil rights of schoolchildren, leaders, and ordinary men and women.

5. Development of Ideas
Magazine profiles show events in time order. Summarize, in time order, the events of the day Parks appeared in court.

That evening, after talking it over with her mother and husband, Rosa Parks agreed to challenge Montgomery's segregation laws. Thirty-five thousand handbills were distributed to all black schools the next morning. The message was simple:

"We are . . . asking every Negro to stay off the buses Monday in protest of the arrest and trial . . . You can afford to stay out of school for one day. If you work, take a cab, or walk. But please, children and grown-ups, don't ride the bus at all on Monday. Please stay off the buses Monday."

Monday came. Rain threatened, yet the black population of Montgomery stayed off the buses, either walking or catching one of the black cabs stopping at every **municipal** bus stop for ten cents per customer—standard bus fare. Meanwhile, Parks was scheduled to appear in court. As she made her way through the throngs at the courthouse, a girl in the crowd caught sight of her and cried out, "Oh, she's so sweet. They've messed with the wrong one now!"

Yes, indeed. The trial lasted thirty minutes, with the expected **conviction and penalty**. That afternoon, the Montgomery Improvement Association was formed. The members elected as their president a **relative newcomer to** Montgomery, the young minister of Dexter Avenue Baptist Church: the Reverend Martin Luther King Jr. That evening, addressing a crowd, King declared in that ringing voice millions the world over would soon thrill to: "There comes a time that people get tired." When he was finished, Parks stood up so the audience could see her. She did not speak; there was no need to. Here I am, her silence said, among you.

And she has been with us ever since—a **persistent** symbol of human dignity in the face of brutal **authority**. The famous **U.P.I.** photo (actually taken more than a year later, on December 21, 1956, the day

Key Vocabulary
- **persistent** *adj.*, continuing in spite of challenges, unchanging
- **authority** *n.*, people with power over others

In Other Words
municipal city
conviction and penalty decision and punishment
relative newcomer to person who hadn't lived long in
U.P.I. United Press International (a news agency)

Montgomery's public transportation system was legally integrated) is a study of calm strength. She is looking out the bus window, her hands resting in the folds of her checked dress. A white man sits calmly in the row behind her. That clear profile, the neat eyeglasses and sensible coat—she could have been my mother, anybody's favorite aunt. History is often portrayed **as a grand opera, all baritone intrigues and tenor heroics**. Some of the most **tumultuous** events, however, have been **provoked** by **serendipity**—the assassination of an archduke spawned World War I, a kicked-over lantern may have sparked the Great Chicago

Rosa

How she sat there,
the time right inside a place
so wrong it was ready.

That trim name with
its dream of a bench
to rest on. Her sensible coat.

Doing nothing was the doing:
the clean flame of her gaze
carved by a camera flash.

How she stood up
when they bent down to retrieve
her purse. That courtesy.

—Rita Dove

Key Vocabulary
provoke *v.*, to force a person or thing to act

In Other Words
as a grand opera, all baritone intrigues and tenor heroics as if it were an exciting drama played out on a stage
tumultuous wild and noisy
serendipity a lucky accident

6. Make Inferences
The author describes the U.P.I. photo of Rosa Parks as "a study of calm strength." What can you infer about Parks, and about heroes, from the picture?

7. Interpret
Read the poem by the author. In your own words, summarize the main idea.

8. Make Inferences

Why does the story of Parks continue to inspire people? Underline phrases in the text that describe her effect on others.

Fire. One cannot help wondering what role Martin Luther King Jr. would have played in the civil rights movement if the opportunity had not presented itself that first evening of the boycott—if Rosa Parks had chosen a row farther back from the outset, or if she had missed the bus altogether. Today, it is the modesty of Rosa Parks's example that **sustains us**. It is no less than the belief in the power of the individual, that **cornerstone** of the American Dream, that she inspires, along with the hope that all of us—even the least of us—could be that brave, that **serenely** human, when crunch time comes. ❖

In Other Words

sustains us gives us hope and support
cornerstone foundation
serenely calmly

Selection Review Rosa Parks

A. Choose one of the story events. How did the action change the world?

> **Event 1:** Rosa Parks refuses to give up her seat on the bus.
>
> **Event 2:** African Americans boycott the city buses.

_____

_____

_____

B. Answer the questions.

1. How does the sequence of events in the magazine profile of Rosa Parks help you understand her influence on the civil rights movement?

_____

_____

_____

2. Why were Rosa Parks's actions on the bus so important?

_____

_____

_____

Reflect and Assess

WRITING: Write About Literature

A. Plan your writing. List examples from both selections that support the theme of overcoming prejudice.

The Woman in the Snow	Rosa Parks

B. What do both selections say about the struggle to overcome prejudice? Write a brief theme statement. Use examples from both selections to support your statement.

_____

_____

_____

_____

_____

_____

_____

_____

_____

_____

_____

Integrate the Language Arts

LITERARY ANALYSIS: Compare Themes

A **theme** is the most important idea in a work of literature. Themes usually deal with issues that all people can relate to, such as looking for love or experiencing loss.

A. Compare the themes of "Hero" by Mariah Carey and "The Woman in the Snow." In the chart, list examples from each selection that deal with the universal theme of heroism.

Hero	The Woman in the Snow
Every person has the ability to be a hero.	Ray Hammond became the first African American driver that Metro hired.

B. Describe what the examples for each selection say about the universal theme of heroism.

"Hero": _____

_____

"The Woman in the Snow": _____

_____

C. How is the theme of heroism similar in both selections? What do you think the authors say about heroism in each selection? Use examples from the text to support your response.

_____

_____

_____

VOCABULARY STUDY: Word Families

Knowing the meaning of one word can help you understand other words that belong in the same **word family**.

A. The following words are in the same word family as words found in the selections. Write what you think each word means. Then use a dictionary to confirm the definition.

Word	What I Think It Means	What It Means
discriminate		
hazard		
provocation		
segregate		
sensible		
tumult		

B. List related words that belong to each word's family below.

hero	differ	depend
heroic, heroine		

C. Look through each of the selections. Find three words. Brainstorm related words that belong to the word's family.

1. _____

_____

2. _____

_____

3. _____

_____

Read for Understanding

1. Genre What kind of text is this passage? How do you know?

_____

_____

_____

_____

_____

2. Topic Write a topic sentence to tell what the text is mostly about.

_____

_____

_____

_____

_____

_____

_____

Reread and Summarize

3. Word Choice Circle three words or phrases that express big ideas in each section. Note why you chose it.

· Section 1: paragraphs 1–6
· Section 2: paragraphs 7–14

4. Summary Use your topic sentence and notes from item 3 to write a summary of the selection.

_____

_____

_____

_____

_____

_____

_____

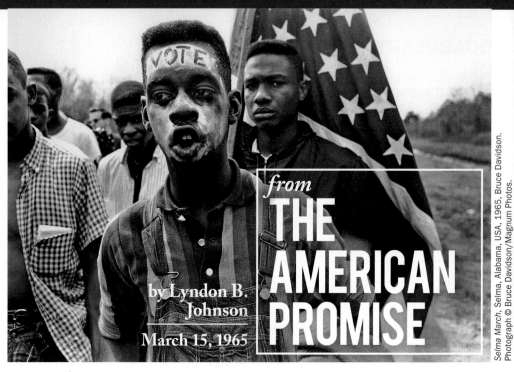

from

THE AMERICAN PROMISE

by Lyndon B. Johnson

March 15, 1965

Selma March, Selma, Alabama, USA, 1965, Bruce Davidson. Photograph © Bruce Davidson/Magnum Photos.

1   . . . **At** times history and fate meet at a single time in a single place to shape a turning point in man's unending search for freedom. So it was at **Lexington and Concord**. So it was a century ago at **Appomattox**. So it was last week in Selma, Alabama.

2   There, long-suffering men and women peacefully **protested** the denial of their rights as Americans. Many were brutally assaulted. One good man, a man of God, was killed. . . .

3   In our time we have come to live with moments of great crisis. Our lives have been marked with debate about great issues; issues of war and peace, issues of prosperity and depression. But rarely in any time does an issue lay bare the secret heart of America itself. Rarely are we met with a challenge, not to our growth or abundance, our welfare or our security, but rather to the values and the purposes and the meaning of our beloved nation.

4   The issue of equal rights for American Negroes is such an issue. And should we defeat every enemy, should we double our wealth and conquer the stars, and still be unequal to this issue, then we will have failed as a people and as a nation. . . .

5   This was the first nation in the history of the world to be founded with a purpose. The great phrases of that purpose still sound in every American

In Other Words

Lexington and Concord the first battles of the American Revolution
Appomattox the last battle of the Civil War

Historical Background

In March 1965, African Americans in Selma, Alabama marched to protest laws preventing them from voting. Authorities attacked the marchers, killing one of them.

heart, North and South: "All men are created equal"—"government by consent of the governed"—"give me liberty or give me death." Well, those are not just clever words, or those are not just empty theories. In their name Americans have fought and died for two centuries, and tonight around the world they stand there as guardians of our liberty, risking their lives.

6 Those words are a promise to every citizen that he shall share in the **dignity** of man. This dignity cannot be found in a man's possessions; it cannot be found in his power, or in his position. It really rests on his right to be treated as a man equal in opportunity to all others. It says that he shall share in freedom, he shall choose his leaders, educate his children, and provide for his family according to his ability and his merits as a human being.

7 To apply any other test—to deny a man his hopes because of his color or race, his religion or the place of his birth—is not only to do injustice, it is to **deny** America and to dishonor the dead who gave their lives for American freedom. . . .

8 Every American citizen must have an equal right to vote. . . .

9 Wednesday I will send to Congress a law designed to eliminate illegal barriers to the right to vote. . . .

10 But even if we pass this bill, the battle will not be over. What happened in Selma is part of a far larger movement which reaches into every section and state of America. It is the effort of American Negroes to secure for themselves the full blessings of American life.

11 Their cause must be our cause too. Because it is not just Negroes, but really it is all of us, who must overcome the crippling legacy of **bigotry** and injustice.

12 And we shall overcome.

13 The real hero of this struggle is the American Negro. His actions and protests, his courage to risk safety and even to risk his life, have awakened the **conscience** of this nation. His demonstrations have been designed to call attention to injustice, designed to provoke change, designed to stir reform.

14 He has called upon us to make good the promise of America. And who among us can say that we would have made the same progress were it not for his **persistent** bravery, and his faith in American democracy. . . . ❖

Reread and Analyze

5. Authors' Viewpoint
Reread paragraphs 3 and 4. Underline text that shows Johnson's viewpoint on equal rights. Explain his viewpoint in your own words.

_____

_____

_____

6. Details Reread paragraphs 5 and 6. Highlight two examples from American history and explain how they support Johnson's viewpoint.

_____

_____

_____

_____

_____

7. Details Reread paragraphs 6–14. Underline important pieces of information that show how equal rights are important to all Americans. Discuss how these details support the author's viewpoint.

_____

_____

_____

Key Vocabulary
● **persistent** _adj.,_ continuing in spite of challenges, unchanging

In Other Words
dignity value and worthiness
deny reject
bigotry hating another person because of ethnic background, racism
conscience sense of right and wrong

Discuss

8. **Synthesize** With the class, identify specific ways that Johnson supports his viewpoint.

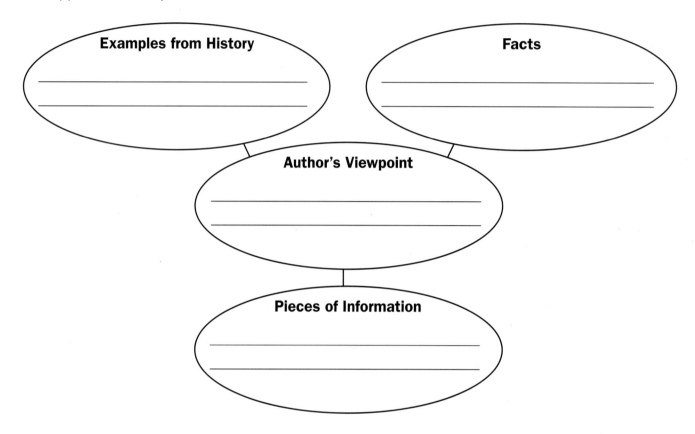

Examples from History

_____

_____

Facts

_____

_____

Author's Viewpoint

_____

_____

Pieces of Information

_____

_____

9. **Write** Use your notes from question 8 to write about how good speakers support their viewpoints. Use details from Johnson's speech to support the points you make. Before writing, use these questions to help you organize your thoughts.

> · What is an author's viewpoint?
>
> · What are three ways that authors support their viewpoints?

_____

_____

_____

_____

_____

_____

Connect with the **EQ** What Makes a Hero?

Consider the relationship between heroism and justice.

10. **Viewpoint** Reread paragraphs 13–14. According to Johnson, who are the true heroes? Explain using specific examples from the text.

_____

_____

_____

_____

_____

11. **Theme** What is Johnson's message about heroes?

_____

_____

_____

_____

_____

Key Vocabulary Review

A. Read each sentence. Circle the word that best fits into each sentence.

1. You might start a(n) (**investigation** / **boycott**) to learn the truth about something.

2. A (**survivor** / **skeptic**) questions what other people believe.

3. A (**persistent** / **prejudiced**) person does not give up.

4. You might behave (**conscientiously** / **desperately**) in a crisis.

5. (**Segregation** / **Tragedy**) does not allow people from different races to live together.

6. A judge is required to be (**genuine** / **just**) in his or her courtroom.

7. Siblings often (**protest** / **provoke**) each other to do silly things.

8. Some people have a(n) (**inherent** / **distracted**) sense of loyalty.

B. Use your own words to write what each Key Vocabulary word means. Then write a synonym for each word.

Key Word	My Definition	Synonym
1. authority		
2. compassion		
3. conscientiously		
4. endure		
5. inhibit		
6. prejudiced		
7. protest		
8. tragedy		

anxiety	conscientiously	endure	• inherent	• persistent	segregation
• authority	desperately	• evidence	• inhibit	prejudiced	skeptic
boycott	• discrimination	genuine	• investigation	protest	• survivor
compassion	distracted	historian	just	provoke	tragedy

• **Academic Vocabulary**

C. Complete the sentences.

1. I am easily **distracted** when _____

_____ .

2. **Evidence** is important to police because _____

_____ .

3. I feel **anxiety** when _____

_____ .

4. Something I would like to see a **boycott** of is _____

_____ .

5. A **survivor** of a serious illness might feel _____

_____ .

6. A **genuine** emerald is valuable because _____

_____ .

7. Some things that a **historian** might do are_____

_____ .

8. Someone I know experienced **discrimination** when _____

_____ .

Prepare to Read

▶ Curtis Aikens and the American Dream
▶ Go For It!

Key Vocabulary

Rating Scale

1 I have never seen this word before.

2 I am not sure of the word's meaning.

3 I know this word and can teach the word's meaning to someone else.

A. How well do you know these words? Circle a rating for each word. Check your understanding of each word by circling the correct synonym. Then complete the sentences. If you are unsure of a word's meaning, refer to the Vocabulary Glossary, page 878, in your student text.

Key Word	Check Your Understanding	Deepen Your Understanding
❶ ambitious (am-**bi**-shus) *adjective* **Rating:** 1 2 3	An **ambitious** person is _____. **satisfied** **determined**	My friend is ambitious because _____ _____ _____ _____ .
❷ cause (**kawz**) *noun* **Rating:** 1 2 3	A **cause** is a/an _____. **difficulty** **idea**	A cause I think is important is _____ _____ _____ _____ .
❸ confession (kun-**fe**-shun) *noun* **Rating:** 1 2 3	A **confession** is a _____. **denial** **declaration**	One reason someone might make a confession is _____ _____ _____ _____ .
❹ discourage (dis-**kur**-ej) *verb* **Rating:** 1 2 3	To **discourage** people is to _____ them. **prevent** **inspire**	A person should discourage a friend from _____ _____ _____ _____ .

Key Word	Check Your Understanding	Deepen Your Understanding
5 **fate** (fāt) *noun* **Rating:** **1 2 3**	The **fate** of something is its _____. **future**　　　**past**	I believe it is my fate to _____ _____ _____ _____ _____.
6 **literacy** (**li**-tu-ru-sē) *noun* **Rating:** **1 2 3**	**Literacy** is a kind of _____. **ignorance**　　　**knowledge**	Literacy is important because _____ _____ _____ _____ _____.
7 **profession** (pru-**fe**-shun) *noun* **Rating:** **1 2 3**	A **profession** is a _____. **hobby**　　　**career**	A profession I would like to know more about is _____ _____ _____ _____ _____.
8 **reputation** (re-pyu-**tā**-shun) *noun* **Rating:** **1 2 3**	A **reputation** is an _____ others have about you. **opinion**　　　**enthusiasm**	I have a reputation for being _____ _____ _____ _____ _____.

B. Use one of the Key Vocabulary words to write about a time your knowledge about something gave you power.

_____

_____

Before Reading Curtis Aikens and the American Dream

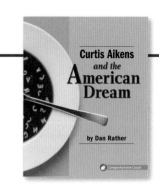

LITERARY ANALYSIS: Analyze Text Structure: Chronology

A biography tells the true story of someone's life, including information about important events and people. Authors often describe events in the order they happened using sequence words, dates, and times. This organization is called **chronological order.**

A. Read the passage below. Find clues that show you this is a biography written in chronological order. Write the clues in the chart.

> **Look Into the Text**
>
> In the third grade, Curtis made a decision that would determine the course of his life. As he sat through a parent-teacher conference, he heard his teacher praise him: "'I just love having your boy in my class,'" Curtis remembers her saying. "'He's a great kid, he's sweet,' and then I heard a 'but.' And I thought, 'Oh no. What's this? But he's dumb? He's stupid?'" Well, no. She didn't say anything close to that, but she did say that he had some reading trouble, and she thought it would be best for him to repeat the third grade.

Type of Clue	Examples in Passage
Dates and times	third grade
Sequence words	
Important event	
Important people	

B. Complete the sentence.

The most important event in Curtis's life was _____

_____

_____ .

FOCUS STRATEGY: Ask Questions

HOW TO SELF-QUESTION

1. **Ask Yourself Questions** Asking questions as you read is a good way to find new information or solve problems.

2. **Make a Question-Answer Chart** Ask *Who, What, Where, When, Why,* and *How* questions.

3. **Reread the Passage** to find the answers. If you can't find the answers in the text, ask a classmate or teacher.

A. Read the passage below. Use the strategies above to self-question as you read. Complete the Question-Answer Chart. Use the 5W/How questions.

Look Into the Text

> "I was shocked. I was floored. I'm thinking to myself, 'Well, I'm not gonna let anyone ever call me dumb or stupid again.' So instead of learning to read, I learned to hide the fact that I couldn't read." Bad choice, as Curtis would find out. Faking it took a good deal more effort than if he had simply asked for help. As he grew older, he felt that if anyone found out his secret, the label "stupid, dumb" would be much bigger and harder to shake. So he dug himself deeper and deeper into a hole.

Question-Answer Chart

My Questions	My Answers

B. Describe how self-questioning helped you understand the passage.

_____

_____

Selection Review Curtis Aikens and the American Dream

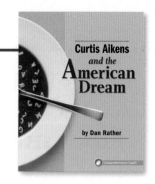

 How Can Knowledge Open Doors?
Consider how learning can give you power.

A. In "Curtis Aikens and the American Dream," you found out how knowledge gave Curtis power. Complete the T Chart with the events in Curtis's life before and after he learned to read and write.

T Chart

Before Curtis Learned to Read and Write	After Curtis Learned to Read and Write
Watching TV and listening to music helped Curtis develop a strong vocabulary and self-confidence to fool people into thinking he could read and write.	His self-confidence increased and was no longer an act.

B. Use the information in the chart to answer the questions.

1. How did Curtis's life change after he learned to read and write?

_____

_____

2. Why does Curtis support the cause of literacy? Use **cause** in your answer.

_____

_____

3. How might your life be different if you could not read or write?

_____

_____

Connect Across Texts

"Curtis Aikens and the American Dream" describes how one person reaches for success by learning. In this essay, what does basketball star Magic Johnson say to people about success in life?

Go For It!

by Earvin "Magic" Johnson
with William Novak

Basketball was my ticket to success. But if I hadn't been good enough at basketball, I would have been successful in something else.

Magic Johnson at the 1992 Olympics in Barcelona, Spain

I would have gone to college, and worked hard, and made something of myself. You can do that, too. Basketball is not the best way to get ahead. It's probably the most difficult path you could take. There are thirty teams in the **NBA**, and each team has twelve players. That makes 360 players who are in the league at any one time. In a country as big as ours, that's not a big number. There are about 1,800 college seniors who play ball, and only a few of them are good enough to be **drafted**. So even if you're good enough and fortunate enough to play in college, what makes you think you're going to play in the NBA? You have to understand that your chances of playing basketball for a living are **miniscule**.

The black community already has enough basketball players. And enough baseball players, and football players. But there are a lot of other people we could really use. We need more teachers. We need more lawyers. We need more doctors. We need more accountants. We need more nurses. We need more pilots. And more scientists. And more carpenters. And more professors. And more police officers. And more bankers. And more computer programmers. And more mechanics. And more **social workers**. And more car dealers. And more politicians.

We need more teachers . . . And more scientists.

And every single one of these **professions** *—including doctor and lawyer— is easier to get into than the NBA.*

If you can possibly go to college, go! I know it's hard. I know that some kids you know will **discourage** you. If you're **ambitious**, if you

Key Vocabulary
- **profession** *n.*, job that requires education or training
- **discourage** *v.*, to make someone not want to do something
- **ambitious** *adj.*, having big goals

In Other Words
NBA National Basketball Association
drafted chosen to play on a professional team
miniscule tiny
social workers people who work for a city or state to help other people

Magic lives up to his name.

Earvin "Magic" Johnson got his nickname in high school after a local sportswriter saw him in action on the basketball court. Johnson went on to play basketball for two years at Michigan State University in East Lansing. Then in 1979, he was drafted by the NBA to play for the Los Angeles Lakers. From there, he went on to make NBA history. He was named to the NBA All-Star team twelve times and was voted both league and NBA Finals Most Valuable Player three times. He retired from the NBA in 1991. Johnson was a member of the USA's famous "Dream Team," which won a gold medal at the 1992 Olympics. He was voted into the Naismith Memorial Basketball Hall of Fame in 2002.

Magic Johnson spends time with students at his computer center in Philadelphia, PA.

His basketball career over, Johnson continues to amaze. He is the head of Magic Johnson Enterprises, a company that tries to bring business to urban areas. It is estimated that he is worth $800 million from his post-basketball activities. But Johnson gives back to the community through his charity, The Magic Johnson Foundation. He provides scholarships and develops community centers and technology training centers. Johnson lives up to his own advice: Go for it!

study hard, if your goals are high, some people may tell you you're "acting white." Stay away from these people! They are not your friends. If the people around you aren't going anywhere, if their dreams are no bigger than hanging out on the corner, or if they're **dragging you down**, get rid of them. Negative people can **sap your energy** so fast, and they can take your dreams from you, too.

In Other Words

dragging you down making it harder for you to succeed

sap your energy take away your desire to reach your goals

Interact with the Text

3. Text Features
Look at the photo and the caption on this page. What information do they provide? Why is a photo a good way to show this information?

4. Interpret
Do you agree that you should not spend time with people who have no dreams for their lives? Why or why not?

5. Question the Author

Underline a sentence that you find confusing or that you think others may find confusing. Ask a question about the author to help you understand his opinion or belief.

I don't mean to tell you it's easy. It's *not* easy. Growing up today is hard. I know that. It's much harder than when I was your age. We've got to quit making excuses. Quit feeling sorry for ourselves. We have to go to college. Think about business. Work hard. Support one another, like other groups do.

The government will not save you.

The black leadership will not save you.

You're the only one who can make the difference.

Whatever your dream is, go for it. ❖

Selection Review Go For It!

A. Choose one of the questions you provided in your answer to question 2 on page 152 or question 5 on this page. Answer the questions below.

1. What was your question?

_____

2. What answer did you find?

_____

_____

3. What evidence in the text supports your answer?

_____

_____

_____

B. Answer the questions.

1. How did the photos and captions help support the author's opinions and beliefs?

_____

_____

2. The author lists things that help people achieve their goals. Which one of these has influenced your life?

_____

Reflect and Assess

▷ Curtis Aikens and the American Dream
▷ Go For It!

WRITING: Write About Literature

A. Plan your writing. List examples from both texts that describe how knowledge can open doors to success in the future.

Curtis Aikens and the American Dream	Go For It!

B. Write a public service announcement that encourages high school students to go to a technical school or college. Include information and quotes from each selection.

_____

_____

_____

_____

_____

_____

_____

_____

_____

_____

_____

Integrate the Language Arts

LITERARY ANALYSIS: Analyze Text Structure: Chronology

Chronology is the order in which events happen. Authors often organize biographies in chronological order.

A. List sequence words that show chronological order.

Sequence Words	
1. first	5.
2.	6.
3.	7.
4.	8.

B. The following events from "Curtis Aikens and the American Dream" are presented out of order. Use the sequence words from the chart to write a paragraph about Aikens and his life in chronological order.

Events:

Curtis learned to read. Curtis started a produce company in California. Curtis dropped out of college. Curtis decided to become a celebrity to promote the cause of literacy. Curtis heard a public service announcement from Literacy Volunteers of America.

_____

_____

_____

_____

_____

C. Think about what you or someone you know did yesterday. Recount those events in chronological order. Use at least five different sequence words.

_____

_____

_____

_____

_____

_____

_____

_____

VOCABULARY STUDY: Dictionary and Jargon

Many English words have an everyday meaning and a specialized meaning. **Jargon** is the specialized language of a career field. Meanings of words also vary according to their parts of speech. Word meanings and parts of speech can be found in a **dictionary**.

A. The words in the chart below are all related to baseball. Look up each word in the dictionary and write the specialized and the everyday meaning.

Word	Specialized Meaning	Everyday Meaning
bat	a solid stick used for hitting a ball	
hit		
pitcher		
run		

B. Brainstorm words that have both a specialized meaning and an everyday meaning, and list each in the chart.

Word	Specialized Meaning	Everyday Meaning

C. Write a sentence for each word in Activity B using one of the meaning types.

1. _____

2. _____

3. _____

4. _____

Prepare to Read

▷ **Superman and Me**
▷ **A Smart Cookie**
▷ **It's Our Story, Too**

Key Vocabulary

A. How well do you know these words? Circle a rating for each word. Check your understanding of each word by circling *yes* or *no*. Then write a definition. If you are unsure of a word's meaning, refer to the Vocabulary Glossary, page 878, in your student text.

Rating Scale	
1	I have never seen this word before.
2	I am not sure of the word's meaning.
3	I know this word and can teach the word's meaning to someone else.

Key Word	Check Your Understanding	Deepen Your Understanding
❶ arrogant (**ar**-u-gunt) *adjective* **Rating:** 1 2 3	A person who is **arrogant** would never brag. **Yes** **No**	My definition: _____ _____ _____ _____
❷ assume (u-**sūm**) *verb* **Rating:** 1 2 3	You might **assume** a very old car will not run. **Yes** **No**	My definition: _____ _____ _____ _____
❸ constant (**kon**-stunt) *adjective* **Rating:** 1 2 3	There is usually **constant** noise at a football game. **Yes** **No**	My definition: _____ _____ _____ _____
❹ disgusted (di-**skus**-tid) *adjective* **Rating:** 1 2 3	Someone might feel **disgusted** by a respectful comment. **Yes** **No**	My definition: _____ _____ _____ _____

Key Word	Check Your Understanding	Deepen Your Understanding
5 prodigy (**prah**-du-jē) *noun* **Rating:** 1 2 3	A **prodigy** might be able to play the piano before learning to tie his or her shoes. **Yes** **No**	My definition: _____ _____ _____ _____ _____
6 recall (rē-**kawl**) *verb* **Rating:** 1 2 3	Someone who loves music might **recall** his or her favorite song. **Yes** **No**	My definition: _____ _____ _____ _____ _____
7 shame (**shām**) *noun* **Rating:** 1 2 3	A person might feel **shame** after lying to a friend. **Yes** **No**	My definition: _____ _____ _____ _____ _____
8 standard (**stan**-durd) *noun* **Rating:** 1 2 3	A restaurant with a high **standard** for excellence would use the best ingredients in its food. **Yes** **No**	My definition: _____ _____ _____ _____ _____

B. Use one of the Key Vocabulary words to write about what you have discovered from reading a favorite book.

_____

_____

LITERARY ANALYSIS: Analyze Text Structure: Cause and Effect

Authors use **cause and effect** to explain how one event (the cause) leads to another event (the effect).

A. Read the passage below. In the Cause-and-Effect Chart, list examples of cause-and-effect relationships in the text.

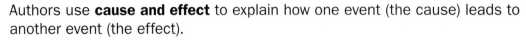

> In a fit of unemployment-inspired creative energy, my father
> built a set of bookshelves and soon filled them with a random
> assortment of books about the Kennedy assassination, Watergate,
> the Vietnam War, and the entire twenty-three-book series of the
> Apache westerns. My father loved books, and since I loved my
> father with an aching devotion, I decided to love books as well.

Cause-and-Effect Chart

Cause	Effect
My father was unemployed.	He built a set of bookshelves.

B. Complete the sentences.

The narrator developed a love for books because _____
_____ .

The narrator's father built a set of bookshelves because _____
_____ .

FOCUS STRATEGY: Ask Questions

How to FIND QUESTION-ANSWER RELATIONSHIPS

1. **Ask Questions** As you read, ask *Who, What, Where, When, Why* and *How* questions to learn how important events are related.

2. **Reread** Go back to find answers that are "right there" in the text.

3. **Read On** Keep reading to find answers later if the answer cannot be found in this section.

A. Read the passage. Use the strategies above to find question-answer relationships as you read. Then answer the questions below.

Look Into the Text

I was three years old, a Spokane Indian boy living with his family on the Spokane Indian Reservation in eastern Washington state. We were poor by most standards, but one of my parents usually managed to find some minimum-wage job or another, which made us middle-class by reservation standards. I had a brother and three sisters. We lived on a combination of irregular paychecks, hope, fear, and government-surplus food.

1. Why was the narrator's family considered to be middle-class by reservation standards?

   _____

   _____

2. Which of the three strategies did you use to answer question 1? Explain.

   _____

   _____

B. Return to the passage above and underline the words or sentences that gave you the answer to the first question. Then ask another 5W or H question. Which strategy did you use to find the answer?

Question: _____

Strategy: _____

Selection Review Superman and Me

 How Can Knowledge Open Doors?
Discover how books can take you places.

A. In "Superman and Me," you found out how reading changed Sherman Alexie's life and opened up doors for him. In the Goal-and-Outcome Chart, list the events that had an effect on the outcome of Alexie's goal.

Goal-and-Outcome Chart

> **Goal:** to not be like the other Native Americans who felt that to be a failure was the only option

Event 1:

Event 2:

Event 3:

Outcome:

B. Use the information in the chart to answer the questions.

1. How did reading affect Alexie's life?

_____

_____

2. What did other people assume about Alexie because he was Native American? Use **assume** in your answer.

_____

_____

3. In the end, Alexie describes students who have given up. Why do you think those students resist learning?

_____

_____

Connect Across Texts

In "Superman and Me," Sherman Alexie describes how a comic book changed his life. Read "A Smart Cookie" and "It's Our Story, Too" to learn how Cisneros's book changed the life of one of her readers.

A Smart Cookie

by Sandra Cisneros

Do words have the power to change lives?
Author Sandra Cisneros's characters (and
her readers) certainly think so.

I could've been somebody, you know? my mother says and sighs. She has lived in this city her whole life. She can speak two languages. She can sing an opera. She knows how to fix a T.V. But she doesn't know which subway train to take to get downtown. I hold her hand very tight while we wait for the right train to arrive.

She used to draw when she had time. Now she draws with a needle and thread, little knotted rosebuds, tulips made of silk thread. Someday she would like to go to the ballet. Someday she would like to see a play. She borrows opera records from the public library and sings with **velvety lungs powerful as morning glories**.

Today while cooking oatmeal she is **Madame Butterfly** until she sighs and points the wooden spoon at me. I could've been somebody, you know? Esperanza, you go to school. Study hard. That Madame Butterfly was a fool. She stirs the oatmeal. Look at my *comadres*. She means Izaura whose husband left and Yolanda whose husband is dead. Got to take care all your own, she says shaking her head.

Then out of nowhere:

Shame is a bad thing, you know. **It keeps you down.** You want to know why I quit school? Because I didn't have nice clothes. No clothes, but I had brains.

Yup, she says **disgusted**, stirring again. I was a smart cookie then.

The Dreamer, 2002, Patssi Valdez. Acrylic on canvas.

▲ **Critical Viewing: Design**
What is the title of this work? How do the colors and light contribute to its meaning?

Key Vocabulary
shame *n.*, a painful feeling that is caused by embarrassment or guilt
disgusted *adj.*, feeling very upset

In Other Words
velvety lungs powerful as morning glories a strong and beautiful voice
Madame Butterfly a famous opera character
comadres very good friends (in Spanish)
It keeps you down. It keeps you from being happy and doing what you want to do.

It's Our Story, Too

by Yvette Cabrera

The Orange County Register (Santa Ana, California)
April 15, 2002

Growing up, I studied books my high school English teachers said were must reads for a well-rounded education. Books like J. D. Salinger's *Catcher in the Rye*, Fyodor Dostoyevsky's *Crime and Punishment*, and Thomas Hardy's *Tess of the d'Urbervilles*.

It was literature with great meaning that taught important lessons. But still, **I felt a disconnection**. *Beowulf* was an epic poem. But as my high school teacher went into great detail explaining what **a mail shirt** was, I wondered what that had to do with my life.

It was that way all through high school. Then one day in college I was assigned to read *The House on Mango Street*.

Mango. The word alone **evoked memories** of childhood weekends. Back then my family and I would pile into our sky-blue Chevrolet Malibu and head to **Olvera Street's plaza** in downtown Los Angeles.

For my sisters and me, the treat for behaving ourselves was a juicy mango on a stick sold at a fruit stand in the plaza. We would squeeze lemon and sprinkle chile and salt over the bright yellow slices.

As an adult, whenever I had a reporting assignment near Olvera Street, I'd always take a minute to stop. Standing amid the smell of sizzling *carne asada*, the sounds of **vendors negotiating** prices in Spanish, and children licking a rainbow of *raspados* (shaved ice treats), I would bite into my mango and feel at home.

That's what *The House on Mango Street* did for me.

Fresh fruit from a fruit stand at the Olvera Street plaza in Los Angeles, California

Interact with the Text

1. Text Structure: Chronology
Highlight the phrase the author uses to show a flashback. Then highlight a phrase that signals another time shift. Explain how these words signal how time changes.

_____
_____
_____
_____
_____
_____
_____
_____
_____

In Other Words
felt a disconnection couldn't relate to the stories
a mail shirt armor in old battles
evoked memories reminded me
Olvera Street's plaza an outdoor shopping area that is famous for its Hispanic products
carne asada grilled steak (in Spanish)
vendors negotiating sellers arguing about

2. Interpret

How did reading *The House on Mango Street* remind the author of her childhood? How do you think the author feels about her childhood?

_____

_____

_____

_____

_____

_____

_____

3. Find Question-Answer Relationships

Underline words and phrases that show why the author felt so connected to Cisneros's book. Explain how you found your answer.

_____

_____

_____

_____

_____

_____

_____

_____

_____

East on the 10, 2001, Frank Romero. Oil on wood, private collection.

▲ **Critical Viewing: Effect** What mood do the colors and lines create? How might this reflect the feeling of a large city like Los Angeles?

On the first page, Esperanza explains how at school they say her name funny, "as if the syllables were made out of tin and hurt the roof of your mouth." I was **hooked**.

I knew nothing of the East Coast **prep schools** or the English **shires** of the books I had read before. But like Esperanza, I could remember how different my last name sounded when it was **pronounced melodically** by my parents but **so haltingly** by everyone else.

Cisneros's hometown of Chicago may have been hundreds of miles away from the palm-tree lined streets of Santa Barbara, California, where I grew up. But in her world I was no longer **the minority**.

In Other Words

hooked so interested I couldn't stop reading it
prep schools expensive private schools
shires villages
pronounced melodically said in a musical way

so haltingly said in a jerky, ugly way
the minority part of the small group that no one seemed to notice or care about

That was a dozen years ago. Today, Latinos are the **majority** in cities like Santa Ana, California, where Cisneros spoke at Valley High School.

Today, these students can pick from bookstore shelves filled with authors such as Julia Álvarez, Victor Villaseñor, and Judith Ortiz Cofer. These are authors who go beyond **census numbers** to explain what U.S. Latino life is about.

Cisneros provided an hour of humorous storytelling that had the students busting with laughter. They crowded in line afterward, **giddily** waiting to get her autograph.

"Everything she explains, what she says is true," Jessica Cordova, a 10th-grader at Valley High School, says of *The House on Mango Street.* "She puts a lot of emotion, feeling, and thought into the book."

Later, as I talk to Cisneros, she explains how much **the literary world** has changed since she finished writing *The House on Mango Street* twenty years ago. Back then, forget trying to get *The New York Times* to review your book if you were Latino—or getting a major bookseller to carry it, she says.

One thing has remained **constant**, something that Cisneros can see by the question that's most asked by students.

The House on Mango Street is a book by Sandra Cisneros. The narrator is a Latina girl named Esperanza, who describes people and events in her neighborhood.

Key Vocabulary
- **constant** *adj.*, the same, without any change

In Other Words
majority group which has the most people
census numbers the official number of people who live in the country
giddily excitedly
the literary world the book-selling and publishing businesses

4. Interpret
Underline the words that show how much time has passed since Cisneros wrote *The House on Mango Street*. What can you conclude about the influence Latino authors have had since then?

5. Text Structure: Chronology
Underline the signal words and phrases that show this is taking place in the present. Explain why the author chose to conclude the memoir in the present tense.

_____

_____

_____

_____

_____

_____

_____

_____

"They want to know, 'Is this real? Did this happen to you?'" Cisneros says. "They're so concerned and want to make sure this is my story, because it's their story, too." ❖

Selection Review   A Smart Cookie; It's Our Story, Too

A. Write a question that you would like to ask either Cisneros or Cabrera about these selections.

Question: _____

Describe how you can find the answers to your questions in the text. _____

_____

_____

B. Answer the questions.

1. Why do the authors use flashbacks to tell their stories? How are they effective?

_____

_____

2. Reread page 164. Describe one way that Esperanza's mother's advice might have opened doors for Esperanza.

_____

_____

Reflect and Assess

WRITING: Write About Literature

A. Plan your writing. List examples of advice that each author gives to struggling students.

Sherman Alexie	Sandra Cisneros	Yvette Cabrera
read whenever possible		

B. Choose one of the struggling students you have read about—one of Alexie's students, Esperanza's mother, or young Yvette Cabrera. Write an e-mail message offering advice about how the student can change his or her attitude toward school and reading. Use examples from each selection.

_____

_____

_____

_____

_____

_____

_____

_____

Integrate the Language Arts

LITERARY ANALYSIS: Analyze Imagery

Imagery is language that appeals to the five senses. It helps readers picture what is being described.

A. Read the excerpt below from "Superman and Me." On a separate sheet of paper, draw a picture of the image.

> . . . Our house was filled with books. They were stacked in crazy piles in the bathroom, bedrooms, and living room. In a fit of unemployment-inspired creative energy, my father built a set of bookshelves and soon filled them with a random assortment of books about the Kennedy assassination, Watergate, the Vietnam War, and the entire twenty-three-book series of the Apache westerns.

B. Choose words or phrases from all three selections that appeal to the five senses. Complete the chart below with the imagery. Cite the page number and the selection.

Sense	Page Number / Selection	Imagery
Sight	page 353, "It's Our Story, Too"	"palm-tree lined streets of Santa Barbara, California"
Taste		
Smell		
Sound		
Touch		

C. Use imagery to describe a place you know well or an experience you have had. Include how things taste, smell, look, feel, or sound.

_____

_____

_____

_____

_____

_____

VOCABULARY STUDY: Multiple-Meaning Words

Many English words are **multiple-meaning words**, or words that have more than one meaning. You can study the context clues near the word to figure out the word's meaning.

A. Read the sentences in the chart. Use context clues to figure out the meaning of each underlined word.

Sentence	Word Meaning
The large crowd at the concert added to my excitement.	
My parents keep a record of every grade I receive on a test.	
My mom asked me to go to the store to buy milk.	
In order to sew a shirt, you need thread.	

B. Write a second meaning for each of the words.

1. crowd _____

2. record _____

3. store _____

4. thread _____

C. Write two sentences for each multiple-meaning word. Use a different meaning for each sentence.

batter _____

_____

practice _____

_____

tense _____

_____

tire _____

_____

Unit 4
Pages 362–383

Prepare to Read
▶ The Fast and the Fuel-Efficient
▶ Teens Open Doors

Key Vocabulary

A. How well do you know these words? Circle a rating for each word. Check your understanding of each word by marking an X next to the correct definition. Then complete the sentences. If you are unsure of a word's meaning, refer to the Vocabulary Glossary, page 878, in your student text.

Rating Scale

1 | I have never seen this word before.
2 | I am not sure of the word's meaning.
3 | I know this word and can teach the word's meaning to someone else.

Key Word	Check Your Understanding	Deepen Your Understanding
1 aggressive (u-**gre**-siv) *adjective* Rating: 1 2 3	☐ motivated ☐ overly energetic or forceful	A situation when you would choose to be aggressive would be when _____ _____ _____ _____ .
2 assemble (u-**sem**-bul) *verb* Rating: 1 2 3	☐ to put together ☐ to move something	If you have wood, nails, and a hammer, you can assemble a _____ _____ _____ _____ .
3 device (di-**vīs**) *noun* Rating: 1 2 3	☐ a decoration ☐ a tool used for a particular job	A device that makes communication easier is _____ _____ _____ _____ _____ .
4 efficient (i-**fi**-shunt) *adjective* Rating: 1 2 3	☐ working at a slower speed than normal ☐ working well without wasting energy	Traveling to a distant place is more efficient when you _____ _____ _____ .

172   Unit 4: Opening Doors

Key Word	Check Your Understanding	Deepen Your Understanding
⑤ environment (in-**vī**-ru-munt) *noun* **Rating:** **1 2 3**	☐ the things that surround you ☐ the things within each person	People can help the environment by _____ _____ _____ _____.
⑥ obstacle (**ahb**-sti-kul) *noun* **Rating:** **1 2 3**	☐ something that can be used as a tool ☐ something that gets in your way	An obstacle you might have when you try to get to class on time is _____ _____ _____ _____.
⑦ solution (su-**lü**-shun) *noun* **Rating:** **1 2 3**	☐ an answer that solves a problem ☐ a way of forgiving a person	One solution to an allergy problem might be _____ _____ _____ _____.
⑧ technology (tek-**nah**-lu-jē) *noun* **Rating:** **1 2 3**	☐ a resolution to a problem or difficulty ☐ scientific knowledge as it is used in the world	Examples of modern technology that I use most often are _____ _____ _____.

B. Use one of the Key Vocabulary words to describe a time when you had to
solve a difficult problem. How did you solve it?

_____

_____

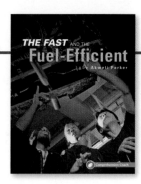

LITERARY ANALYSIS: Analyze Text Structure: Problem and Solution

Some nonfiction authors use a **problem and solution** text structure. The author introduces a problem and then explains how it is solved.

A. Read the passage below. In the Sequence Chart, write the steps the students took to solve the problem.

> **Look Into the Text**
>
> A student got under the car to pop the axle in. Kinsler yanked on the suspension to create clearance. But, after many tries, it hadn't connected.
>
> Quietly, Calvin Cheeseboro . . . took over. . . .
>
> First, the wheel-facing side popped into place. Then, with Kinsler again pulling on the suspension, the inboard side connected with the transmission with a satisfying clunk . . .
>
> The team had hopefully resolved their most difficult problem. They'd find out soon if their solution had worked.

Sequence Chart

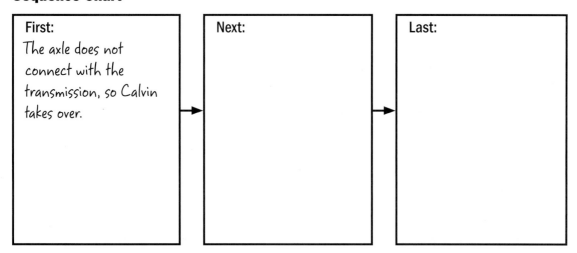

First:	Next:	Last:
The axle does not connect with the transmission, so Calvin takes over.		

B. Answer the question about the team's solution to their problem.

What problem did the team members face, and how did they solve it?

_____

_____

_____

FOCUS STRATEGY: Ask Questions

HOW TO FIND QUESTION-ANSWER RELATIONSHIPS

1. **"Right There" or "Think and Search" Questions** These are the types of questions you can find right in the text.

2. **"Author and You" Questions** Use what you have already read to figure out an answer. Check that your answers make sense with the rest of the author's ideas.

A. Read the passage. Use the strategies above to find question-answer relationships. Then answer the questions below.

Look Into the Text

> The ideas that come out of West Philly's auto shop aren't rocket science, Hauger says, but they do require imagination and some risk-taking—traits he thinks Detroit could use. He dreams of the high school program sharing the team's know-how of building hybrid cars cheaply. No major automaker sells a performance car that gets such outrageously high mileage. With oil prices high and demand for hybrids soaring, the timing could not be better.
>
> Developing a car model costs automakers about $1 billion. Even adding back the discounts and freebies the school team received—such as carbon-fiber body panels and custom wheels—the Attack would still have clocked in well under $100,000. Hauger estimated their two-seater, if mass-produced, could sell for about $50,000.

1. What is the auto shop trying to accomplish?

_____

_____

2. Which of the two strategies did you use to answer question 1?

_____

_____

B. Return to the passage above and underline the words or sentences that gave you the answer to the question.

Selection Review The Fast and the Fuel-Efficient

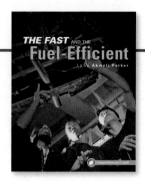

 How Can Knowledge Open Doors?
Explore how knowledge changes the world.

A. In "The Fast and the Fuel-Efficient," you learned how a group of students overcame many problems and discovered that knowledge and hard work can open doors. Write the events of the competition and the final outcome in the chart.

Goal-and-Outcome Chart

Goal:	Teachers wanted to instill the values of hard work and responsibility to a group of students whose environment outside of school encouraged the opposite.

Event 1:

Event 2:

Event 3:

Outcome:

B. Use the information in the chart to answer the questions.

1. How did the problems along the way eventually help the team?

_____

_____

2. Explain how the students' environment was or was not an obstacle to winning the competition. Use **environment** and **obstacle** in your answer.

_____

_____

3. How might this high-school experience benefit these students in the future?

_____

_____

_____

Teens Open Doors

by Richard Thompson

Connect Across Texts

*The students in "The Fast and the Fuel-Efficient" found that the **technology** they used could change the world. As you read this article, consider how technology can open all sorts of doors.*

Getting through high school can be challenging for any teenager. For junior Molly Rizk, who has **cerebral palsy**, one of the most difficult tasks is not taking tests at Whittier Regional Vocational Technical High School. It's opening her locker.

That should change in the fall, thanks to the skill of four classmates who have designed and produced a locker remote control. It will allow Rizk to get into her locker as quickly as other students.

Assistive Technology: Resources that help people with disabilities to become more independent.

Examples:
- wheelchairs, crutches, and other equipment
- hearing aids, text phones, and captioned TV

The wheels of the iBot wheelchair can lift a person to standing height.

The remote control took less than two months to complete. It was one of four entries last month at the University of Massachusetts-Lowell's Assistive Technology Design Fair. The fair is a noncompetitive event that gives **engineering experience** to high school students who complete projects that help people with special needs or disabilities.

Since it began in 2002, the fair has grown. Now it includes more than 100 students from a dozen schools across the country.

Interact with the Text

1. Interpret
Highlight the sentence that tells what the students in the school did for Molly. How do you think this made her feel?

Key Vocabulary
- **technology** *n.*, scientific knowledge as it is used in the world

In Other Words
cerebral palsy a condition that affects the central nervous system
engineering experience experience in designing, building, and using machines

2. Development of Ideas

Underline the exact words that someone said about the benefits of the project. How does this quotation elaborate on the ideas in the article?

_____

_____

_____

_____

_____

_____

_____

_____

3. Find Question-Answer Relationships

What other school departments were involved in this project? Circle the answer in the text. Then tell which strategy you used to answer this question.

_____

_____

_____

_____

_____

_____

_____

_____

_____

For juniors Zachary Drapeau and Tom Smallwood, and seniors Casey Hansen and Nathan Lindberg, their work could make getting through college easier to afford. If they choose to **enroll** at University of Massachusetts-Lowell, each student will be able to apply for a $2,000 grant for each of the four years.

"We tried to run this like it was a real-world project that an engineering company would go through," said Paul Moskevitz, a machine technology instructor who was a **mentor** to the group.

More than a dozen students at Whittier contributed to the final product, Moskevitz said. He added that he liked how a variety of the school's programs, including carpentry, electronics, robotics, and metal fabrication, were involved.

"We have lots of capabilities at this school, and it was good for folks to see the other **disciplines**," Moskevitz said.

Students must use keys to unlock their lockers at Whittier. The **device** developed by the four students lets Rizk use a remote control. It automatically slides the bolt out of the lock. They have also given her a specially designed key. It is molded to fit her grasp, in case the batteries in the remote stop working.

The remote control uses **an infrared signal**. It ensures that if more than one is used in a hallway, the signal will only be able to open the locker **programmed to the same encryption**.

Assistive Technology:
Resources that help people with disabilities to become more independent.
More examples:
- voice recognition, Braille, and other touch technology
- symbols-based computer software, switch technology, speech-generators
- prosthetic limbs

High school senior Ryan Patterson invented a glove that deaf people can wear to send messages to a screen for others to read.

Key Vocabulary
- **device** _n._, machine or tool that is used to do a particular job

In Other Words
enroll go to school
mentor teacher and guide
disciplines types of classes and studies
an infrared signal a powerful beam of light
programmed to the same encryption that has the same code

Molly Rizk tests the new device.

Interact with the Text

4. Interpret
Why do you think the author chose to write about this project?

_____

_____

_____

_____

_____

_____

_____

_____

5. Find Question-Answer Relationships
Who else do the students hope to help with their invention? Underline the answer in the text. Which strategy would help you determine how this product might help those people?

_____

_____

_____

_____

_____

_____

_____

_____

_____

_____

_____

"There was a lot of **trial and error** along the way," Smallwood said. "Especially trying to fit the parts together and trying to get things to work and to have everything centered so the **deadbolt** would come across and strike the plate at the right time."

In the last few weeks, the students have been in the process of **patenting** their device. David Cunningham, the school's technology chairman, said he hopes that the device could have **broader application**. It's a realistic possibility, he said, given that the setup can be easily **duplicated and maintained**.

Next year, school officials plan to "check with local **nursing homes** . . . to see if this device could be used" to help **their residents**, Cunningham said.

Mike Hart, president of the Haverhill Rotary Club, saw the remote control in action last month when the students sat in on one of his

In Other Words
trial and error testing new ideas and then fixing them if they didn't work
deadbolt metal bar in the lock
patenting getting ownership of
broader application many more uses

duplicated and maintained made again and taken care of
nursing homes homes for people with very serious health problems
their residents the people who live there

6. Development of Ideas
Highlight Molly's words on this page. What do her words tell you about her previous experiences with people, especially her peers?

group's weekly meetings. Hart said he was "very impressed." The presentation "really added a lot to the meeting . . . I was amazed at **the sophistication and the complexity of** the device," he said. "It was just beyond what you would've expected their achievements to be."

Rizk said she was moved by the commitment of her classmates.

"When I first saw the actual locker, I was touched that the kids had built this for me," said Rizk. "I really appreciated that they took the time out of their busy schedules to do this for me, and I've learned that people can be very caring once you get to know them." ❖

In Other Words
the sophistication and the complexity of
the professional quality and hard work that was shown in

Selection Review Teens Open Doors

A. Choose one of the questions below, and answer it by using one of the question-answer strategies. Next to your answer, write the strategy you used.

Question 1: Why did the students want to build this device for Molly?
Question 2: How will the students benefit from this project?

_____

_____

_____

_____

B. Answer the questions.

1. What did the quotations in the text help you understand?

_____

_____

2. What are other challenges that Molly might face at school? What are ways that these might be solved?

_____

_____

_____

Reflect and Assess

WRITING: Write About Literature

A. Plan your writing. Think about the work that the West Philly team and the students at Whittier High School did as described in these selections. Write which project you think is more important in the center oval. Then support your choice with examples from the text in the outer ovals.

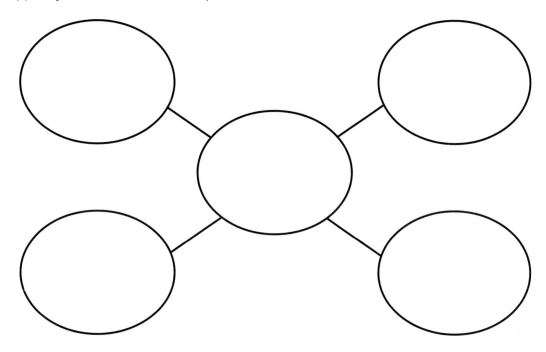

B. What is your opinion? Which group's work is more important? Write an opinion statement. Explain your opinion and support it with examples from both selections.

_____

_____

_____

_____

_____

_____

_____

_____

_____

_____

_____

_____

_____

_____

LITERARY ANALYSIS: Analyze Text Structure: Problem and Solution

Some nonfiction authors use a **problem and solution** text structure. The author introduces a problem and then describes how the problem is solved.

A. Write the main problem in "The Fast and the Fuel-Efficient." Then list the smaller problems that had to be solved along the way.

Main Problem	Smaller Problems

B. Write a brief paragraph describing how the main and the smaller problems were solved in "The Fast and the Fuel-Efficient."

_____

_____

_____

_____

_____

_____

C. Describe a problem that the students in "Teens Open Doors" struggled with. What was their solution?

_____

_____

_____

_____

_____

VOCABULARY STUDY: Multiple-Meaning Words

Many **multiple-meaning words** have specialized meanings in different subject areas.

A. For each word, look in a dictionary to find a specialized definition in two subject areas. Write the subject areas and the definitions below.

1. area

_____

_____

2. difference

_____

_____

3. formula

_____

_____

B. Brainstorm words you know that have two or more multiple meanings, and write them in the chart below. Then write two or more specialized definitions. Use a dictionary to help you, if needed.

Word	Specialized Meanings

C. Write two sentences for each word in the chart above using each meaning.

1. _____

_____

2. _____

_____

3. _____

_____

The Sky Is Not the Limit

Read for Understanding

1. Genre What kind of text is each part? How do you know?

_____

_____

_____

_____

_____

2. Topic Write a topic sentence to tell what these texts are mostly about.

_____

_____

_____

_____

_____

_____

Reread and Summarize

3. Key Ideas Circle three words or phrases that best express the key ideas in each part of the selection. Note why each word or phrase is important.

· Part 1: pages 184–185
· Part 2: pages 186–187

4. Summary Use your topic sentence and notes to write a summary of the whole selection.

_____

_____

_____

_____

_____

_____

_____

_____

_____

_____

110th CONGRESS
    1st Session
H. RES. 661

House Calendar No. 158

RESOLUTION

1   _Honoring the accomplishments of Barrington Antonio Irving, the youngest pilot and first person of African descent ever to fly solo around the world._

2   **Whereas** Barrington Irving was born in 1983 in Kingston, Jamaica, and raised in inner-city Miami, Florida;

3   Whereas Irving discovered his passion for aviation at the age of 15 when Captain Gary Robinson, a Jamaican airline pilot who has since served as his mentor, took him to tour the **cockpit of a Boeing 777**;

4   Whereas Irving overcame financial hardship to pursue his dream to become a pilot by working miscellaneous jobs and working for private aircraft owners in exchange for flying lessons;

5   Whereas Irving was the recipient of a joint Air Force/Florida Memorial University Flight Awareness Scholarship to cover college tuition and flying lessons for his tireless volunteer efforts and commitment to community service;

6   Whereas in 2003, Irving contacted companies including aircraft manufacturer Columbia, which agreed to provide him with a plane to fly around the world if he could secure **donations and components**;

7   Whereas over several years, Irving visited **aviation trade shows** throughout the country and secured more than $300,000 of cash and donated components including the engine, tires, cockpit systems, and seats for a Columbia 400, one of the world's fastest single-engine piston airplanes;

In Other Words

Whereas Since
cockpit of a Boeing 777 steering area of a large airplane
donations and components money and parts
aviation trade shows meetings of companies that sell airplane parts

Social Studies Background

Resolutions are documents created by members of the United States Congress. Unlike bills, simple resolutions are not laws. Instead, they may give advice, honors, or opinions.

8   Whereas in the process of pursuing his dream of an around the world flight, Irving founded a nonprofit organization in 2005 to address the significant shortage of youth pursuing careers in aviation and aerospace;

9   Whereas Irving's efforts have **garnered** widespread community support and sponsorship as an effective model to expose young people and underrepresented groups to opportunities in aviation;

10 Whereas on March 23, 2007, Irving embarked from Miami, Florida, on a 24,600-mile flight around the world in an airplane named "Inspiration" at 23-years of age while still a senior majoring in aerospace at Florida Memorial University;

11 Whereas on June 27, 2007, Irving concluded his flight in Miami, Florida, after stopping in 27 cities throughout the world; and

12 Whereas Irving continues to inspire youth and adults alike with his achievements and work to increase the accessibility of opportunities in aviation and aerospace: Now, therefore, be it

13   Resolved, that the House of Representatives—

14   (1) honors the accomplishments of Barrington Irving, the youngest pilot and first person of African **descent** ever to fly solo around the world and founder of a nonprofit organization that inspires youth to pursue careers in aviation and aerospace;

15   (2) encourages young people and minorities to pursue educational opportunities in preparation for careers in aviation and related industries; and

16   (3) encourages museums throughout the Nation related to aviation to commemorate the historic achievements of Captain Barrington Irving.

In Other Words
garnered gotten
descent ancestry

Reread and Analyze

5. Text Structure: Chronology   Reread paragraphs 1 and 2. Underline dates or ages that give clues about the sequence of events. Which event happens first?

6. Text Structure: Chronology   Reread paragraphs 3–11 and highlight more dates, ages, and sequence words that tell about the chronology of events. What did Irving do before he flew around the world?

7. Text Features   Review paragraphs 13–16. What text features help to show the most important parts of the resolution?

8. Text Structure: Chronology Reread paragraphs 4–6. Highlight sequence words or phrases that help signal chronological order.

9. Text Structure: Chronology Reread paragraph 7 and look for clues that tell about sequence. Then write numbers beside the events below to show the order in which they happened.

_____ Irving started Experience Aviation.

_____ Irving learned how to fly planes using simulator software.

_____ Irving decided to give back to his community.

10. Text Features Circle the quotation on this page that states Irving's exact words. Why do you think the author includes this quotation?

_____
_____
_____
_____
_____
_____

http://myNGconnect.com/Pilot

HOME **NEWS** SPORTS ENTERTAINMENT BUSINESS LIVING OPINION JOBS

Posted on Tuesday, 06.05.12   A **A** | ✚ Share   **21**   email   print   comment   reprints

Miami Pilot Makes History, Inspires Others

2007, John Ross.

Barrington Irving

BY DANIELA GUZMAN
The Miami Herald

1 As a young man at Miami Northwestern Senior High School, Barrington Irving knew he had **potential**. He imagined a football scholarship to a state school would fulfill that potential. When the Opa-locka **native** was offered a full **ride** to the University of Florida, he was set.

2 But another dream took off. Before turning 29 years old, Irving became the youngest person and the first black pilot to fly around the world, the founder of a non-profit organization and most recently, one of 15 National Geographic Emerging Explorers in 2012.

3 His journey began in Miami, long before he took off on his first flight.

4 Irving was sixteen and working at his parents' bookstore in Miami Gardens when he met Gary Robinson, a customer and a commercial pilot. Robinson told Irving about the life of a pilot. Although the **salary was intriguing**, Irving didn't feel he was smart enough.

5 "I never had that confidence," Irving said.

6 But his confidence soared when Robinson invited Irving to take a test flight with him in a training plane from the Opa-locka airport. Flying above his own neighborhood, from the airport he lived so close to, Irving **became enamored** with aviation. Robinson gave Irving a handheld radio that could tune into airport traffic control, helping Irving tune into his own calling. Upon graduating, Irving rejected the UF football scholarship and started working odd jobs. He cleaned pools. He bagged groceries. But he dreamed of the skies. While he saved up, Irving started studying aeronautical science at Florida Memorial University in Miami Gardens.

In Other Words
potential the ability to become successful
native resident
ride scholarship
salary was intriguing pay was interesting
became enamored fell in love

7   With the help of his mentor, Irving started learning how to fly planes, first with simulator software, which he now uses with students grades 3 through 12 in his after-school and summer camp program, Experience Aviation. The non-profit educational program is based at Opa-locka Airport and the newly restored Glen Curtiss Mansion in Miami Springs. Through the program, which he started in 2008, he has mentored hundreds of students in the South Florida area. Because of Irving's success in aviation, he decided to give back by encouraging young people to pursue careers in science, **technology**, engineering and mathematics.

8   "My ultimate goal is to show young people that they can do amazing things," said Irving.

9   It's something that Irving showed the world when he flew around the world in a plane put together from over $300,000 worth of donated parts. Irving reached out to aviation companies, telling them about his passion for flying and aerospace engineering. The companies saw the young man's effort as remarkable. The airplane, a Cessna 400, is named the "Inspiration," and was manufactured and **assembled** by the Columbia Aircraft Mfg. Co. in 2005. Without a de-icing system or weather radar, the 23-year-old pilot took off from Miami making the unprecedented journey around the globe.

10   Upon landing, Irving felt the accomplishment would not be complete without teaching minority youth that they could do the same. Under his guidance, 60 high school students built a plane in 10 weeks—from scratch. Then, Barrington tested it out with a flight over Miami. The program evolved into Experience Aviation. There are some students in the program that are coming straight from jail, and some that are straight-A students. But according to Irving, you wouldn't be able to tell the difference when they're learning how to fly on a simulator, or building an engine.

11   Daniel Diaz, 14, an incoming ninth-grader at Coral Park Senior High, has participated in Experience Aviation for three years. While he had never seen aviation as a **field** before, he has his mind set on being an aeronautical engineer.

12   "I have a chance to do things that a lot of people my age don't have," said Diaz, who flew with Irving in a small plane last year, sealing his love for flying. "I never thought I could feel what it's like to be in the sky. Now that's all I want to do." ❖

Reread and Analyze

11. Text Features   Underline the quotation on this page that states Irving's exact words.

12. Text Features   Why does the author include this quotation?

_____

_____

_____

_____

_____

_____

_____

13. Text Structure: Chronology   Reread paragraphs 9–10. Highlight clues that show the sequence of events.

14. Text Structure: Chronology   Summarize the three most important events of paragraphs 9–10 in chronological order.

_____

_____

_____

_____

_____

_____

_____

Key Vocabulary
- **technology** _n._, scientific knowledge as it is used in the world
- **assemble** _v._, to put something together

In Other Words
field career option

CLOSE READING   The Sky Is Not the Limit

Discuss

15. **Synthesize** With the class, discuss how both selections use text
structures and features. Identify the text structure of each selection
and include specific examples of signal words and phrases. Then list
text features that help convey information and key ideas.

Selection	Text Structure	Text Features

Then, with the class, discuss how nonfiction writers use text structures
and features to organize and present information. Make notes.

_____

_____

_____

16. **Write** Write a paragraph to explain how nonfiction authors use text
structures and features to present information. Use your notes from
item 15 and the questions below to help you organize your thoughts. If
you need more space, continue your writing on another piece of paper.

> · What text structure is used in both selections?
>
> · What types of words and phrases signal the text structure?
>
> · What text features are used in the selections?
>
> · How do text features give more information about the topic?

_____

_____

_____

_____

_____

Connect with the **EQ** How Can Knowledge Open Doors?
Investigate the role of knowledge in reaching your goals.

17. **Opinion** Review the resolution and online news article to identify important details about Barrington Irving's life. Would Irving agree with the idea that knowledge can open doors? Use evidence from the text to support your response.

_____

_____

_____

_____

_____

_____

_____

_____

_____

18. **Theme** What do the two texts in "The Sky Is Not the Limit" show about the ways that people can change their own lives and the lives of others? Be sure to cite evidence from the texts to support your answer.

_____

_____

_____

_____

_____

_____

_____

_____

_____

Key Vocabulary Review

A. Read each sentence. Circle the word that best fits into each sentence.

1. It may be your (**fate** / **device**) to work with children in the future.

2. The (**disgusted** / **ambitious**) woman worked long hours and went to night classes so she could get a promotion.

3. Without (**literacy** / **confession**) it is nearly impossible to get a good job.

4. You should not let other people (**recall** / **discourage**) you from trying new things.

5. The man chose law as a (**profession** / **reputation**), so he could help other people.

6. The (**reputation** / **prodigy**) could solve complex math problems when she was five years old.

7. You may need to overcome a(n) (**obstacle** / **cause**) to achieve your goals.

8. She felt (**shame** / **fate**) after she told the teacher a lie.

B. Use your own words to write what each Key Vocabulary word means. Then write a synonym for each word.

Key Word	My Definition	Synonym
1. assemble		
2. assume		
3. cause		
4. confession		
5. constant		
6. disgusted		
7. efficient		
8. standard		

Unit 4 Key Vocabulary

aggressive	• assume	• device	• environment	prodigy	shame
ambitious	cause	discourage	fate	• profession	solution
arrogant	confession	disgusted	literacy	recall	standard
• assemble	• constant	efficient	obstacle	reputation	• technology

• **Academic Vocabulary**

C. Answer the questions using complete sentences.

1. How does **technology** make your life easier?

_____

_____

2. Name one **solution** to a problem in your community.

_____

_____

3. How might an **arrogant** person treat other people?

_____

_____

4. What happy memory do you **recall** from the past?

_____

_____

5. What is your **reputation**?

_____

_____

6. Describe a **device** you use every day.

_____

_____

7. What can you do to improve the **environment**?

_____

_____

8. Why might **aggressive** people achieve their goals?

_____

_____

Prepare to Read

▶ The Interlopers
▶ An Interview with the King of Terror

Key Vocabulary

A. How well do you know these words? Circle a rating for each word. Check your understanding of each word by circling *yes* or *no*. Then complete the sentences. If you are unsure of a word's meaning, refer to the Vocabulary Glossary, page 878, in your student text.

Rating Scale

1	I have never seen this word before.
2	I am not sure of the word's meaning.
3	I know this word and can teach the word's meaning to someone else.

Key Word	Check Your Understanding	Deepen Your Understanding
❶ boundary (**bown**-du-rē) *noun* **Rating:** 1 2 3	A fence is sometimes a **boundary** between two houses. Yes No	An example of a boundary is _____ _____ _____ _____ _____ .
❷ feud (**fyūd**) *noun* **Rating:** 1 2 3	Friends who have a **feud** get along well with each other. Yes No	One time I had a feud with _____ _____ _____ _____ _____ .
❸ grant (**grant**) *verb* **Rating:** 1 2 3	Many organizations **grant** money to people who need help. Yes No	My parents grant me permission to _____ _____ _____ _____ _____ .
❹ identification (ī-den-tu-fu-**kā**-shun) *noun* **Rating:** 1 2 3	People have trouble feeling an **identification** with others who are like them. Yes No	I feel a sense of identification with _____ _____ _____ _____ _____ .

Key Word	Check Your Understanding	Deepen Your Understanding
5 obvious (**ob**-vē-us) *adjective* **Rating:** 1 2 3	Solutions to problems are always **obvious.** **Yes** **No**	It is obvious that I _____ _____ _____ _____ .
6 reconciliation (re-kun-si-lē-**ā**-shun) *noun* **Rating:** 1 2 3	An argument usually comes after a **reconciliation.** **Yes** **No**	Once, I had a reconciliation with _____ _____ _____ _____ .
7 release (rē-**lēs**) *verb* **Rating:** 1 2 3	A careless person could accidentally **release** a bird from its cage. **Yes** **No**	I release stress by _____ _____ _____ _____ .
8 terror (**ter**-rur) *noun* **Rating:** 1 2 3	News of a tornado could spread **terror** through a small town. **Yes** **No**	I felt great terror when _____ _____ _____ _____ .

B. Use one of the Key Vocabulary words to write about a scary experience you have had because of an unexpected situation.

_____

_____

Before Reading The Interlopers

LITERARY ANALYSIS: Analyze Structure: Plot

Plot structure is the pattern of events in fiction: exposition (the introduction, or the part of the story where the characters and setting are introduced), conflict, (the main problem), complications (smaller problems), climax (the turning point), and resolution (how the story ends).

A. Read the passage below. Find the characters, setting, and plot in this introduction. Then complete the chart.

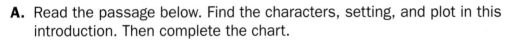

Look Into the Text

> In a forest of mixed growth somewhere in the eastern Carpathian Mountains, a man stood one winter night. He was watching and listening, as though waiting for some beast of the woods to come within the range of his vision . . . and his rifle. But the game he sought could not be found in any sportsman's guide. Ulrich von Gradwitz searched the dark forest on the hunt for a human enemy.

Elements of Exposition	Text Clues
Characters	
Setting	
Plot	

B. Answer the question about the exposition.

In what ways does the author create a frightening introduction?

_____

_____

FOCUS STRATEGY: Make Connections

A. Read the passage. Use the strategies above to make connections as you read. Then answer the questions below.

Look Into the Text

> The narrow strip of woodland around the edge of the Gradwitz forest was not remarkable, but its owner guarded it more jealously than all his other possessions. Long ago, the court had granted the land to his grandfather, taking it away from the illegal possession of a neighboring family. The family who had lost the land had never agreed with the court's decision. Over time, they began poaching trips and caused scandals that started a feud between the families which had lasted for three generations.

1. How does Gradwitz, the owner, feel about his land?

_____

_____

2. How does relating the story to your experience help you answer the question?

_____

_____

B. Return to the passage above and circle the words and phrases that helped you to answer the first question.

Selection Review The Interlopers

EQ **What Makes Something Frightening**
Think about the power of the unexpected.

A. In "The Interlopers," you found out how two enemies reconciled because of an unexpected natural event. Complete the Plot Diagram by describing the conflict, the climax, and the resolution.

Plot Diagram

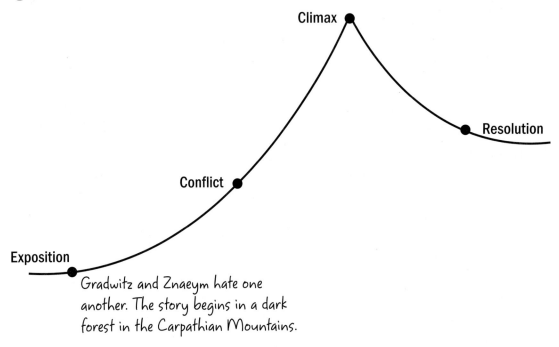

Climax

Resolution

Conflict

Exposition

Gradwitz and Znaeym hate one another. The story begins in a dark forest in the Carpathian Mountains.

B. Use the information in the Plot Diagram to answer the questions.

1. What is the climax of the story? Why is it the most important event?

_____

_____

2. In what way is terror an important part of the plot of the story?
Use **terror** in your answer.

_____

_____

3. Do you think the story would be more or less frightening if the author had described what happens to the men after the wolves reach them? Why?

_____

_____

_____

An Interview with the King of

Terror

by Bryon Cahill

Connect Across Texts

In "The Interlopers," two enemies come face to face with the unexpected. As you read this interview, think about how writers can use the unexpected to reach our greatest fears.

Stephen King is one of the world's most famous horror writers. Over his career he has sold more than 80 million copies of his spine-tingling books, and the movies based on his stories chill audiences in their seats. His subjects range from the outright **terror** of *Carrie* and *The Shining* to the mysteries of the **supernatural** in *The Dead Zone* and *The Green Mile*. The "King of Terror" has said, "I am Halloween's answer to Santa Claus." What makes him so popular?

Q: What makes a scary story really scary?

A: I don't know. That's a really tough question. That's like asking someone: "What makes a funny story really funny?" Scary things are personal. People come up to me sometimes and say, "You know I really love that book *IT* because I was always terrified of clowns." But other people come up to me and say, "Why would you say such mean things about clowns? I'm married to a guy who's a clown. Children love [them]! It's so mean to say that about clowns." When I was a kid, clowns just scared me and I've seen other kids cry about clowns and to me there's something scary, something **sinister** about such a figure of happiness and fun being evil. **Lon Chaney** once said,

Interact with the Text

1. Word Choice: Analogy
Highlight Stephen King's analogy. Why did he make this analogy? What does it mean?

2. Make Connections
Circle the two different views of clowns that King mentions. Which view is most like your own? Explain.

Key Vocabulary
terror *n.*, feeling of great fear

In Other Words
supernatural things that are not part of this world, like unusual powers and abilities
sinister threatening and evil
Lon Chaney An actor who starred in many classic horror movies

3. Make Connections
Underline what King believes makes something scary. Describe something you have seen or know from personal experience that supports King's belief.

4. Summarize
Highlight King's main point on this page. In your own words, summarize what King means by this statement.

"Nobody laughs at a clown at midnight." So I guess that sometimes what makes a scary thing scary is that when we realize there's something sinister behind a nice face.

I think things are scarier when there's some sensory deprivation, when we take away our ability to sense things, when we take away escape—that makes things scary. We're afraid of things that are different than we are. A lot of times what somebody does when they're writing scary stories is they're giving us permission to **be politically incorrect**, to say, "It's all right to be afraid of things that are different than you are." And people will say, "You have to be nice to people that are different than you are." And we understand that that's true and we try to do it but **nevertheless**, there's always that little bit of fear that says, "Maybe they're going to eat us up." And the person who writes a scary story says that it's all right to feel that way because you have to find a place to get rid of that.

Friendly or scary? The clown from the movie *IT* may change your mind.

Q: What, if anything, scares you?

A: Well clowns **freak me out** and scare me. I think that any kind of situation that I'm trapped in, certainly

In Other Words
be politically incorrect say or do things that might insult other people
nevertheless even though we know it's wrong
freak me out terrify me

claustrophobia or turbulence at 40,000 feet, freaks me out a lot. I hate that. Any kind of a situation where I'm not in control and somebody else is. Those things freak me out.

Q: **Would you like to talk about building suspense in a book?**

A: The most important thing about building suspense is building **identification** with character. You have to take some time and make your reader care about the characters in the story. There's a difference between horror and terror. You can go to a movie and you can be horrified because you don't know what terrible things are going to happen or who's going to get their head chopped off and that's horrible. But you don't necessarily know any of those people. They're very **two-dimensional**.

But if you take somebody and you put them in a situation . . . and little by little you get to know this guy and you get to understand him a little bit and you get to see different **aspects** of him and you start to feel for him . . . this person. Then you start to **empathize with** him and you start to put yourself in his shoes and then you start to be very, very afraid because you don't want anything to happen to him. It isn't a question anymore of *when* will something happen to him. It's a question that you're saying, "I don't want anything to happen." But because it's the kind of story that it is, you know that something **is gonna**, so one by one you close off the exits and things get more and more nerve wracking until finally there's an explosion. You know that's going to

> There's a difference between horror and **terror.**

Key Vocabulary
  identification *n.*, feeling that you know and understand someone else's experiences and feelings

In Other Words
claustrophobia or turbulence feeling trapped on a small, bumpy plane ride
two-dimensional unrealistic
aspects sides
empathize with care about and understand
is gonna is going to happen

Interact with the Text

5. Make Connections
Underline King's statement about identifying with characters. What connection can you make to this statement that helps you understand what he means?

6. Make Connections

Underline the words and phrases that show what King thinks is the most important element of storytelling. Describe the kind of writing that encourages you to read the way he wants you to.

_____

_____

_____

_____

_____

_____

_____

_____

_____

7. Word Choice: Analogy

Highlight the analogy King makes about himself. In your own words, describe what you think this comparison means.

_____

_____

_____

_____

_____

_____

_____

_____

_____

_____

_____

happen. The other thing is that there's a **format to** these stories where we all understand that things are going to build up to some kind of climax. And that adds to the suspense.

Q: What is the most important element of storytelling to you?

A: They all have their part to play but for me the most important thing is I want the reader to turn the page. So I would say that it's **an almost intangible thing that adds up to readability**. That makes somebody want to sit down and read the story that you wrote. It's a kind of modesty almost where you say to yourself this is not about me, this is about the person who reads my stories. It's not **psychoanalysis**, it's not about showing off (although it always is, we know that). You just hope that it goes out to somebody who's going to connect with what you said. And that you're going to tell them the story that makes them want to continue to read. Different writers feel different ways about this. I want to make a connection with them that's emotional. I want them to read the story and I want to make them sweat a little bit, laugh, and cry. I'm less interested in their thought processes than I am **their lower emotion**.

> I want the reader to **turn the page.**

Q: You once said, "I am the literary equivalent of a Big Mac and fries."

A: Yeah, and I'm still paying for that. What I meant by that is I'm tasty. I go down smooth. And I don't think that a steady diet of Stephen King

In Other Words

format to set pattern for
an almost intangible thing that adds up to readability something about a good story that is hard to describe
psychoanalysis figuring out how the mind works

their lower emotion in how they feel
the literary equivalent of a writer who is like

would make anybody a healthy human being. I think that you **oughtta** eat your vegetables, and you oughtta find other things, you oughtta **find some Dickens, some Ian McEwan** . . . you oughtta range widely and read all kinds of different stuff. You shouldn't just settle on one thing. I'd feel the same way about people that said they didn't read

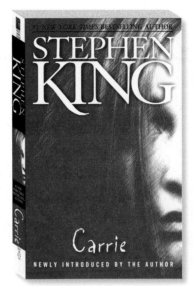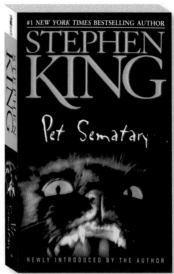

Many of King's books have been made into movies and TV shows.

anything but *Harry Potter*. I'd say, "There's something wrong with you, buddy." If you're gonna read fiction, read all kinds of things and challenge yourself, read some stuff that's really tough.

Q: If you were a teacher, what is the most important lesson you would **impart** to your students? What writing advice do you have for our readers?

A: As writers, I'd say write every day. If you want to write and you want to write well, do it a lot. Practice it. The same way that you would anything else that you want to do all the time. Baseball players know about it, trombone players know about it, swimmers know about it. Use it or lose it. Get better. Work at it. Feel comfortable with it. Feel comfortable with sentences, feel comfortable with paragraphs until those things just roll off your fingertips. And the better you feel about it, the better it's going to go for you.

In Other Words
oughtta should (slang)
find some Dickens, some Ian McEwan read a
  mix of classics and good modern books
Harry Potter popular books for young people
impart teach, share with

8. Interpret

Underline the words and phrases on page 201 that describe King's view on reading fiction. Do you agree or disagree with King?

_____

_____

_____

_____

_____

_____

_____

Q: **After you were hit by a van in '99, rumors were circulating that you would never write again. If that tragedy couldn't stop you, do you think you'll ever retire?**

A: Sure, I'll die. Or I'll get a horrible disease, or something. You see, I'm a horror writer, I can think of all sorts of nasty reasons to stop. ❖

In Other Words
rumors were circulating people were saying
retire stop writing as your job

Selection Review   An Interview with the King of Terror

A. In this interview, King says he turns nice things, like clowns, sinister. What connection can you make to this statement and how is this useful to you in understanding the text?

_____

_____

_____

B. Answer the questions.

1. Why do you think King uses analogies to discuss the process of writing about terror?

_____

_____

2. What are three strategies King uses to write his stories? Give specific examples from the interview.

_____

_____

_____

WRITING: Write About Literature

A. Plan your writing. Read the story starter in your student text on page 431. Complete the Plot Diagram with details about a scary story that you can write that begins with the story starter.

Plot Diagram

Climax

Complication

Complication

Complication

Conflict

Exposition

Resolution

Nick is walking alone in his neighborhood at night.

B. Now write your own tale of terror. Use the ideas you listed in the Plot Diagram to tell your story.

_____

_____

_____

_____

_____

_____

_____

_____

_____

_____

_____

LITERARY ANALYSIS: Analyze Irony

Verbal irony contrasts what a character says with what he or she really means. **Situational irony** contrasts what we expect to happen with what really happens.

A. Read the examples from "The Interlopers" that show how Saki uses verbal irony. Then explain how the underlined dialogue is ironic.

Examples of Verbal Irony	How the Dialogue is Ironic
"Trapped. What a joke! Ulrich von Gradwitz trapped in his stolen forest. That's justice for you."	
"What a useful idea," said Ulrich fiercely. "My men have orders to follow me. When they get me out, I will remember your idea."	

B. Find examples from "The Interlopers" that show how Saki uses situational irony. Then explain how each situation is ironic.

Examples of Situational Irony	How the Situation is Ironic
"He was watching and listening, as though waiting for some beast of the woods to come within the range of his vision."	The wolves are the beasts watching and listening.

C. Write about a TV show or film you have seen that used verbal or situational irony. Explain why you think the writer or director used it.

_____

_____

_____

VOCABULARY STUDY: Synonyms

Synonyms are related words that have the same, or nearly the same, meaning. Knowing the exact meaning of a synonym helps you use words more precisely.

A. Use a dictionary to find the meanings of these synonyms for the word *fear*. Write the definition in your own words in the chart below. Then rank the words from 1 (most intense) to 4 (least intense).

Synonyms	Meaning	Rank
dread		
fright		
panic		
terror		

B. Use a thesaurus to find synonyms for the words in the chart.

Word	Synonyms
answer	
drink	
gloomy	
misfortune	
silent	

C. Write sentences using the synonyms you listed in the chart above. Make sure the synonym you choose fits the precise meaning of your sentence.

answer _____

drink _____

gloomy _____

misfortune _____

silent _____

Prepare to Read

▷ **The Baby-Sitter**
▷ **Beware: Do Not Read This Poem**

Key Vocabulary

A. How well do you know these words? Circle a rating for each word. Check your understanding of each word by marking an *X* next to the correct definition. Then complete the sentences. If you are unsure of a word's meaning, refer to the Vocabulary Glossary, page 878, in your student text.

Rating Scale	
1	I have never seen this word before.
2	I am not sure of the word's meaning.
3	I know this word and can teach the word's meaning to someone else.

Key Word	Check Your Understanding	Deepen Your Understanding
1 capable (**kā**-pu-bul) *adjective* **Rating:** 1 2 3	☐ able to do something ☐ easily influenced	If I work hard, I am capable of _____ _____ _____ _____ .
2 precision (pri-**si**-zhun) *noun* **Rating:** 1 2 3	☐ confusion or error ☐ exactness or accuracy	One thing I do with precision is _____ _____ _____ _____ .
3 rely (ri-**lī**) *verb* **Rating:** 1 2 3	☐ to complete something ☐ to depend on something	One person I rely on for help is _____ _____ _____ _____ .
4 resist (ri-**zist**) *verb* **Rating:** 1 2 3	☐ to fight against something ☐ to focus on something	It is hard for me to resist _____ _____ _____ _____ .

Key Word	Check Your Understanding	Deepen Your Understanding
5 **ritual** (**ri**-chu-wul) *noun* **Rating:** 1　2　3	☐ a formal way of doing something ☐ the wrong way to do something	My morning ritual is _____ _____ _____ _____ _____ .
6 **subside** (sub-**sīd**) *verb* **Rating:** 1　2　3	☐ interpret ☐ to become less strong	To make my anger subside, I _____ _____ _____ _____ _____ .
7 **trace** (**trās**) *noun* **Rating:** 1　2　3	☐ a tool that helps a person to do their job ☐ a small sign or evidence	If you are at a campsite, you might find a trace of _____ _____ _____ _____ .
8 **vulnerable** (**vul**-nu-ru-bul) *adjective* **Rating:** 1　2　3	☐ helpless or easily hurt ☐ tired and lazy	People are vulnerable when _____ _____ _____ _____ .

B. Use one of the Key Vocabulary words to write about a fear you have overcome.

_____

_____

Before Reading The Baby-Sitter

LITERARY ANALYSIS: Analyze Word Choice: Mood and Tone

Mood is the feeling of a story. Sometimes, the mood of a story will change. **Tone** is how the author feels about the subject, the characters, or you, the reader.

A. Read the passage below. Find details that create a mood and reveal the author's tone. Write the details in the T Chart below.

> **Look Into the Text**
>
> Hilary hated baby-sitting at the Mitchells' house, though she loved the Mitchell twins. The house was one of those old, creaky Victorian horrors, with a dozen rooms and two sets of stairs . . .
>
> There was a long, dark hallway upstairs, and the twins slept at the end of it. Each time Hilary checked on them, she felt as if there were things watching her from behind the closed doors of the other rooms or from the walls. She couldn't say what exactly, just *things*.

T Chart

Mood	Tone
The Mitchells' house is an old, creaky, Victorian horror.	Hilary hates babysitting at the Mitchells' house.

B. Use the information in the T Chart to complete the sentence.

The author's tone creates a mood of _____

_____ .

FOCUS STRATEGY: Make Connections

HOW TO MAKE CONNECTIONS

Focus Strategy

1. **Read aloud** with a partner.

2. **Pause** to make connections to the text.

3. **Talk** with your partner about your connections.

4. **Discuss and evaluate** whether or not your connections help you understand the story.

A. Read the passage. Use the strategies above to make connections as you read. Answer the questions below.

Look Into the Text

> After she smoothed the covers over the sleeping boys, Hilary always drew in a deep breath before heading down the long, uncarpeted hall. It didn't matter which stairs she headed for, there was always a strange echo as she walked along, each footstep articulated with precision, and then a slight *tap-tapping* afterward. She never failed to turn around after the first few steps. She never saw anything behind her.

1. Why does Hilary feel nervous?

   _____

   _____

2. What connections did you make when you read about Hilary walking through the hallway?

   _____

   _____

B. Return to the passage above and circle the words or phrases that gave you the answer to the first question.

What Makes Something Frightening?
Explore how fears can become reality.

A. In "The Baby-Sitter," you found out how Hilary's fears about the Mitchells' old house become reality. Complete the Sequence Chart with the events of the story.

Sequence Chart

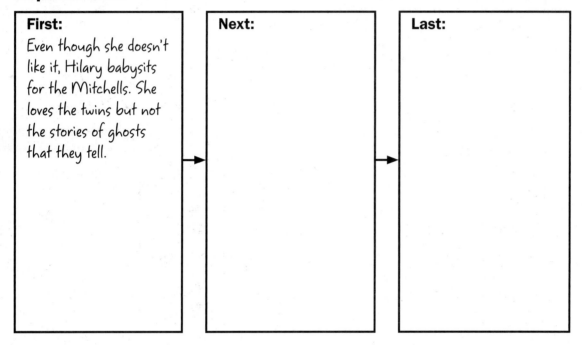

First:	Next:	Last:
Even though she doesn't like it, Hilary babysits for the Mitchells. She loves the twins but not the stories of ghosts that they tell.		

B. Use the information in the Sequence Chart to answer the questions.

1. How does the mood of the story change by the end?

_____

_____

2. Why do the man's screams subside? Use **subside** in your answer.

_____

_____

3. How might Hilary feel about babysitting at the Mitchell house in the future?

_____

_____

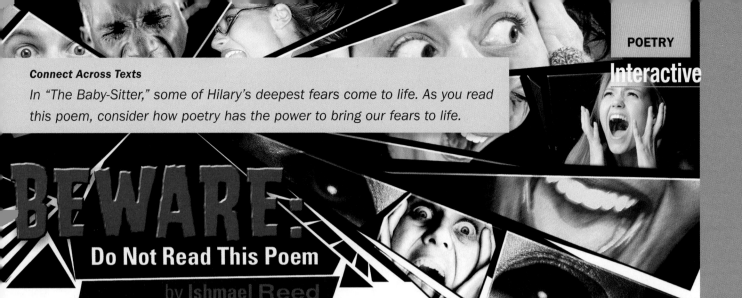

Connect Across Texts

In "The Baby-Sitter," some of Hilary's deepest fears come to life. As you read this poem, consider how poetry has the power to bring our fears to life.

BEWARE:
Do Not Read This Poem
by Ishmael Reed

tonite, *thriller* was
abt an ol woman, so vain she
surrounded her self w/
    many mirrors
5 It got so bad that finally she
locked herself indoors & her
whole life became the
    mirrors
one day the villagers broke
10 into her house, but she was too
swift for them. she disappeared
      into a mirror
each tenant who bought the house
after that, lost a loved one to
15   the ol woman in the mirror:
      first a little girl
      then a young woman
        then the young woman/s husband
the hunger of this poem is legendary
20 it has taken in many victims

Interact with the Text

1. Word Choice: Mood
Underline the words that tell you about the woman. What mood does the poet's word choice create?

_____

_____

_____

_____

_____

_____

2. Make Connections
Circle a phrase that tells how the woman affects people in the house. What connections can you make to this part of the poem?

_____

_____

_____

_____

In Other Words
thriller the spooky TV show
vain pleased with herself, focused on her looks
swift quick
tenant person living there
legendary so famous, well-known

3. Word Choice: Mood
List words and phrases that describe the image. Then explain how this image adds to the poem's mood.

▲ Critical Viewing: Effect What effect is the artist trying to create with this image? How does it make you feel? Explain your response.

back off from this poem
it has drawn in yr feet
back off from this poem
it has drawn in yr legs
25   back off from this poem
it is a greedy mirror
you are into this poem. from
      the waist down
nobody can hear you can they?
30   this poem has had you up to here
            belch
this poem aint got no manners
you cant call out frm this poem
relax now & go w/ this poem
35   move & roll on to this poem

            do not resist this poem
            this poem has yr eyes
            this poem has his head
            this poem has his arms
40   this poem has his fingers
            this poem has his fingertips

this poem is the reader & the
      reader this poem

statistic: the us bureau of missing persons reports

45   that in 1968 over 100,000 people disappeared
            leaving no solid clues
                  nor trace   only
      a space   in the lives of their friends

Interact with the Text

4. Interpret
Circle the metaphor that explains the relationship between the reader and the poem. What is the poem capable of doing? Use the word **capable** in your response.

_____
_____
_____
_____
_____
_____
_____
_____

5. Word Choice: Mood
Highlight the phrases that include facts. Why does the poet use this statistic? What effect does this have on the mood of the poem?

_____
_____
_____
_____
_____
_____
_____
_____
_____
_____
_____
_____
_____

Selection Review   Beware: Do Not Read This Poem

A. In the chart, list the lines of the poem you made connections to.
Then tell how your connections helped you understand the poem.

Lines from the Poem	My Connection	My Understanding
"she disappeared / into a mirror"	I once read about a girl who entered another world through a wardrobe.	The connection reminds me to use my imagination to find meaning.

B. Answer the questions.

1. How did the poet's words, repetition, or syntax help create the mood of the poem?

_____

_____

2. How might this poem bring people's fears to life?

_____

_____

Reflect and Assess

WRITING: Write About Literature

A. Plan your writing. Read the opposing opinions. Put an *X* next to the opinion you agree with. Then list examples from each text to support it.

☐ **Opinion 1:** Scenes that are shown are the most frightening.

☐ **Opinion 2:** Scenes that rely on the reader's imagination are the most frightening.

Selection	Events That Are Shown	Events That Aren't Shown
"The Baby-Sitter"		
"Beware: Do Not Read This Poem"		

B. Which events are more frightening—scenes that are shown, or scenes that rely on the reader's imagination? Write an opinion statement. Remember to use the text evidence you listed in the chart to support your statement.

_____

_____

_____

_____

_____

LITERARY ANALYSIS: Analyze Foreshadowing

Authors use **foreshadowing** when they give hints or clues about events that will happen later in the story.

A. Jane Yolen foreshadows events in "The Baby-Sitter" by giving clues. Write one clue for each of these events.

Event	Clue
the attack by "Them"	
The intruder gets in the house.	

B. Read each clue below from "The Baby-Sitter." Write what the clue foreshadows.

Clue	What the Clue Foreshadows
Hilary feels as if there are things watching her.	
Hilary is a stubborn girl.	
She counts what cookies remain— there are thirteen.	
The twins have a ritual their grandma taught them.	

C. Choose one detail from "Beware: Do Not Read This Poem," and write a brief paragraph explaining how it foreshadows later events.

_____

_____

_____

VOCABULARY STUDY: Thesaurus

A **thesaurus** lists words with their synonyms and antonyms. Using a thesaurus helps writers avoid repeating the same words.

A. Use a thesaurus and write two synonyms for each word.

creaky _____

imagine _____

ritual _____

strange _____

stubborn _____

B. Complete the chart below by writing one synonym and one antonym for each word.

Word	Synonym	Antonym
disappeared		
legendary		
nuzzle		
rapidly		
screaming		

C. Write sentences using either the synonym or antonym for the words in the chart above.

1. _____

_____

2. _____

_____

3. _____

_____

4. _____

_____

5. _____

_____

Prepare to Read

▶ The Tell-Tale Heart
▶ The Raven

Key Vocabulary

A. How well do you know these words? Circle a rating for each word. Check your understanding of each word by circling the synonym. Then write a definition. If you are unsure of a word's meaning, refer to the Vocabulary Glossary, page 878, in your student text.

Rating Scale	
1	I have never seen this word before.
2	I am not sure of the word's meaning.
3	I know this word and can teach the word's meaning to someone else.

Key Word	Check Your Understanding	Deepen Your Understanding
1 burden (**bur**-din) *noun* **Rating:** 1 2 3	A **burden** is a _____. load secret	My definition: _____ _____ _____ _____ _____
2 cease (sēs) *verb* **Rating:** 1 2 3	To **cease** making noise is to _____ making noise. start stop	My definition: _____ _____ _____ _____ _____
3 dread (dred) *noun* **Rating:** 1 2 3	If you feel **dread**, you feel _____. funny fear	My definition: _____ _____ _____ _____ _____
4 ominous (**ah**-mu-nus) *adjective* **Rating:** 1 2 3	An **ominous** sky is a _____ sky. threatening clear	My definition: _____ _____ _____ _____ _____

Key Word	Check Your Understanding	Deepen Your Understanding
5 **ponder** (**pon**-dur) *verb* Rating: 1 2 3	To **ponder** carefully is to _____ carefully. speak think	My definition: _____ _____ _____ _____ _____
6 **prophet** (**pro**-fut) *noun* Rating: 1 2 3	A **prophet** is a person who is a _____. poet predictor	My definition: _____ _____ _____ _____ _____
7 **relevance** (**re**-lu-vuns) *noun* Rating: 1 2 3	When something has **relevance**, it has _____. importance insignificance	My definition: _____ _____ _____ _____ _____
8 **suspect** (su-**spekt**) *verb* Rating: 1 2 3	To **suspect** something means to _____ it. know suppose	My definition: _____ _____ _____ _____ _____

B. Use one of the Key Vocabulary words to write about a time you or someone else imagined something that frightened you.

_____

_____

Before Reading The Tell-Tale Heart

LITERARY ANALYSIS: Analyze Structure: Suspense

Writers often build **suspense** in their stories to keep readers interested. Techniques include raising questions, slowing down or speeding up the action, putting characters in dangerous situations, hinting that the narrator is not trustworthy, and giving clues about things that may happen later.

A. Read the passage below. Find examples that the narrator is not trustworthy, and list them in the chart. Then explain how each example makes you feel.

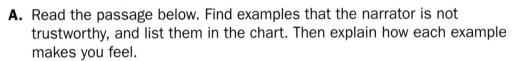

Look Into the Text

> True! I had been and still am very nervous—very, very dreadfully nervous. But why *will* you say that I am mad? The disease had made my senses sharper. It had not destroyed or dulled them. Above all, my sense of hearing was sharp. I heard all things in the heaven and in the earth. How, then, can you say I am mad? Listen! You shall see how healthy and calm I am as I tell you the whole story.

Example	My Feelings
The narrator is very nervous.	This makes me feel worried. What bad thing does the narrator think will happen?

B. Complete the sentence.

This text was suspenseful because _____

_____.

FOCUS STRATEGY: Make Connections

> ## HOW TO MAKE CONNECTIONS
> Focus Strategy
>
> 1. **Look** for words, phrases, and ideas that are important to understanding the story.
>
> 2. **Make a connection** between these ideas and your own life, other texts, and the world.
>
> 3. **Explain** how these connections help you to understand the text.

A. Read the passage. Use the strategies above to make connections as you read. Then answer the questions below.

> **Look Into the Text**
>
> I smiled—for what did I have to fear? I greeted the officers warmly. The scream, I said, was my own. I had had a bad dream. The old man, I said, was on vacation in the country. I took my visitors all over the house. I told them to search—search *well*. Finally, I took them to *his* room. I showed them his belongings, safe and undisturbed. Feeling very confident, I even brought chairs into the room. I told the officers to rest for a while. Quite sure of myself, I even put my own chair right over the old man's body.

1. How does this text compare to things you may have seen in movies, television, or read in other books?

   _____

   _____

2. What does making this connection help you understand about the narrator's actions?

   _____

   _____

B. Return to the passage above and circle the words, phrases, or ideas that describe what the narrator does to convince the officers that he is innocent.

Selection Review The Tell-Tale Heart

 What Makes Something Frightening?
Consider the role of imagination.

A. In "The Tell-Tale Heart," you learned how a writer can use suspense to make a story frightening. Complete the chart below with examples of each technique the author uses and the effect each example had on you as you read.

Technique	Example	Effect
Raising questions	The narrator questions why others think he is mad.	I knew there must be a reason why others thought he was crazy.
Slowing down or speeding up the action		
Putting characters in dangerous situations		
Hinting that the narrator is not reliable		
Giving clues about things that may happen later		

B. Use the information in the chart to answer the questions.

1. Which technique worked best to make this story suspenseful? Why?

_____

_____

2. Why does the narrator believe the officers suspect him? Use **suspect** in your answer.

_____

_____

3. Imagine that the police officers suspect the narrator. How might the ending be different?

_____

_____

The Raven
by Edgar Allan Poe

Once upon a midnight dreary, while I pondered, weak and weary,
Over many an old and curious book filled with forgotten lore—
While I sat there, nearly napping, suddenly there came a tapping,
As of someone gently rapping, rapping at my bedroom door.
5   "It is some visitor," I muttered, "tapping at my bedroom door—
Only this, and nothing more."

Ah, clearly I remember it was in cold and dark December,
And each separate dying ember formed a ghost upon the floor.
Eagerly I wished for tomorrow—I had tried but failed to borrow
10   Help from books to cease my sorrow—sorrow for the lost Lenore—
For the rare and beautiful maiden whom the angels name Lenore—
Nameless here for evermore.

Interact with the Text

1. Word Choice: Imagery and Repetition
Highlight words and phrases that help to create a picture in your mind. Describe the picture.

2. Make Connections
Why do you think the poet repeats the name Lenore?

Key Vocabulary
ponder *v.*, to think carefully about
● **cease** *v.*, to stop

In Other Words
dreary that was gloomy, dark, and sad
forgotten lore knowledge that was taught long ago
rapping knocking
ember glowing coal
for evermore forever

3. Interpret

What is the speaker trying to convince himself of in lines 13–18? Underline the phrase that helps you figure out the answer.

4. Word Choice: Imagery and Repetition

Circle the words or phrases in lines 25–35 that create pictures in your mind. Describe the image the poet is creating.

And the silken, sad, uncertain rustling of each purple curtain
Thrilled me—filled me with fantastic terrors never felt before;
15   So that now, to still the beating of my heart, I stood repeating,
"It's some visitor entreating entrance at my bedroom door—
Some late visitor entreating entrance at my bedroom door—
                    That is it and nothing more."

Very soon my soul grew stronger; hesitating then no longer,
20   "Sir," said I, "or Madam, truly your forgiveness I ask for;
The fact is that I was napping, and so gently you came rapping,
And so faintly you came tapping, tapping at my bedroom door,
That I was not sure I heard you." Then I opened wide the door—
                    Darkness there and nothing more.

25   Deep into that darkness peering, long I stood there wondering, fearing,
Doubting, dreaming dreams no man had ever dared to dream before;
But the silence was unbroken, and the stillness gave no token,
And the only word there spoken was the whispered word, "Lenore!"
This I whispered, and an echo murmured back the word "Lenore!"
30   Only this and nothing more.

Back into the bedroom turning, all my soul within me burning,
Soon again I heard a tapping somewhat louder than before.
"Surely," I said, "surely that is something at my glass pane;
Let me see, then, what could be there, and this mystery explore—
35   Let my heart be still a moment and this mystery explore—
                    It is the wind and nothing more!"

In Other Words
entreating asking for
hesitating pausing, waiting
peering looking and searching
token hint of what was out there

Open wide I flung the shutter, when, with many a flit and flutter,

In there stepped a noble Raven from the ancient days of yore.

Not the smallest greeting made he; not a minute stopped or stayed he;

40 But, with look of lord or lady, perched above my bedroom door—

Perched upon a bust of Pallas just above my bedroom door—

Perched, and sat, and nothing more.

Then this ebony bird beguiling my sad spirit into smiling,

By the serious appearance of the expression that it wore,

45 "Though your crown is short and shaven, you," I said, "are sure no craven,

Terrible, grim, and ancient Raven wandering from the Nightly shore—

Tell me what your lordly name is on the Night's so ghostly shore!"

Said the Raven, "Nevermore."

I was amazed by this ungainly bird to hear it speak so plainly,

50 Though its answer little meaning—little relevance it bore;

For we cannot help agreeing that no living human being

Ever yet was blessed with seeing bird above his bedroom door—

Bird or beast upon the sculptured bust above his bedroom door,

With such name as "Nevermore."

Key Vocabulary
- **relevance** *n.*, importance that connects to something else

In Other Words
days of yore past
bust of Pallas statue of the head of the Greek goddess, Athena
beguiling charming
craven coward
Nevermore Never again

Australian Raven, 2005, Kate Breakey. Handcolored silver gelatin photograph, Courtesy of Stephen Clark Gallery.

Corvus coronoides, Australian Raven

▲ Critical Viewing: Mood Study the artist's use of color, shadow, and light. What mood do these elements make you feel?

55　But the Raven, sitting lonely on the silent bust, spoke only

That one word, as if his soul in that one word he did outpour.

Nothing further then he uttered—not a feather then he fluttered—

Till I scarcely more than muttered "Other friends have flown before—

On the morrow *he* will leave me, as my hopes have flown before."

60　　　　　　　　　　　Then the bird said, "Nevermore."

Startled at the stillness broken by reply so clearly spoken,

"Surely," I said, "what it utters is a trick and nothing more,

Caught from some unhappy master whom a terrible Disaster

Followed fast and followed faster till his songs one burden bore—

65　Till the sad songs of his Hope that even sadder burden bore

　　　　　　　　　Of 'Never—nevermore.'"

But the Raven still beguiling all my spirit into smiling,

Soon I wheeled a cushioned seat in front of bird and bust and door;

Then, while into the cushion sinking, in my mind I started linking

70　Idea to idea, all the time thinking what this ominous bird of yore—

What this grim, ungainly, ghastly, gaunt and ominous bird of yore

　　　　　　　　Meant in croaking, "Nevermore."

So I sat engaged in guessing, but without a word expressing

To the bird whose fiery eyes now burned into my spirit's core;

75　This and more I sat divining, with my head at ease reclining

On the cushion's velvet lining which the lamp-light shined all over,

But whose velvet violet lining with the lamp-light shining o'er,

　　　　　　　　She shall touch, ah, nevermore!

Key Vocabulary
burden *n.*, something heavy or difficult
　that one has to carry
ominous *adj.*, threatening

In Other Words
uttered said
On the morrow Tomorrow
bore carried
divining guessing

6. Make Connections
Reread this page. What connection can you make? Underline the text you made a connection to. Then explain the connection and how it helps you understand the poem better.

_____
_____
_____
_____
_____
_____
_____

7. Interpret
Reread the last line. What is the speaker upset about?

_____
_____
_____
_____
_____
_____
_____
_____
_____
_____

8. Word Choice: Imagery and Repetition

Underline repeated phrases on this page. What kind of mood does Poe create by repeating these phrases?

9. Make Connections

Reread the last two stanzas on this page. The speaker asks the raven to tell him if he will ever see Lenore again. Have you ever wanted something so badly that you would not take *no* for an answer? How does this help you understand the text?

Then, I thought, the air grew denser, perfumed from an unseen censer
80   Swung by angels whose soft foot-falls tapped so lightly on the floor.
"Wretch," I cried "your God has lent you—by these angels he has sent you
Relief—relief and cure from your memories of Lenore;
Drink, oh drink this kind cure and forget this lost Lenore!"
                    Said the Raven, "Nevermore."

85   "Prophet!" I said, "thing of evil!—still a prophet, bird or devil!—
Did the Tempter or the tempest storm toss you to this shore?
All alone yet all undaunted, on this desert land enchanted—
On this home by Horror haunted—tell me truly, I ask for—
Is there—is there relief from sorrow? tell me—truth, I ask you for!"
90   Said the Raven, "Nevermore."

"Prophet! I said, "thing of evil!—still a prophet, bird or devil!
By that Heaven that bends above us—by that God we both adore—
Tell this soul with sorrow laden if, within the distant Aidenn,
It shall clasp again a maiden whom the angels name Lenore—
95   Clasp a rare and beautiful maiden whom the angels name Lenore."
                    Said the Raven, "Nevermore."

"Be that word our sign of parting, bird or fiend!" I yelled, upstarting—
"Then get yourself back into the tempest and the Night's ghostly shore!
Leave no feather as a token of that lie your soul has spoken!
100 Leave my loneliness unbroken!—leave the bust above my door!
Take your beak out of my heart, and take your form off of my door!"
                    Said the Raven, "Nevermore."

Key Vocabulary
prophet *n.*, someone who predicts what will happen in the future

In Other Words
censer container for burning incense
Wretch Poor, unhappy person
distant Aidenn long-ago Garden of Eden
fiend evil creature, devil
tempest storm

And the Raven, never flitting, still is sitting, *still* is sitting

On the pale bust of Pallas just above my bedroom door;

105 And his eyes have all the seeming of a demon's that is dreaming,

And the lamp-light over him streaming throws his shadow on the floor;

And my soul from out of that shadow that lies floating on the floor

Shall be lifted—nevermore!

10. Interpret
Underline the words and phrases that the poet uses to describe what the raven does to him. What can you conclude about the speaker?

_____

_____

_____

_____

_____

_____

_____

Selection Review The Raven

A. Choose and answer one question about "The Raven." Give examples from the poem to support the connections you make. Then explain how making this connection helps you understand the text better.

Question 1: How does the poem remind you of "The Tell-Tale Heart"?

Question 2: How does the situation the speaker finds himself in remind you of your own life?

I chose question _____

_____

_____

_____

_____

_____

Selection Review, continued

B. In the T chart, list examples of imagery and repetition from the poem. Then answer the questions.

T Chart

Imagery	Repetition
raven	"nevermore"

1. How does imagery and repetition help to build suspense in the poem? Write a paragraph. Give examples from the poem to support your answers.

   _____
   _____
   _____
   _____
   _____

2. What do you think happened to Lenore? How does imagining what happened to Lenore make this poem more frightening? Support your opinion with examples from the poem.

   _____
   _____
   _____
   _____

Reflect and Assess

WRITING: Write About Literature

A. Plan your writing. List the most frightening details from each selection.

The Tell-Tale Heart	The Raven
The old man's eye is like the eye of a vulture.	Someone or something will not stop tapping at the narrator's door.

B. How do you think Poe would answer the question, "What makes something frightening?" Write a short response giving your opinion. Give details from both texts to support your answer.

_____

_____

_____

_____

_____

_____

_____

_____

_____

_____

_____

Integrate the Language Arts

LITERARY ANALYSIS: Analyze Mood, Tone, and Symbolism

Mood is the feeling that a reader gets from a story. **Tone** is the author's attitude toward his or her topic. A **symbol** is something that stands for something else. Writers use symbolism to make their stories more interesting.

A. Read the words and phrases from "The Tell-Tale Heart" that help create the mood and tone of the story. Then write how the words and phrases make you feel.

Words and Phrases	How It Makes Me Feel
"I knew he had no idea that every night, just at midnight, I looked upon him while he slept."	
"It was the unseen shadow of Death that made the old man feel my closeness."	
"The noise grew louder—louder—louder!"	

B. Answer the questions.

1. How would you describe the mood of this story?

   _____

2. How would you describe the story's tone?

   _____

3. How does Poe's choice of words create mood and tone?

   _____

4. What do you think the old man's eye symbolizes? Explain.

   _____

C. Sunrise is often used in literature. List more examples of symbols you have read in books or short stories and what they mean.

_____

_____

VOCABULARY STUDY: Analogies

An **analogy** is a comparison between two pairs of words to show relationships.

> Example: "School is to education as restaurant is to food" can be written as school : education :: restaurant : food.

A. Complete the analogies. Circle the letter of the correct answer.

1. fearful : brave :: _____
  a. cat : mouse
  b. happy : joyful
  c. loud : quiet

2. raven : bird :: _____
  a. oak : tree
  b. skirt : shirt
  c. tall : short

3. month : December :: _____
  a. find : lose
  b. season : summer
  c. snow : rain

4. dreary : gloomy :: _____
  a. first : last
  b. earth : moon
  c. funny : humorous

B. Explain the relationships between the pairs of words for each analogy above.

1. _____

2. _____

3. _____

4. _____

C. Complete each analogy. Then explain the relationship.

1. happy : joyful :: _____

Relationship: _____

2. exciting : boring :: _____

Relationship: _____

3. desk : office :: _____

Relationship: _____

4. write : paper :: _____

Relationship: _____

Read for Understanding

1. Genre What kind of text is this selection? How do you know?

_____

_____

_____

_____

2. Topic Write a topic sentence to tell what the text is mostly about.

_____

_____

_____

_____

_____

Reread and Summarize

3. Key Ideas In each section, circle three words or phrases that express the key ideas in that section. Note next to each word or phrase why you chose it.

· Section 1: paragraphs 1–8
· Section 2: paragraphs 9–25

4. Summary Use your topic sentence and notes from item 3 to write a summary of the selection.

_____

_____

_____

_____

_____

_____

_____

_____

Puddle

by Arthur Porges

1 A great poet promised to show us fear in a handful of dust. If ever I doubted that such a thing were possible, I know better now. In the past few weeks **a vague**, terrible memory of my childhood suddenly came into sharp focus after staying **tantalizingly** just beyond the edge of recall for decades. Perhaps the high fever from a recent virus attack opened some blocked pathways in my brain, but whatever the explanation, I have come to understand for the first time why I see fear not in dust, but water.

2 It must seem quite absurd: fear in a shallow puddle made by rain; but think about it for a moment. Haven't you ever, as a child, gazed down at such a little pool on the street, seen the reflected sky, and experienced the illusion, very strongly, so that it brought a **shudder**, of endless depth a mere step away—**a chasm** extending downward somehow to the heavens? A single stride to the center of the glassy puddle, and you would fall right through. Down? Up? The direction was indefinable, a weird blend of both. There were clouds beneath your feet, and nothing but that shining surface between. Did you dare to take that critical step and **shatter the illusion**? Not I. Now that memory has returned, I recall being far too scared of the consequences. I carefully skirted such wet patches, no matter how casually my playmates splashed through.

In Other Words
a vague an unclear
tantalizingly in a teasing way
shudder fearful shaking
a chasm an opening
shatter the illusion prove yourself wrong

Literary Background
"I will show you fear in a handful of dust" is a line from the famous poem "The Wasteland," by T.S. Eliot.

3   Most of my acquaintances tolerated this weakness in me. After all, I was a sturdy, active child, and **held my own** in the games we played. It was only after Joe Carma appeared in town that my own little hell materialized, and I lost status.

4   He was three years older than I, and much stronger; thickset, muscular, dark—and perpetually surly. He was never known to smile in any joyous way, but only to laugh with a kind of *schadenfreude*, the German word for **mirth** provoked by another's misfortunes. Few could stand up to him when he **hunched his blocky frame** and bored in with big fists **flailing**, and I wasn't one of the elect; he terrified me as much by his **demeanor** as his physical power.

5   Looking back now, I discern something grim and evil about the boy, fatherless, with a weak and **querulous** mother. What he did was not the thoughtless, basically merry mischief of the other kids, but full of malice and cruelty.

6   Somehow Joe Carma learned of my phobia about puddles, and my torment began. On several occasions he meant to go so far as to **collar me**, hold my writhing body over one of the bigger pools, and pretend to drop me through—into that terribly distant sky beyond the sidewalk.

7   Each time I was saved at the last moment, nearly hysterical with fright, by Larry Dumont, who was taller than the bully, at least as strong, and thought to be more agile. They were bound to clash eventually, but so far Carma had **sheered off**, hoping, perhaps, to find and exploit some weakness in his opponent that would give him an edge. Not that he was a coward but just coldly careful; one who always **played the odds**.

8   As for Larry, he was good-natured, and not likely to fight at all unless pushed into it. By grabbing Carma with his lean, wiry fingers that could bend thick nails, and half-jokingly arguing with him, Dumont would bring about my release without forcing a **showdown**. Then they might scuffle a bit, with Larry smiling and Joe darkly sullen as ever, only to separate, newly respectful of each other's strength.

9   One day, after a heavy rain, Carma caught me near a giant puddle— almost a pond—that had appeared behind the Johnson barn at the north end of town. It was a lonely spot, the hour was rather early, and ordinarily

5. Text Structure: Foreshadowing Reread paragraph 5. Highlight clues and hints about Joe Carma's character.

What events do these clues foreshadow later in the story?

6. Text Structure: Foreshadowing Reread section 1 and underline examples of foreshadowing.

What later events does the author foreshadow in paragraphs 1–8?

In Other Words

held my own was a strong participant
mirth happiness, laughter
hunched his blocky frame bent his large body
flailing moving wildly
demeanor personality
querulous complaining

collar me grab me by the neck
sheered off gotten away
played the odds made sure he would win
showdown fight

7. Text Structure:
Suspense Reread
paragraphs 10–11.
Highlight the sentence that
shows the narrator in a
dangerous situation.

How does the author
use this scene to build
suspense?

Joe would not have been about, as he liked to sleep late on weekends. If I had **suspected** he might be around, that was the last place in the world I'd have picked to visit alone.

10   Fear and fascination often go together. I stood by the huge puddle, but well away from the edge, peering down at the blue sky, quite cloudless and so far beneath the ground where it should not have been at all; and for the thousandth time tried to gather enough nerve to step in. I *knew* there had to be solid land below—jabs with a stick had proved this much before in similar cases—yet I simply could not make my feet move.

11   At that instant brawny arms seized me, lifted my body into the air, and tilted it so that my **contorted** face was parallel to the pool and right over the glittering surface.

12   "Gonna count to ten, and then drop you right through!" a rasping voice taunted me. "You been right all along: it's a long way down. You're gonna fall and fall, with the wind whistling past your ears; turning, tumbling, faster and faster. You'll be gone for good, kid, just sailing down forever. You're gonna scream like crazy all the way, and it'll get fainter and fainter. Here we go: one! two! three!—"

8. Text Structure:
Suspense Reread
paragraphs 13–15.
Underline details that
show the narrator is in real
danger.

How does the author use
this situation to increase
the feeling of suspense?

13   I tried to scream but my throat was sealed. I just made husky noises while squirming desperately, but Carma **held me fast**. I could feel the heavy muscles in his arms all knotted with the effort.

14   "—four! five! Won't be long now. Six! seven!—"

15   A thin, whimpering sound broke from my lips, and he laughed. My vision was blurring; I was going into shock, it seems to me now, years later.

16   Then help came, swift and effective. Carma was jerked back, away from the water, and I fell free. Larry Dumont stood there, white with fury.

17   "You're a dirty skunk, Joe!" he gritted angrily. "You need a lesson, your own kind."

18   Then he did an amazing thing. Although Carma was heavier than he, if shorter, Larry whipped those lean arms around the bully, snatched him clear of the ground and with a single magnificent heave threw him fully six feet into the middle of the water.

Key Vocabulary
suspect *v.*, to believe that something
  may be different from what it seems

In Other Words
contorted fearful
held me fast kept hold of me

19   Now I wonder about my memory; I have to. Did I actually see what I now recall so clearly? It's quite impossible, but the vision persists. Carma fell full-length, face down, in the puddle, and surely the water could not have been more than a few inches deep. But he went on through! I saw his body twisting, turning, and shrinking in size as it dropped away into that cloudless sky. He screamed, and it was exactly as he had described it to me moments earlier. The terrible, shrill cries grew fainter, as if dying away in the distance; the flailing figure became first a tiny doll, and then a mere dot; an unforgettable thing, surely, yet only a dream-memory for so long.

20   I looked at Larry; he was **gaping**, his face drained of all blood. His long fingers were still hooked and tense from that mighty toss.

21   That's how I remember it. Perhaps we **probed** the puddle; I'm not sure, but if we did, surely it was inches deep.

22   On recovering from my illness three weeks ago, I hired a good private detective to make a check. The files of the local paper are unfortunately not complete, but one item for August 20, 1937, when I was eight, begins:

23   NO CLUES ON DISAPPEARANCE OF CARMA BOY
        After ten days of police investigation, no trace has been found of Joe Carma, who vanished completely on the ninth of this month. It is not even known how he left town, if he did, since there is no evidence that he went by either bus or train. Martin's Pond, the only deep water within many miles, was **dragged**, but without any result.

24   The detective assures me that Joe Carma never returned to town and that the name is unlisted in army records, with the FBI, or indeed any national roster from 1937 to date.

25   These days, I skin dive, sail my own little **sloop**, and have even **shot** some of the worst Colorado River rapids in a rubber boat. Yet it still takes almost more courage than I have to slosh through a shallow puddle that mirrors the sky. ❖

In Other Words
gaping staring
probed poked
dragged searched
sloop sailboat
shot floated down

9. Text Structure: Plot
Reread paragraph 19. Summarize what happens.

_____

_____

_____

_____

How does this event relate to what the author foreshadowed earlier in the story?

_____

_____

_____

_____

_____

_____

_____

10. Text Structure: Plot
Reread paragraphs 20–25. How did the author foreshadow these events earlier in the story?

_____

_____

_____

_____

_____

_____

_____

_____

_____

_____

CLOSE READING Puddle

Discuss

11. **Synthesize** With the class, discuss how fiction authors use text structures to build suspense. Discuss how each example adds to the tone of suspense. Take notes about your discussion using specific examples from "Puddles."

	Examples from the Short Story	How They Increase Suspense
Foreshadowing		
Dangerous Situations		

Then, with the class, discuss how story authors build suspense.
Take notes.

_____

_____

_____

12. **Write** Use your notes from question 11 to write a paragraph that explains how authors of short stories build suspense. If you need more space, continue your writing on another piece of paper.

_____

_____

_____

_____

_____

_____

_____

_____

Connect with the EQ What Makes Something Frightening?
Consider what makes fear real.

13. **Opinion** Think about the experience the narrator had with puddles of water and the bully. According to this story, what creates fear? Use evidence from the text to support your response.

_____

_____

_____

_____

_____

_____

_____

_____

_____

_____

14. **Theme** Reread the two quotations on page 404. Which quotation best matches the story? Be sure to cite evidence from the text to support your answer.

_____

_____

_____

_____

_____

_____

_____

_____

_____

_____

Unit 5

Key Vocabulary Review

A. Use the words to complete the paragraph.

dread ominous subside trace
obvious resist suspect vulnerable

Tina began to _____ (1) something was wrong when it became _____ (2) that she was alone in the cemetery. She could not find a single _____ (3), or sign, of her friends. She was filled with _____ (4) and felt _____ (5) and helpless. When she heard an _____ (6) noise, she could barely _____ (7) the urge to scream. Finally, she saw her friends, and her fear began to _____ (8).

B. Use your own words to write what each Key Vocabulary word means. Then write a synonym for each word.

Key Word	My Definition	Synonym
1. boundary		
2. cease		
3. feud		
4. grant		
5. release		
6. relevance		
7. rely		
8. ritual		

Unit 5 Key Vocabulary

boundary	dread	• obvious	prophet	• rely	suspect
burden	feud	ominous	reconciliation	resist	terror
• capable	• grant	ponder	• release	ritual	• trace
• cease	identification	• precision	• relevance	subside	vulnerable

• Academic Vocabulary

C. Answer the questions using complete sentences.

1. If you could meet a **prophet**, what would you ask him or her?

_____

_____

2. Describe someone from a book or movie whom you feel a strong **identification** with.

_____

_____

3. What is an example of a task that requires **precision**?

_____

_____

4. When have you felt **terror**?

_____

_____

5. Describe one thing you are very **capable** of doing on your own.

_____

_____

6. What are two things that people often **ponder** in books and movies?

_____

_____

7. How do you feel after you have a **reconciliation** with someone?

_____

_____

8. Describe a **burden** that some people have in their lives.

_____

_____

Prepare to Read

▶ Ad Power
▶ What's Wrong with Advertising?

Key Vocabulary

A. How well do you know these words? Circle a rating for each word. Check your understanding of each word by circling *yes* or *no*. Then complete the sentences. If you are unsure of a word's meaning, refer to the Vocabulary Glossary, page 878, in your student text.

	Rating Scale
1	I have never seen this word before.
2	I am not sure of the word's meaning.
3	I know this word and can teach the word's meaning to someone else.

Key Word	Check Your Understanding	Deepen Your Understanding
❶ advertising (**ad**-vur-tīz-ing) *noun* **Rating:** 1 2 3	Commercials are examples of **advertising** on television. **Yes**　　**No**	I notice advertising when it appears _____ _____ _____ _____ .
❷ appeal (u-**pēl**) *verb; noun* **Rating:** 1 2 3	Products that come in unattractive packaging will **appeal** to consumers. **Yes**　　**No**	To appeal to teens, a TV commercial should have _____ _____ _____ _____ .
❸ consumer (kun-**sū**-mur) *noun* **Rating:** 1 2 3	A **consumer** is the buyer of a company's product. **Yes**　　**No**	A healthy person might be a consumer of _____ _____ _____ _____ .
❹ convince (kun-**vins**) *verb* **Rating:** 1 2 3	It is easy to **convince** a person to buy a bad product. **Yes**　　**No**	I want to convince my friends that _____ _____ _____ _____ .

Key Word	Check Your Understanding	Deepen Your Understanding
5 impact (**im**-pakt) *verb* **Rating:** **1 2 3**	Advertisers use commercials to **impact** buyers' shopping habits. **Yes No**	I know I impact my grade when I _____ _____ _____ _____ _____ .
6 manipulate (mu-**ni**-pyū-lāt) *verb* **Rating:** **1 2 3**	A factual article about wildlife can **manipulate** children. **Yes No**	A salesperson can manipulate a shopper by _____ _____ _____ _____ _____ .
7 persuasive (pur-**swā**-siv) *adjective* **Rating:** **1 2 3**	A salesperson uses **persuasive** techniques to sell a product. **Yes No**	I can be very persuasive when I _____ _____ _____ _____ .
8 profit (**prah**-fut) *noun* **Rating:** **1 2 3**	Businesses make a **profit** when their sales decline. **Yes No**	A student group could use the profit they make in a fundraiser to _____ _____ _____ _____ .

B. Use one of the Key Vocabulary words to write about how an advertisement influenced you.

_____

_____

Before Reading Ad Power

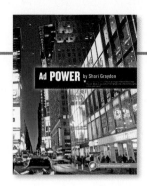

LITERARY ANALYSIS: Evaluate Evidence

An **argument** gives a writer's point of view about an issue or problem. A writer supports an argument with **evidence**, such as facts, statistics, data, and quotations.

A. Read the passage below. Find the evidence that supports the writer's argument. Complete the diagram with the evidence.

Look Into the Text

> People in Ghana, a country in West Africa, have a saying: *To the fish, the water is invisible.* In other words, when you're surrounded by something all the time, you don't notice it. . . .
>
> In parts of the world where people have a lot of modern conveniences and up-to-date technology, you could say that advertising has become "the water in which we swim." There's so much of it that we hardly notice it anymore. In fact, some experts estimate that a young person growing up in North America is likely to see between 20,000 and 40,000 TV commercials every year. When you add in all the advertisements from other media— up to 16,000 a day!—it's easy to see how you'd begin to stop noticing, and just keep swimming.

Main-Idea Diagram

Argument:	There is so much advertising that we hardly notice it anymore.

Evidence:
Evidence:

B. Answer the question.

Is the author's evidence reliable? Why or why not?

_____

_____

FOCUS STRATEGY: Synthesize

How to Draw Conclusions

Focus Strategy

1. **Note** the writer's claims.

2. **Add the writer's evidence** that supports each claim.

3. **Add your background knowledge** and experience.

4. **Synthesize,** or combine, your ideas with the writer's ideas.

5. **Draw a conclusion** that makes a judgment, gives an opinion, or shows new understanding.

A. Read the passage. Use the strategies above to draw conclusions as you read. Then answer the questions below.

Look Into the Text

> Every time you put on a T-shirt or a pair of jeans that shows a company's logo, you become a walking billboard. You're "advertising" the company's products.
>
> Think about the exchange. You get a T-shirt. The company gets the money you paid for the shirt plus the exposure that comes from you wearing it. Your willingness to wear the company's name on your body is the same as you personally endorsing the product.

1. What claim does the writer make about logos?

_____

_____

2. What is your personal experience with clothes and logos?

_____

_____

B. Draw a conclusion about the author's claim.

_____

_____

Selection Review Ad Power

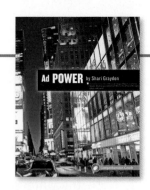

EQ **How Do the Media Shape the Way People Think?**
Explore how advertising changes our opinions.

A. In "Ad Power," you learned how advertising influences people. List the facts, statistics, data, and quotations the writer uses to support her argument that ads have become so common that people no longer notice them.

Facts	Statistics/Data	Quotations/Expert Opinions
Ads surround us. They are on the radio, signs, billboards, posters, logos, the Internet, magazines, and TV.		

B. Use the information in the chart to answer the questions.

1. How reliable is the writer's evidence? Based on her evidence and your experience, do you agree or disagree with her claim? Why or why not?

_____

_____

_____

_____

2. What kind of consumer is the writer trying to convince readers to be? Use **consumer** or **convince** in your response.

_____

_____

_____

3. Will you look at advertising differently from now on? Why or why not?

_____

_____

_____

_____

What's Wrong with Advertising?
by David Ogilvy

Connect Across Texts

"Ad Power" examines how **advertising** **impacts** *our lives. In this essay, an ad executive explains how he feels about the work he does.*

David Ogilvy, the "Father of Advertising," began his career by selling kitchen stoves door-to-door. In 1949, Ogilvy only had $6,000, but he used it to open **an advertising agency** with two partners. Their company went on to create advertising for many of the world's largest companies. Forty years later, the Ogilvy Group was sold for $864 million. *Time* magazine called Ogilvy "the most sought-after wizard in the advertising industry."

Ogilvy once said, "Never write an advertisement which you wouldn't want your family to read. You wouldn't tell lies to your own wife. Don't tell them to mine." Here are more of David Ogilvy's ideas from his book *Ogilvy on Advertising*.

Is Advertising Evil?

A professor in New York teaches his students that "advertising is . . . **intellectual and moral pollution**. . . . It is **undermining** our faith in our nation and in ourselves."

Holy smoke, is *that* what I do for a living?

Some of the defenders of advertising are equally guilty of **overstating** their case. Said Leo Burnett, the great Chicago advertising man: "Advertising is not the noblest creation of man's mind . . . It does not,

Key Vocabulary
advertising *n.*, work that encourages people to buy, do, or use things
- **impact** *v.*, to influence and affect

In Other Words
an advertising agency a company that creates advertisements
intellectual and moral pollution destroying our minds and values
undermining weakening and damaging
overstating exaggerating

Interact with the Text

1. Draw Conclusions
Highlight the words and phrases that describe Ogilvy's success. Think about your knowledge and experience. What do you think his position on advertising will be?

2. Word Choice
Underline the professor's quote. Why do you think Ogilvy begins the essay with a negative quote about advertising?

3. Word Choice

Underline the information that makes advertising seem as though it helps people. What words and ideas does Ogilvy use to appeal to readers' emotions?

single-handedly, **sustain the whole structure of capitalism and democracy and the free world**. . . . We are merely human, trying to do a necessary human job **with dignity, with decency, and with competence**."

My view is that advertising is no more and no less than a reasonably efficient way to sell. Procter & Gamble spends about $600,000,000* a year on advertising. Howard Morgens, their former president, is quoted as saying, "We believe that advertising is the most effective and efficient way to sell to the consumer. If we should ever find better methods of selling our type of products to the **consumer**, we'll leave advertising and turn to these other methods."

Few of us advertising professionals lie awake nights feeling guilty about the way we earn our living. We don't feel bad when we write advertisements for toothpaste. If we do it well, children may not have to go to the dentist so often.

*This was Proctor & Gamble's advertising **budget** in 1983. Today, the manufacturing company spends about $2 billion a year on advertising.

4. Draw Conclusions

Circle the advertising categories in the chart that affect you the most. What conclusion can you draw about the amount of advertising money that is spent in these industries?

ADVERTISING DOLLARS SPENT

Large companies spend a large percentage of their budgets on advertising. Look at these products. Do they sound familar to you? Have you bought or used any of them yourself? Maybe these advertising dollars are well spent after all.

Top Advertising Categories *January–September 2005*	
Industry	**Ad Expenditu** (billions)
Automobile (foreign and domestic brands)	$12.4
Financial Services (banks, credit cards, car loans, etc.)	$5.7
Telecommunications (phone, Internet)	$5.5
Personal Care Products (cosmetics, shampoo, etc.)	$4.2
Travel and Tourism	$4.0

Source: TNS Media Intelligence Report, December 2005

⚠ **Interpret the Chart** Why do you think automobile companies spend more on advertising than companies that sell personal care products?

Key Vocabulary
- **consumer** *n.*, someone who buys or uses something

In Other Words

sustain the whole structure of capitalism and democracy in the free world keep the free world running
with dignity, with decency, and with competence with pride, good taste, and skill
budget cost

I did not feel bad when I wrote advertisements promoting travel to Puerto Rico. They helped **attract industry** and tourists to a country that had been in poverty for 400 years.

I do not think that I am wasting my time when I write advertisements for the World Wildlife Fund.

My children were grateful when I wrote an advertisement that recovered their dog Teddy from **dognappers**.

Nobody suggests that the printing press is evil because it is used to print pornography. It is also used to print the Bible. Advertising is only evil when it advertises evil things.

Some **economists** say that advertising tempts people to waste money on things they don't need. Who are they to decide what you need? Do you *need* a dishwasher? Do you *need* a deodorant? Do you *need* a trip to Rome? I **feel no qualms of conscience** about persuading you that you do. What the economists don't seem to know is that buying things can be one of life's more innocent pleasures, whether you need them or not.

If advertising were **abolished**, what would be done with the money? Would it be spent on public works? Or **distributed to stockholders**? Or given to the media for the loss of **their largest source of revenue**? Perhaps it could be used to reduce prices to the consumer—*by about 3 percent.*

Reports show that Americans spent more money than they earned in 2005. Advertisers fight for their attention—and their money.

Interact with the Text

5. Draw Conclusions
Circle the argument that some economists make against advertising. Then circle Ogilvy's response. Make a conclusion based on this information and what you know.

_____

_____

_____

_____

_____

_____

_____

_____

_____

_____

_____

In Other Words

attract industry bring businesses, jobs
dognappers the people who stole him
economists experts who study how people spend money
feel no qualms of conscience don't feel ashamed or guilty

abolished stopped
distributed to stockholders given to people who own parts of a company
their largest source of revenue the way they make most of their money

6. Draw Conclusions
Highlight the writer's main point in the first paragraph. Based on your experience, do you agree or disagree? Explain.

6. Draw Conclusions
Highlight the writer's main point in the first paragraph. Based on your experience, do you agree or disagree? Explain.

_____

_____

_____

_____

_____

_____

_____

_____

_____

7. Interpret
Underline the main idea behind subliminal advertising. Why would it be wrong for advertisers to use this method?

_____

_____

_____

_____

_____

_____

_____

_____

_____

_____

Can Advertising Sell Bad Products?

It is often charged that advertising can persuade people to buy inferior products. So it can—*once*. But the consumer sees that the product is inferior and never buys it again. This is expensive for the manufacturer, whose **profits** come from *repeat* purchases.

The best way to increase the sale of a product is to *improve the product*. This is particularly true of food products. The consumer is amazingly quick to notice an improvement in taste and buy the product more often.

Manipulation?

You may have heard it said that advertising is "manipulation." I know of only two examples, and neither of them actually happened. In 1957, a **market researcher** called James Vicary **hypothesized** that it might be possible to flash commands on television screens so fast that the viewer would not **be conscious of** seeing them. However, the viewer's *unconscious* mind *would* see the commands—and obey them. He called this gimmick "subliminal" advertising, but he never even got around to testing it, and no advertiser has ever used it.

I myself once came near to doing something so diabolical

The best way to increase the sale of a product is to improve the product.

Key Vocabulary
profit *n.*, the money a company makes after expenses

In Other Words
market researcher man who studied how consumers spend their money
hypothesized guessed
be conscious of realize he or she was

that I hesitate to confess it even now, thirty years later. Suspecting that *hypnotism* might be an element in successful advertising, I hired a professional hypnotist to make a commercial. When I saw it in the projection room, it was so powerful that I had visions of millions of **suggestible consumers** getting up from their armchairs and rushing like **zombies** through the traffic on their way to buy the product at the nearest store. Had I invented the *ultimate* advertisement? I burned it,

TRUTH IN ADVERTISING?

Advertisers want their products to appear attractive and appealing. Many times, this includes removing distracting objects and "touching up" photos. Which of these photos gives a more appealing glimpse of a vacation getaway?

Original Photo

Touched-Up Photo

Interact with the Text

8. Word Choice
Highlight what Ogilvy did that he describes as "diabolical." Why do you think he confesses this?

_____

_____

_____

_____

_____

In Other Words

hypnotism controlling people's unconscious so they will do whatever they are told to do
suggestible consumers buyers who didn't know what they were doing
zombies half-dead people

9. Interpret

Highlight the important words and phrases in the conclusion. What is Ogilvy's final point about advertising?

_____

_____

_____

_____

_____

and never told my client how close I had come to **landing him in a national scandal**.

One way or another, the odds against your being manipulated by advertising are now very long indeed. Even if I wanted to manipulate you, I wouldn't know how to get around the **legal regulations**. ❖

In Other Words
landing him in a national scandal making him and his company look bad
legal regulations laws that prevent untruthful or deceptive ads

---

Selection Review What's Wrong with Advertising?

A. List two ways the writer tries to appeal to the reader's emotions. Explain the effect each appeal had on you.

1. _____

_____

2. _____

_____

B. Answer the questions.

1. In your own words, state the writer's main idea. Then use your own experience and knowledge to draw a conclusion about his claim.

_____

_____

2. Imagine you are writing a letter to David Ogilvy. What would you tell him about the conclusions you drew about his essay?

_____

_____

WRITING: Write About Literature

A. Plan your writing. Collect definitions and other information about advertising from each selection.

Ad Power	What's Wrong with Advertising?

B. What is advertising? Use the information given in both texts, add what you know, and synthesize your own definition. Write your definition below. Support your definition with examples from the texts.

_____

_____

_____

_____

C. Use what you have learned about advertising to write your own ad.

_____

_____

_____

_____

_____

_____

_____

_____

LITERARY ANALYSIS: Compare Authors' Purposes and Viewpoints

The reason an author writes a selection is known as the **author's purpose**.
An author's perspective reflects his or her background, experiences, and
viewpoint.

A. Write what you think the author's purpose and viewpoint are for
each selection.

Selection	Author's Purpose	Author's Viewpoint
"Ad Power"		
"What's Wrong with Advertising?"		

B. Read the excerpt from "Ad Power." Then answer the questions.

> Advertising is basically anything someone does to grab your attention and hold on to it
> long enough to tell you how cool, fast, cheap, tasty, fun, rockin', or rad whatever they're
> selling is. Some people have a different definition. They argue that advertising is trickery
> used to shut down your brain just long enough to convince you to open your wallet!

1. What is the author's purpose?

_____

_____

2. Does the author have an agenda?

_____

_____

3. What effect does the author's purpose have on you?

_____

_____

C. Think about an ad that you have read or seen on television. Write two or
three sentences describing the purpose of the ad and if there is a bias
that affects how the ad is presented.

_____

VOCABULARY STUDY: Latin and Greek Roots

Many English words are made up of **Latin and Greek roots** with other word parts added. Knowing the meaning of a root can help you understand the meaning of the entire word.

A. The chart below shows some common Latin and Greek roots and their meanings. Complete the chart by listing words you've used that contain each root.

Root	Meaning	Words I've Used
fin	end	
sume	to take	
uni	one	
voc	call	

B. Read the paragraph below. Underline words you find that contain the Latin and Greek roots from the chart above.

My friends and I began talking one day about how much energy we consume in our daily lives. Leaving a light on or a stereo playing after you have left the room are ways we waste energy. We started thinking about some ideas that can be used universally to make our planet a better place to live. I decided that my vocation would be to help save our environment. I am so glad that I finally figured out a meaningful way to live my life!

C. Write a meaning for each word with a Latin or Greek root that you found in the paragraph above. Use the root meanings in Activity A to help you.

1. _____
2. _____
3. _____
4. _____

Prepare to Read
▷ **A Long Way to Go: Minorities and the Media**
▷ **Reza: Warrior of Peace**

Key Vocabulary

A. How well do you know these words? Circle a rating for each word. Check your understanding of each word by marking an *X* next to the correct definition. Then complete the sentence. If you are unsure of a word's meaning, refer to the Vocabulary Glossary, page 878, in your student text.

Rating Scale

1	I have never seen this word before.
2	I am not sure of the word's meaning.
3	I know this word and can teach the word's meaning to someone else.

Key Word	Check Your Understanding	Deepen Your Understanding
1 alternative (awl-**tur**-nu-tiv) *adjective* Rating: 1 2 3	☐ different from what is usual ☐ what is expected	I enjoy alternative _____ _____ _____ _____ .
2 expand (ik-**spand**) *verb* Rating: 1 2 3	☐ to grow larger ☐ to make smaller	I can expand my vocabulary by _____ _____ _____ _____ .
3 influence (**in**-flū-uns) *verb* Rating: 1 2 3	☐ to ignore something ☐ to affect someone or something	People who influence me in a positive way are _____ _____ _____ _____ .
4 media (**mē**-dē-u) *noun* Rating: 1 2 3	☐ a means of communication ☐ a means of hiding information	For me, two of the most important sources of media are _____ _____ _____ _____ .

Key Word	Check Your Understanding	Deepen Your Understanding
5 **minority** (mu-**nor**-u-tē) *noun, adjective* **Rating:** **1 2 3**	☐ a large group or crowd ☐ a small group of people	One minority group I would like to know more about is _____ _____ _____ _____ .
6 **racism** (**rā**-si-zum) *noun* **Rating:** **1 2 3**	☐ prejudice against a race ☐ a contest	A judge would be accused of racism if she _____ _____ _____ _____ _____ .
7 **stereotype** (**ster**-ē-u-tīp) *noun* **Rating:** **1 2 3**	☐ a fact or statistic ☐ an idea about a group of people	One stereotype of teenagers is _____ _____ _____ _____ _____ .
8 **token** (**tō**-kun) *adjective* **Rating:** **1 2 3**	☐ representing a larger group ☐ representing individuals	A company might hire a token woman if it had _____ _____ _____ _____ _____ .

B. Use one of the Key Vocabulary words to write about a TV show that affects your worldview.

_____

_____

Before Reading A Long Way to Go: Minorities and the Media

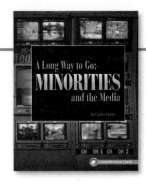

LITERARY ANALYSIS: Evaluate Evidence

Persuasive writers support their claims with **evidence**, such as facts, examples, data, and statistics. Readers should evaluate evidence by asking: *Is it relevant? Is it sufficient? Is it accurate?*

A. Read the passage below. Evaluate the evidence that supports the writer's claim that minorities are making slow progress in the media. Complete the chart.

> **Look Into the Text**
>
> Minorities have traditionally had only a small presence in the media. The national popularity of Bryant Gumbel, Connie Chung, and Geraldo Rivera on television is very recent. While these breakthroughs are certainly welcome, progress is slow. For example, only about 40 percent of the nation's 1,600 daily newspapers have *any* minorities as editors.

Writer's Evidence	My Evaluation of the Evidence
The national popularity of Bryant Gumbel, Connie Chung, and Geraldo Rivera is very recent.	

B. Answer the question.

Why is it important to evaluate the evidence that a writer uses to support his or her opinion?

_____

_____

FOCUS STRATEGY: Synthesize

> ## HOW TO COMPARE OPINIONS
>
> Focus Strategy
>
> 1. **Record Ideas** List each important claim.
>
> 2. **Add Texts** Read another selection on the same topic.
>
> 3. **Compare** Determine how the claims are alike and different. Combine the ideas.
>
> 4. **Read On** Add more claims to your notes.

A. Read the passage. Use the strategies above to compare opinions as you read. Then answer the questions below.

> **Look Into the Text**
>
> The entertainment media have a fascination with Latino gangs. The news media also like to show them often. At the same time, the entertainment media rarely show other Latino characters. And the news media rarely show other Hispanic topics, except for such "problem" issues as immigration and language. The result has been a Latino public image—better yet, a stereotype—in which gangs are an important part.

1. What is the writer's opinion about the media's fascination with Latino gangs?

_____

_____

2. Based on your own experience, do you agree with the writer's claim?

_____

_____

3. How will comparing this author's opinion with another author's opinion help you understand the topic better?

_____

_____

B. Return to the passage above, and underline the words or phrases that helped you answer the first question.

Selection Review   A Long Way to Go: Minorities and the Media

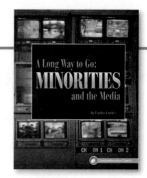

 How Do the Media Shape the Way People Think?
Consider the ways media shape our worldview.

A. In "A Long Way to Go: Minorities and the Media," you learned how the media can influence the way minorities are portrayed. Complete the diagram below.

Main-Idea Diagram

Author's Main Point:
The few minorities in the media are shown as stereotypes. Minorities resent the stereotypes and want change.

Evidence:

Evidence:

Evidence:

Evidence:

B. Use the information in the chart to answer the questions.

1. What kinds of evidence does the writer use in his essay? Is his evidence relevant and accurate? Why or why not?

_____

_____

2. How might racism play a role in how the media portray minorities? Use **racism** in your answer.

_____

_____

3. Do you think the media have a responsibility to portray minorities fairly? Explain.

_____

_____

Connect Across Texts

"A Long Way to Go" argues that the **media** have a negative effect on people's perception by casting minorities only in **token** roles. This photo-essay shows how photography can change people's minds.

Reza: WARRIOR OF PEACE

by AMY OSTENSO

Photographs are just pretty pictures, right? Not always! Photographs have the power to change the way people see the world.

Photojournalist Reza Deghati has been using the power of photography to change people's minds for 40 years. Reza captures images that portray suffering and injustice and show people the whole truth about the events of our world. In this way, his images **influence** the way people see the world and move them to seek solutions to the world's problems. Reza felt compelled to pursue this line of work because, he says, "As a **witness**, I could make a difference."

April 1983, Afghanistan. An old man sitting on a bench reads the Koran near the Pakistani border. He and his family are refugees fleeing the Soviet invasion.

Interact with the Text

1. Argument
Highlight words and phrases that show the writer's argument about the power of photography. How does the quotation from Reza support the claim?

_____

_____

_____

_____

_____

_____

_____

_____

_____

_____

Key Vocabulary
- **media** *n.*, ways people communicate
- **token** *adj.*, only symbolic
- **influence** *v.*, to affect

In Other Words
Photojournalist A person who takes photographs in order to tell about events
witness person who sees an event

2. Argument
Underline words and phrases that tell how the government of Iran responded to Reza's photographs. How do these words support Ostenso's claim that photographs have the power to change worldviews?

_____

_____

_____

_____

_____

_____

_____

_____

_____

_____

3. Critical Viewing: Effect
Circle the photo of the sign from Saudi Arabia. What message do you think this sends to photographers?

_____

_____

_____

_____

_____

_____

_____

_____

_____

_____

As a student in the 1970s, Reza began to photograph the political struggles in Iran, his native country. He used only his first name to remain anonymous. The Iranian government felt threatened by the images he displayed and felt that the photos could jeopardize their power. They arrested him and sent him to prison. Then, in 1981, Reza was **exiled from** his home country because of his photography.

A sign prohibiting photography

1980, Banneh, Kurdistan, Iran. Following a bombing by the Iranian army, a family learns of the death of their nine-year-old son, Payman, and his twelve-year-old sister.

In Other Words
exiled from forced to leave and never return to

2010–2011, Luxembourg Metro Station, Paris, France. This exhibition presents the work of Reza and his son Delazad. It is an invitation to think about the importance of education and commitment in a changing society.

4. Argument
Highlight words and phrases that show the effect that Reza's photos of Afghanistan have on their viewers. Why does the author include these details?

Now Reza takes his camera around the world to **document** and report the horrors of war and disaster by capturing the suffering of the people. One place he returns to again and again is Afghanistan.

In 1991, a United Nations official told Reza, "Your photographs are the reason why we're so drawn to Afghanistan." Reza's images portray the whole story of events in Afghanistan. They show people's joys and the sorrows, not just events from the latest news headlines. Because of this, the photos help the viewer to connect with and to show care towards the people there.

In Other Words
document make a record of

5. Compare Opinions
Underline ideas that connect with Carlos Cortés's opinions in "A Long Way to Go." How do they compare?

_____

_____

_____

_____

_____

_____

But Reza's influence doesn't stop with his own photos. He **founded an NGO** called *Aina* (Mirror), enabling the women and children of Afghanistan to tell their own stories in photographs and other visual media. Giving these people their own voice **empowers** them to join the fight for equality, freedom, and peace.

One day an Aina photographer may change the world through her photos, just as Reza has done with his images. ❖

In Other Words
founded an NGO began a non-governmental organization or group
empowers gives power to

Selection Review Reza: Warrior of Peace

A. Complete the diagram for "Reza: Warrior of Peace."

Argument and Evidence Diagram

Argument
"Photographs have the power to change the way people see the world."

Evidence	Evidence	Evidence

Does the evidence in the photo-essay effectively support the author's claim? Use specific examples from the text to support your opinion. _____

_____

B. List each writer's claim. Then compare their opinions, and draw a conclusion about the topic.

1. "A Long Way to Go": _____

2. "Reza: Warrior of Peace" _____

3. My Opinion: _____

_____

Reflect and Assess

WRITING: Write About Literature

A. Plan your writing. List reasons why you think people should care about the way the media shape the way people think. Then list examples from both texts.

Reasons	Examples from Texts

B. Why should people care about the way the media change people's viewpoints? Write an opinion statement. Use your own reasons and examples from both texts to support your opinion.

_____

_____

_____

_____

_____

_____

_____

_____

_____

_____

_____

_____

LITERARY ANALYSIS: Persuasive Text Structures

Persuasive writing is organized into **text structures** that make the writer's ideas easy to follow. Some common structures are strength of arguments, claim-counterclaim, and problem/solution.

A. In "Reza: Warrior of Peace," the author uses the claim-counterclaim persuasive text structure. Write two of the author's counterclaims in the chart below.

Claim	Author's Counterclaim
Some people claim that photographs are just pretty pictures.	

B. Using information from the selections, write a solution to each problem listed below.

Problem: Many minority roles on television promote stereotypes.

Solution: _____

_____

_____

Problem: Minorities do not have much say in the media.

Solution: _____

_____

_____

C. Choose a topic from one of the selections and write the central argument. Restructure the author's points using a "strength of argument" text structure.

Argument: _____

Idea 1: _____

Idea 2: _____

Idea 3: _____

VOCABULARY STUDY: Latin and Greek Roots

Many English words are made up of **Latin and Greek roots** with other word parts added. Knowing the meaning of the roots can help you figure out the meaning of the entire word.

A. *Meter* is a common Greek root that means "measure." Write what you think each word means. Confirm the definition for each word in the dictionary.

Word	What I Think It Means	Definition
barometer		
geometry		
pentameter		
thermometer		

B. The chart below shows some common Latin and Greek roots and their meanings. Complete the chart by listing words you've heard that contain each root.

Root	Meaning	Words I've Used
cred	believe	
graph	write	
oper	work	
pop	people	

C. Write sentences using the words you listed in Activity B.

1. _____
2. _____
3. _____
4. _____

Unit 6
Pages 562–581

Prepare to Read

▷ What Is News?
▷ How to Detect Bias in the News

Key Vocabulary

A. How well do you know these words? Circle a rating for each word. Check your understanding of each word by circling the correct synonym. Then write a definition. If you are unsure of a word's meaning, refer to the Vocabulary Glossary, page 878, in your student text.

Rating Scale

1	I have never seen this word before.
2	I am not sure of the word's meaning.
3	I know this word and can teach the word's meaning to someone else.

Key Word	Check Your Understanding	Deepen Your Understanding
❶ access (**ak**-ses) *noun* **Rating:** 1 2 3	If you have **access** to a building, you have a means of _____. **entry** **opposition**	My definition: _____
❷ bias (**bī**-us) *noun* **Rating:** 1 2 3	A person who shows **bias** shows _____. **awareness** **prejudice**	My definition: _____
❸ deliberate (di-**lib**-u-rut) *adjective* **Rating:** 1 2 3	If something is **deliberate** it is _____. **planned** **impulsive**	My definition: _____
❹ detect (di-**tekt**) *verb* **Rating:** 1 2 3	To **detect** something is to _____ it. **notice** **ignore**	My definition: _____

268 Unit 6: Are You Buying It?

Key Word	Check Your Understanding	Deepen Your Understanding
5 distorted (dis-**tor**-tid) *adjective* Rating: 1　2　3	A **distorted** picture is _____. misleading　　　true	My definition: _____ _____ _____ _____ _____
6 engaged (en-**gājd**) *adjective* Rating: 1　2　3	If you are **engaged** in an activity, you are _____. frustrated　　　absorbed	My definition: _____ _____ _____ _____ _____
7 objectivity (ub-jek-**tiv**-u-tē) *noun* Rating: 1　2　3	If you show **objectivity**, you show _____. enthusiasm　　　neutrality	My definition: _____ _____ _____ _____ _____
8 priority (prī-**or**-u-tē) *noun* Rating: 1　2　3	A **priority** is something that has high _____. insignificance　　　importance	My definition: _____ _____ _____ _____ _____

B. Use one of the Key Vocabulary words to describe a recent news story that affected you. How did it make you feel?

_____

_____

LITERARY ANALYSIS: Analyze Viewpoint: Tone

Tone is the writer's attitude about the topic or reader. A writer sometimes uses a persuasive tone to convince readers to believe his or her opinions and ideas.

A. Read the passage below. Find words and phrases that show the writer's attitude. Write the word choices in the web.

Look Into the Text

> With the pervasiveness of news today, it is important to take a look at how news affects our lives. We have come a long way from the days when the nightly news was reported at 6 p.m. on the "Big 3" broadcast networks.
>
> Today, we have access to news whenever we want—from a variety of 24-hour cable news channels, to "news when you want it" from the Internet, to instant news on one's PDA device. Instant news is just part of our lives.

Details Web

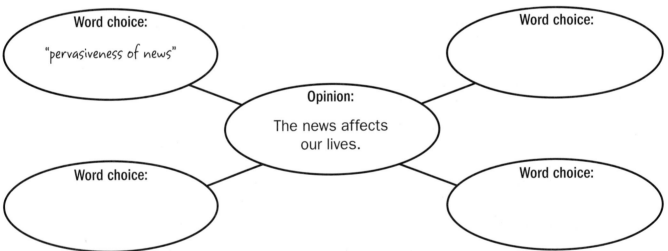

B. Look at the words and phrases the writer uses. Describe the writer's tone. Why do you think the writer chose this tone?

_____

_____

FOCUS STRATEGY: Synthesize

How to FORM GENERALIZATIONS

Focus Strategy

1. **Record Clues** List details, word choice, and organization that show the author's tone.

2. **Combine the Information** Form a statement about the author's purpose and tone.

A. Read the passage. Use the strategies above to form generalizations as you read. Then answer the questions below.

> **Look Into the Text**
>
> News has two priorities: it must be current, and it must mean something to people. A story about the environment and a story about the Super Bowl are both newsworthy, but for different reasons.
>
> On the surface at least, the objective of news is to inform the audience. It's the job of all the news media to tell people what's going on in their community—locally, nationally or globally. In this sense, the news media provide a valuable public service.

B. Return to the passage and circle words and phrases that help you understand the writer's tone and purpose.

C. Use your notes to form generalizations about the passage.

1. What generalization is the author making in the passage?

_____

_____

2. How did recording the clues about the author's tone and purpose help you form a generalization?

_____

_____

Selection Review   What Is News?

How Do the Media Shape the Way People Think?
Discover how the news media affect our understanding of events.

A. In "What Is News?" you found out how the news affects the way we think about events. Read the quotes from the text. Write notes about the author's opinions and tone.

Quote from the Text	Author's Opinion	Author's Tone
"Examining the news is important . . . so many elements, resources, and dollars go toward supporting the news."	People in our country value news, so it is important to examine the information.	straightforward, logical
"History needs to be presented in an interesting way. And there is still work to be done in order for print and electronic news to be effective."		
"When taken to these extremes, 'news' can become just another type of sensational entertainment. Understanding the use of the media then becomes even more important to viewers."		

B. Use the information in the chart to answer the questions.

1. Based on your answers in the chart, how would you describe the author's attitude toward the readers and the subject?

_____

_____

2. What are some ways the news media show bias? Use the word **bias** in your answer.

_____

_____

3. How might the media have more objectivity? Give two suggestions.

_____

_____

How to Detect Bias in the News

by Jeffrey Schank

Connect Across Texts

"What Is News?" raises questions about **objectivity** *in today's news coverage. This how-to article gives tips on how to* **detect** *and judge* **bias** *in the news that comes our way.*

Bias or Objectivity?

At one time or other we all complain about "bias in the news." Despite the journalistic goal of "objectivity," every news story is influenced by the attitudes and background of its interviewers, writers, photographers, and editors. Not all bias is deliberate. But you can watch for journalistic techniques that allow bias to "creep in" to the news.

1. Study selections and omissions.

An editor can express a bias by choosing to use or not to use specific information. These decisions give readers or viewers a different opinion about the events reported. If a few people boo during a speech, the reaction can be described as "remarks greeted by **jeers**." On the other hand, they can be ignored as "a handful of **dissidents**." Bias through omission is difficult to identify. In many cases, it can only be observed by comparing multiple news reports.

Interact with the Text

1. Author's Purpose
Underline the sentence that tells the writer's purpose. What does the writer think about bias in the news?

2. Logical Order
Preview the rest of the article. How is the information in this how-to article arranged? Why do you think it is organized this way?

Key Vocabulary
- **objectivity** *n.*, view that is not influenced by opinions
- **detect** *v.*, to discover or notice
- **bias** *n.*, opinions that affect the way you see or present things

In Other Words
journalistic techniques that the ways that journalists
omissions the things that are left out
jeers rude comments
dissidents people who make it known they don't agree with the speaker

3. Generalizations

Underline the main idea in Step 2. Explain how this step supports the purpose of the article.

_____

_____

_____

_____

_____

_____

_____

_____

_____

4. Logical Order

What does the writer want readers to do in Step 3? Circle the most important ideas in this step. Summarize this step in your own words.

_____

_____

_____

_____

_____

_____

_____

_____

_____

_____

_____

_____

When filmmaker Michael Moore gave a **controversial speech** at the 2003 Academy Awards, the news gave very different reports:

The London Daily: *"He was both applauded and booed by the assembled celebrities."*

CNN: *"The speech won him icy stares and undeniable celebrity . . . "*

ABC News: *"Moore achieved what some may have considered impossible— getting a largely Democratic Hollywood crowd to boo."*

TV Guide: *"That's not what I saw," Moore insisted. "I saw the entire place stand up and applaud . . . "*

2. Look at item placement.

Readers of papers judge first-page stories to be more significant than those in the back. Television and radio newscasts run the most important stories first and leave the less significant for later. Where a story is placed influences what a reader or viewer thinks about its importance.

3. Consider headlines.

Many people read only the headlines of a news item. Most people **scan** nearly all the headlines in a newspaper. Headlines are the most-read part of a paper. They also can present carefully hidden bias and prejudices. They can **convey excitement where little exists**. They can express approval or **condemnation**.

In 2005, Kellenberg Memorial High School in New York canceled its prom. How do these different headlines show bias?

In Other Words

controversial speech speech that made some people upset and others happy
scan quickly look over, skim over
convey excitement where little exists make a story sound exciting even if it isn't
condemnation strong disapproval

The Boston College Observer: N.Y. Catholic School Cancels Prom
MTV News: Principal Cancels Prom, Saying "The Prom Culture Is Sick"
The Kansas City Star: Booze and Sex Sink a Prom in NY
Fox News: High School Institutes "No Prom Zone"

4. Look at names and titles.

News media often use labels and titles to describe people, places, and events. A person can be called an "ex-convict" or someone who "served time for **a minor offense**." Whether a person is described as a "terrorist" or a "freedom fighter" is another example of bias.

5. Study photos, camera angles, and captions.

Some pictures **flatter a person**. Others make the person look unpleasant. For example, a paper can choose photos to influence opinion about a candidate for election. The captions newspapers run below photos are also sources of bias.

⚠ Interpret the Photo Photos can indicate a newswriter's attitude about a subject. Which photo might go with a positive article about actress Jennifer Lopez? Explain.

In Other Words
Institutes Establishes, Sets up
a minor offense a crime that is not too serious
flatter a person make a person look good

Interact with the Text

5. Logical Order
According to Step 4, why should a reader look at names and titles? Circle an example of a biased title or name in this step

6. Generalizations
Underline the sentences that tell how a photo can show bias. How does Step 5 support the purpose of the article?

7. Interpret

Why do companies supply news outlets with their own photos?

_____

_____

_____

_____

_____

_____

6. Consider sources.

To detect bias, always consider where the news item "comes from." Is the information from a reporter, an eyewitness, police or fire officials, executives, or government officials? Each may have a particular bias that influences the story. Companies often supply **news outlets** with **news releases**, photos, or videos. ❖

In Other Words

news outlets newspapers, magazines, and TV stations

news releases statements or stories they want the media to cover

Selection Review How to Detect Bias in the News

A. Review the six steps on how to detect bias in the news. Write a statement that summarizes what readers should do to detect bias.

_____

_____

_____

B. Answer the questions.

1. Form a statement about the purpose of the article and the procedure it describes.

_____

_____

2. The how-to article showed how to find bias in news items. Is it possible to communicate the news with complete objectivity?

_____

_____

_____

Key Word	Check Your Understanding	Deepen Your Understanding
5 distorted (dis-**tor**-tid) *adjective* **Rating:** 1 2 3	A **distorted** picture is _____. misleading true	My definition: _____ _____ _____ _____ _____
6 engaged (en-**gājd**) *adjective* **Rating:** 1 2 3	If you are **engaged** in an activity, you are _____. frustrated absorbed	My definition: _____ _____ _____ _____ _____
7 objectivity (ub-jek-**tiv**-u-tē) *noun* **Rating:** 1 2 3	If you show **objectivity**, you show _____. enthusiasm neutrality	My definition: _____ _____ _____ _____ _____
8 priority (prī-**or**-u-tē) *noun* **Rating:** 1 2 3	A **priority** is something that has high _____. insignificance importance	My definition: _____ _____ _____ _____ _____

B. Use one of the Key Vocabulary words to describe a recent news story that affected you. How did it make you feel?

_____

_____

Before Reading What Is News?

LITERARY ANALYSIS: Analyze Viewpoint: Tone

Tone is the writer's attitude about the topic or reader. A writer sometimes uses a persuasive tone to convince readers to believe his or her opinions and ideas.

A. Read the passage below. Find words and phrases that show the writer's attitude. Write the word choices in the web.

> ### Look Into the Text
>
> With the pervasiveness of news today, it is important to take a look at how news affects our lives. We have come a long way from the days when the nightly news was reported at 6 p.m. on the "Big 3" broadcast networks.
>
> Today, we have access to news whenever we want—from a variety of 24-hour cable news channels, to "news when you want it" from the Internet, to instant news on one's PDA device. Instant news is just part of our lives.

Details Web

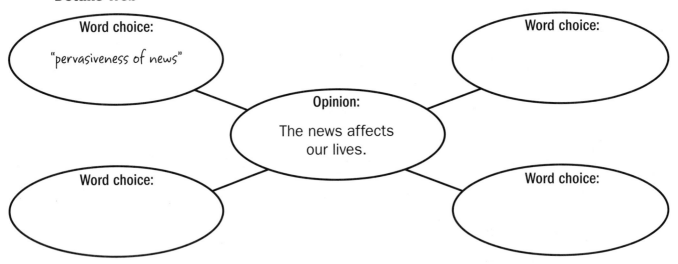

B. Look at the words and phrases the writer uses. Describe the writer's tone. Why do you think the writer chose this tone?

_____

_____

FOCUS STRATEGY: Synthesize

> ## HOW TO FORM GENERALIZATIONS
>
> 1. **Record Clues** List details, word choice, and organization that show the author's tone.
> 2. **Combine the Information** Form a statement about the author's purpose and tone.

A. Read the passage. Use the strategies above to form generalizations as you read. Then answer the questions below.

> **Look Into the Text**
>
> News has two priorities: it must be current, and it must mean something to people. A story about the environment and a story about the Super Bowl are both newsworthy, but for different reasons.
>
> On the surface at least, the objective of news is to inform the audience. It's the job of all the news media to tell people what's going on in their community—locally, nationally or globally. In this sense, the news media provide a valuable public service.

B. Return to the passage and circle words and phrases that help you understand the writer's tone and purpose.

C. Use your notes to form generalizations about the passage.

1. What generalization is the author making in the passage?

_____

_____

2. How did recording the clues about the author's tone and purpose help you form a generalization?

_____

_____

Selection Review What Is News?

EQ **How Do the Media Shape the Way People Think?**
Discover how the news media affect our understanding of events.

A. In "What Is News?" you found out how the news affects the way we think about events. Read the quotes from the text. Write notes about the author's opinions and tone.

Quote from the Text	Author's Opinion	Author's Tone
"Examining the news is important . . . so many elements, resources, and dollars go toward supporting the news."	People in our country value news, so it is important to examine the information.	straightforward, logical
"History needs to be presented in an interesting way. And there is still work to be done in order for print and electronic news to be effective."		
"When taken to these extremes, 'news' can become just another type of sensational entertainment. Understanding the use of the media then becomes even more important to viewers."		

B. Use the information in the chart to answer the questions.

1. Based on your answers in the chart, how would you describe the author's attitude toward the readers and the subject?

_____

_____

2. What are some ways the news media show bias? Use the word **bias** in your answer.

_____

_____

3. How might the media have more objectivity? Give two suggestions.

_____

_____

How to Detect Bias in the News

by Jeffrey Schank

Connect Across Texts

"What Is News?" raises questions about **objectivity** *in today's news coverage. This how-to article gives tips on how to* **detect** *and judge* **bias** *in the news that comes our way.*

Bias or Objectivity?

At one time or other we all complain about "bias in the news." Despite the journalistic goal of "objectivity," every news story is influenced by the attitudes and background of its interviewers, writers, photographers, and editors. Not all bias is deliberate. But you can watch for journalistic techniques that allow bias to "creep in" to the news.

1. Study selections and omissions.

An editor can express a bias by choosing to use or not to use specific information. These decisions give readers or viewers a different opinion about the events reported. If a few people boo during a speech, the reaction can be described as "remarks greeted by **jeers**." On the other hand, they can be ignored as "a handful of **dissidents**." Bias through omission is difficult to identify. In many cases, it can only be observed by comparing multiple news reports.

Interact with the Text

1. Author's Purpose
Underline the sentence that tells the writer's purpose. What does the writer think about bias in the news?

_____

_____

_____

_____

2. Logical Order
Preview the rest of the article. How is the information in this how-to article arranged? Why do you think it is organized this way?

_____

_____

_____

_____

_____

_____

Key Vocabulary
- **objectivity** *n.*, view that is not influenced by opinions
- **detect** *v.*, to discover or notice
- **bias** *n.*, opinions that affect the way you see or present things

In Other Words
journalistic techniques that the ways that journalists
omissions the things that are left out
jeers rude comments
dissidents people who make it known they don't agree with the speaker

When filmmaker Michael Moore gave a **controversial speech** at the 2003 Academy Awards, the news gave very different reports:

The London Daily: "He was both applauded and booed by the assembled celebrities."

CNN: "The speech won him icy stares and undeniable celebrity . . ."

ABC News: "Moore achieved what some may have considered impossible— getting a largely Democratic Hollywood crowd to boo."

TV Guide: "That's not what I saw," Moore insisted. "I saw the entire place stand up and applaud . . ."

2. Look at item placement.

Readers of papers judge first-page stories to be more significant than those in the back. Television and radio newscasts run the most important stories first and leave the less significant for later. Where a story is placed influences what a reader or viewer thinks about its importance.

3. Consider headlines.

Many people read only the headlines of a news item. Most people **scan** nearly all the headlines in a newspaper. Headlines are the most-read part of a paper. They also can present carefully hidden bias and prejudices. They can **convey excitement where little exists**. They can express approval or **condemnation**.

In 2005, Kellenberg Memorial High School in New York canceled its prom. How do these different headlines show bias?

In Other Words
controversial speech speech that made some people upset and others happy
scan quickly look over, skim over
convey excitement where little exists make a story sound exciting even if it isn't
condemnation strong disapproval

The Boston College Observer: N.Y. Catholic School Cancels Prom

MTV News: Principal Cancels Prom, Saying "The Prom Culture Is Sick"

The Kansas City Star: Booze and Sex Sink a Prom in NY

Fox News: High School Institutes "No Prom Zone"

4. Look at names and titles.

News media often use labels and titles to describe people, places, and events. A person can be called an "ex-convict" or someone who "served time for **a minor offense**." Whether a person is described as a "terrorist" or a "freedom fighter" is another example of bias.

5. Study photos, camera angles, and captions.

Some pictures **flatter a person**. Others make the person look unpleasant. For example, a paper can choose photos to influence opinion about a candidate for election. The captions newspapers run below photos are also sources of bias.

◢ Interpret the Photo Photos can indicate a newswriter's attitude about a subject. Which photo might go with a positive article about actress Jennifer Lopez? Explain.

In Other Words
Institutes Establishes, Sets up
a minor offense a crime that is not too serious
flatter a person make a person look good

Interact with the Text

5. Logical Order
According to Step 4, why should a reader look at names and titles? Circle an example of a biased title or name in this step

6. Generalizations
Underline the sentences that tell how a photo can show bias. How does Step 5 support the purpose of the article?

7. Interpret

Why do companies supply news outlets with their own photos?

_____

_____

_____

_____

_____

_____

6. Consider sources.

To detect bias, always consider where the news item "comes from." Is the information from a reporter, an eyewitness, police or fire officials, executives, or government officials? Each may have a particular bias that influences the story. Companies often supply **news outlets** with **news releases**, photos, or videos. ❖

In Other Words

news outlets newspapers, magazines, and TV stations

news releases statements or stories they want the media to cover

Selection Review How to Detect Bias in the News

A. Review the six steps on how to detect bias in the news. Write a statement that summarizes what readers should do to detect bias.

_____

_____

_____

B. Answer the questions.

1. Form a statement about the purpose of the article and the procedure it describes.

_____

_____

2. The how-to article showed how to find bias in news items. Is it possible to communicate the news with complete objectivity?

_____

_____

_____

Reflect and Assess

WRITING: Write About Literature

A. Plan your writing. Which news medium—newspaper, TV news show, or radio broadcast—does the best job of covering the news? List the advantages and disadvantages of each medium based on what you read in each selection.

Medium	Advantages	Disadvantages
Newspaper		
Radio		
Television		

B. Think about the advantages and the disadvantages of each news medium. Write a sentence stating your conclusion. Then explain how you arrived at that conclusion.

My conclusion: I think that _____

_____

because _____

_____

_____

_____

LITERARY ANALYSIS: Analyze Viewpoint: Tone

Tone is the writer's attitude toward the topic or the reader. A persuasive writer often chooses a tone that will convince the audience to believe the writer's opinions and ideas.

A. Read the examples below from "What Is News?" Then describe the authors' tone.

Examples	Tone
"Instant news is just part of our lives."	conversational
"Media cater to their audiences. They report stories they think their consumers want to see, hear, or read about."	
"But a steady exposure to these images can give us a distorted view of what goes on in the world."	
"By knowing how the news industry works, we can find out how to reach the people who shape the news. Then we can begin to change reporting that reflects stereotyping or bias."	

B. Answer the questions.

1. What do the examples say about the author's attitude toward the news media? _____

    _____

    _____

2. What is the author's attitude toward the reader? _____

    _____

    _____

C. Write a brief paragraph to a government leader expressing your attitude toward an issue in your community. Use words that express a serious tone to make your argument.

_____

_____

_____

_____

VOCABULARY STUDY: Denotations and Connotations

The **denotation** of a word is its dictionary meaning. The **connotations** of a word are the various feelings, images, and memories that may be associated with it.

A. Read the words below and write the denotation and connotation of each word.

Word	Denotation	Connotation
manipulate		
mix		
stroll		
territory		
underfoot		

B. Read the words below. For each, write a word that has the same denotation but a different connotation.

1. animal _____

2. big _____

3. excited _____

4. instruct _____

5. tired _____

C. Brainstorm five word pairs that have the same denotations but different connotations. List them below.

1. _____

2. _____

3. _____

4. _____

5. _____

Read for Understanding

1. Genre What kind of text is this selection? How do you know?

2. Topic Write a topic sentence to tell what the text is mostly about.

Reread and Summarize

3. Key Ideas Circle three words or phrases that express the key ideas in each section. Note why you chose them.

· Section 1: paragraphs 1–4
· Section 2: paragraphs 5–11

4. Summary Use your topic sentence and notes from item 3 to write a summary of the text.

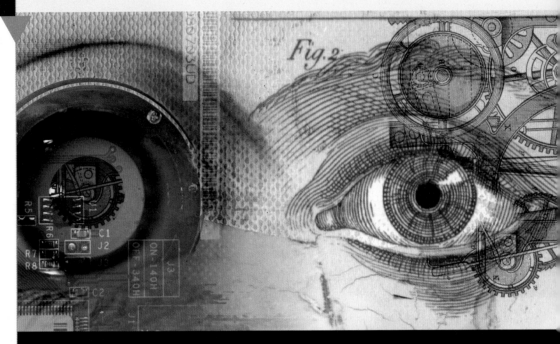

IS GOOGLE MAKING US STUPID?
by Nicholas Carr

1   Over the past few years I've had an uncomfortable sense that someone, or something, has been tinkering with my brain, remapping the **neural circuitry**, reprogramming the memory. My mind isn't going—so far as I can tell—but it's changing. I'm not thinking the way I used to think. I can feel it most strongly when I'm reading. Immersing myself in a book or a lengthy article used to be easy. My mind would get caught up in the narrative or the turns of the argument, and I'd spend hours strolling through long stretches of prose. That's rarely the case anymore. Now my concentration often starts to drift after two or three pages. I get **fidgety**, lose **the thread**, begin looking for something else to do. I feel as if I'm always dragging my wayward brain back to the text. The deep reading that used to come naturally has become a struggle.

In Other Words
neural circuitry nerve pathways
fidgety restless
the thread focus

2   I think I know what's going on. For more than a decade now, I've been spending a lot of time online, searching and surfing and sometimes adding to the great databases of the Internet. The Web has been a **godsend** to me as a writer. Research that once required days in the stacks or periodical rooms of libraries can now be done in minutes. A few Google searches, some quick clicks on hyperlinks, and I've got the telltale fact or pithy quote I was after. Even when I'm not working, I'm as likely as not to be foraging in the Web's info-thickets, reading and writing e-mails, scanning headlines and blog posts, watching videos and listening to podcasts, or just tripping from link to link to link. (Unlike footnotes, to which they're sometimes likened, hyperlinks don't merely point to related works; they propel you toward them.)

3   For me, as for others, the Net is becoming a universal medium, the **conduit** for most of the information that flows through my eyes and ears and into my mind. The advantages of having immediate **access** to such an incredibly rich store of information are many, and they've been widely described and duly applauded. "The perfect recall of silicon memory," *Wired's* Clive Thompson has written, "can be an enormous **boon** to thinking." But that boon comes at a price. As the **media** theorist Marshall McLuhan pointed out in the 1960s, **media** are not just passive channels of information. They supply the stuff of thought, but they also shape the process of thought. And what the Net seems to be doing is chipping away my capacity for concentration and contemplation. My mind now expects to take in information the way the Net distributes it: in a swiftly moving stream of particles. Once I was a scuba diver in the sea of words. Now I zip along the surface like a guy on a Jet Ski.

4   I'm not the only one. Some of the bloggers I follow have also begun mentioning the phenomenon. Scott Karp, who writes a blog about online media, recently confessed that he has stopped reading books altogether. "I was a **lit** major in college, and used to be [a] **voracious** book reader," he wrote. "What happened?" He speculates on the answer: "What if I do all my reading on the Web not so much because the way I read has changed, **i.e.** I'm just seeking convenience, but because the way I THINK has changed?"

Reread and Analyze

5. Author's Viewpoint
Reread paragraph 3. Highlight Nicholas Carr's claim about how the Internet is changing the way he thinks.

6. Evidence Underline the ideas of Marshall McLuhan. How do these ideas support the author's claim?

_____

_____

_____

_____

_____

_____

_____

7. Evidence Reread paragraph 4. Underline the key ideas from Scott Karp. How do Karp's experiences support the author's claim?

_____

_____

_____

_____

_____

_____

_____

_____

_____

_____

_____

_____

Key Vocabulary
• **access** *n.*, the ability to get and use something
• **media** *n.*, different ways people use to communicate, inform, and entertain

In Other Words
godsend huge benefit
conduit passageway
boon help, benefit
lit literature
voracious very enthusiastic
i.e. in other words

8. Evidence Reread paragraphs 5 and 6. Underline evidence that is relevant to the author's claim about the Internet. How do the study results support the author's claim?

_____

_____

_____

_____

_____

What makes this evidence seem reliable?

_____

_____

_____

_____

9. Evidence Underline another person's view in section 2. Why is it relevant to the author's argument?

_____

_____

_____

_____

_____

What would make this person's view more reliable?

_____

_____

_____

_____

5   **Anecdotes** alone don't prove much. And we still await the long-term **neurological and psychological** experiments that will provide a definitive picture of how Internet use affects **cognition**. But a recently published study of online research habits, conducted by scholars from University College London, suggests that we may well be in the **midst of a sea change** in the way we read and think. The authors of the study report:

6   It is clear that users are not reading online in the traditional sense; indeed there are signs that new forms of "reading" are emerging as users "power browse" horizontally through titles, contents, pages, and abstracts going for quick wins. It almost seems that they go online to avoid reading in the traditional sense.

7   The idea that our minds should operate as high-speed data-processing machines is not only built into the workings of the Internet, it is the network's **reigning** business model as well. The faster we surf across the Web—the more links we click and pages we view—the more opportunities Google and other companies gain to collect information about us and to feed us advertisements. Most of the proprietors of the commercial Internet

> *...users "power browse" horizontally through titles, contents, pages, and abstracts going for quick wins.*

have a **financial stake in** collecting the crumbs of data we leave behind as we flit from link to link—the more crumbs, the better. The last thing these companies want is to encourage leisurely reading or slow, concentrated thought. It's in their economic interest to drive us to distraction.

8   Maybe I'm just a **worrywart**.

9   Just as there's a tendency to glorify technological progress, there's a countertendency to expect the worst of every new tool or machine. In Plato's *Phaedrus*, Socrates **bemoaned** the development of writing. He feared that, as

In Other Words

Anecdotes Personal stories
neurological and psychological physical and mental
cognition thought
midst of a sea change middle of a big change

reigning ruling, governing
financial stake in money-related reason for
worrywart person who worries unnecessarily
bemoaned complained about

people came to rely on the written word as a substitute for the knowledge they used to carry inside their heads, they would, in the words of one of the dialogue's characters, "cease to exercise their memory and become forgetful." And because they would be able to "receive a quantity of information without proper instruction," they would "be thought very knowledgeable when they are for the most part quite ignorant." They would be "filled with the conceit of wisdom instead of real wisdom." Socrates wasn't wrong—the new technology did often have the effects he feared—but he was shortsighted. He couldn't foresee the many ways that writing and reading would serve to spread information, spur fresh ideas, and **expand** human knowledge (if not wisdom).

10   Then again, the Net isn't the alphabet, and although it may replace the printing press, it produces something altogether different. The kind of deep reading that a sequence of printed pages promotes is valuable not just for the knowledge we acquire from the author's words but for the intellectual vibrations those words set off within our own minds. In the quiet spaces opened up by the sustained, undistracted reading of a book, or by any other act of contemplation, for that matter, we make our own associations, draw our own inferences and analogies, foster our own ideas. Deep reading, as Maryanne Wolf argues, is indistinguishable from deep thinking.

11   If we lose those quiet spaces, or fill them up with "content," we will **sacrifice** something important not only in our selves but in our culture. ❖

National Public Works Week 2007 Poster ©Gordon St[...]

▷ **Critical Viewing: Theme** How does the artist connect people and machines in this painting? Do you think the artist sees these connections as positive? Why or why not?

Key Vocabulary
● **expand** *v.*, to increase or grow larger

In Other Words
sacrifice give up

Reread and Analyze

10. Word Choice   Reread paragraph 7, focusing on words and phrases that appeal to emotions. Is the phrase "flit from link to link" positive or negative? How does it help convey the author's viewpoint about using the Internet?

_____

_____

_____

_____

_____

11. Word Choice   Highlight other words and phrases in section 2 that appeal to emotions. Explain how one specific example appeals to the emotions and helps convey the author's viewpoint.

_____

_____

_____

_____

_____

_____

_____

_____

_____

_____

_____

_____

_____

_____

Discuss

12. **Synthesize** With the class, discuss how authors use evidence and word choice to make persuasive arguments. Discuss how examples from the selection help make the essay more persuasive. Take notes about your discussion.

	Examples from the Selection	How They Make Selection More Persuasive
Evidence		
Word Choice		

With the class, discuss which techniques are the most effective in supporting an author's arguments. Make notes.

_____

_____

_____

13. **Write** Use your notes from question 12 to write a paragraph that explains how persuasive writers use evidence and word choice to make their arguments more persuasive. If you need more space, continue your writing on another piece of paper.

_____

_____

_____

_____

_____

_____

_____

_____

Connect with the EQ   How Do the Media Shape the Way People Think?

Consider whether the Internet changes the way we think.

14. **Opinion** Think about the argument Nicholas Carr makes in his essay. According to Carr, how does the Internet change the way we read and think? Use evidence from the text to support your response.

_____

_____

_____

_____

_____

_____

_____

_____

_____

_____

15. **Theme** Reread the quotation by Nicholas Johnson on page 506. Instead of television, could it also apply to Carr's view of the Internet? Why or why not? Be sure to cite evidence from the text in your answer.

_____

_____

_____

_____

_____

_____

_____

_____

_____

_____

Key Vocabulary Review

A. Read each sentence. Circle the word that best fits into each sentence.

1. Someone who is listening closely is (**persuasive** / **engaged**).

2. If you buy groceries, you are a (**consumer** / **minority**).

3. You can often (**detect** / **manipulate**) how someone feels by watching how they behave.

4. Many restaurants offer (**distorted** / **alternative**) choices for people who do not eat meat.

5. Editorials are a type of opinion article that show (**racism** / **bias**).

6. Volunteering is one way to (**impact** / **expand**) your community.

7. Commercials are an example of (**objectivity** / **advertising**).

8. Some companies try to increase their (**profit** / **priority**) by lowering their prices and selling more products.

B. Use your own words to write what each Key Vocabulary word means. Then write a synonym for each word.

Key Word	My Definition	Synonym
1. access		
2. appeal		
3. convince		
4. distorted		
5. influence		
6. objectivity		
7. persuasive		
8. token		

Unit 6 Key Vocabulary

- access
  advertising
- alternative
  appeal

- bias
- consumer
- convince
  deliberate

- detect
- distorted
  engaged
- expand

- impact
  influence
- manipulate
- media

  minority
- objectivity
  persuasive
- priority

  profit
  racism
  stereotype
  token

• **Academic Vocabulary**

C. Complete the sentences.

1. The **media** I rely on most frequently are _____

   _____ .

2. When I hear a **stereotype** about teenagers, it makes me feel _____

   _____ .

3. If I could **expand** the school building, I would add _____

   _____ .

4. One time I was in the **minority** was when _____

   _____ .

5. An example of a **deliberate** action is _____

   _____ .

6. My number one **priority** this week is to _____

   _____ .

7. One way to combat **racism** is by _____

   _____ .

8. When someone tries to **manipulate** me, I react by _____

   _____ .

▷ **A Raisin in the Sun**
▷ **My Father Is a Simple Man**
▷ **My Mother Pieced Quilts**

Prepare to Read

Key Vocabulary

A. How well do you know these words? Circle a rating for each word. Check your understanding of each word by circling *yes* or *no*. Then write a definition. If you are unsure of a word's meaning, refer to the Vocabulary Glossary, page 878, in your student text.

Rating Scale

1	I have never seen this word before.
2	I am not sure of the word's meaning.
3	I know this word and can teach the word's meaning to someone else.

Key Word	Check Your Understanding	Deepen Your Understanding
① bond (**bond**) *noun* **Rating:** 1 2 3	Many people often have a special **bond** with their dogs. **Yes** **No**	My definition: _____ _____ _____ _____
② collapse (ku-**laps**) *verb* **Rating:** 1 2 3	People might **collapse** after they hear bad news. **Yes** **No**	My definition: _____ _____ _____ _____
③ integrity (in-**te**-gru-tē) *noun* **Rating:** 1 2 3	A woman shows **integrity** when she lies to a friend. **Yes** **No**	My definition: _____ _____ _____ _____
④ invest (in-**vest**) *verb* **Rating:** 1 2 3	People can **invest** in real estate by buying a house. **Yes** **No**	My definition: _____ _____ _____ _____

Key Word	Check Your Understanding	Deepen Your Understanding
5 loyalty (**loi**-ul-tē) *noun* Rating: 1 2 3	Your friends can show their **loyalty** by disappearing when you need them. **Yes**　　　**No**	My definition: _____ _____ _____ _____ _____
6 pretense (**prē**-tens) *noun* Rating: 1 2 3	Talking about your everyday life is showing **pretense**. **Yes**　　　**No**	My definition: _____ _____ _____ _____ _____
7 provider (pru-**vī**-dur) *noun* Rating: 1 2 3	A good **provider** does not care when there is not enough food for the family. **Yes**　　　**No**	My definition: _____ _____ _____ _____ _____
8 successful (suk-**ses**-ful) *adjective* Rating: 1 2 3	Most **successful** people meet their goals. **Yes**　　　**No**	My definition: _____ _____ _____ _____ _____

B. Use one of the Key Vocabulary words to write about a member of your family who you think holds your family together.

_____

_____

_____

Before Reading A Raisin in the Sun

LITERARY ANALYSIS: Compare Representations: Script and Performance

Drama is a story that is performed for an audience. A **script** is the written text of a drama. Actors interpret the script when they take on the roles of the characters to put on a **performance** of the drama for an audience.

A. Read this passage from Scene 1 of the script of *A Raisin in the Sun* and study the photo from a performance of the same scene, which shows Travis, his mother Ruth, and his grandmother. Then complete the chart to compare the script to the performance.

Look Into the Text

TRAVIS. Mama, my teacher says we're supposed to bring fifty cents to school today for our field trip.

RUTH. We don't have it, baby.

TRAVIS. Aw, come on.

RUTH. I'm sorry, honey. Here, give me a hug.

[TRAVIS *hugs his mom and hurries off to school.*]

	Script	Performance
What I Learn About Travis	wants 50 cents for field trip	seems happy
What I Learn About Ruth, Travis's Mother		
What I Learn About Travis's Grandmother		

B. Use the details you listed to complete the sentence.

I think this play will be about _____

_____ .

FOCUS STRATEGY: Visualize

HOW TO FORM MENTAL IMAGES

1. Pay attention to the dialogue and stage directions.

2. Look for descriptive words and phrases to help you form mental images.

3. Make a simple sketch of the characters and actions.

A. Read the passage. Use the strategies above to form mental images as you read. Use the space beside the script to draw a simple sketch of the scene. Then answer the questions below.

Look Into the Text

> **RUTH.** It *is* your money. Just think—$10,000! What would *you* like to do with it?
>
> **MAMA.** Maybe we can buy a little house somewhere, with a yard for Travis.
>
> **RUTH.** Lord knows we've put enough rent into this rattrap to pay for four houses by now.
>
> [MAMA *looks around sadly.*]
>
> **MAMA.** A rattrap. Yes, that's all it is. I remember when Big Walter and I moved in here. We didn't plan to stay more than a year. I guess dreams sometimes get put on hold.
>
> [RUTH *starts ironing a big pile of clothes.* MAMA *washes the breakfast dishes. It's the beginning of another busy day.*]

1. Describe your mental image of the characters, their actions, and the setting.

_____

_____

2. Which strategies did you use to answer question 1?

_____

_____

B. Return to the passage above, and underline the words or sentences that helped you answer the first question.

Selection Review A Raisin in the Sun

 What Holds Us Together? What Keeps Us Apart?
Consider how families hold us together.

A. In "A Raisin in the Sun," you read about how the Youngers struggle to stay together through difficult times. Complete the T Chart by comparing Walter's actions with Mama's actions.

T Chart

Walter's Actions	Mama's Actions
Walter wants to buy a liquor store with Mama's money.	

B. Use the information in the chart to answer the questions.

1. Which character succeeds in holding the family together? Why?

_____

_____

2. Why does Beneatha tell Walter he doesn't have any integrity? Use **integrity** in your answer.

_____

_____

3. What would you have done if you had to make the same decision as Walter? Explain.

_____

_____

Connect Across Texts
"A Raisin in the Sun" describes what happens when a family deals with sudden wealth. In these poems, parents share lessons about a different kind of wealth.

Family BONDS

Interact with the Text

1. Interpret
Look at the photo. Read the title and "Connect Across Texts." What do you predict these poems will be about?

Key Vocabulary
- **bond** *n.*, connection between people or things

My Father Is a Simple Man

by Luis Omar Salinas

I walk to town with my father
to buy a newspaper. He walks slower
than I do so I must slow up.
The street is filled with children.

5   We argue about the price
of pomegranates, I convince
him it is the fruit of scholars.
He has taken me on this journey
and it's been lifelong.

10   He's sure I'll be healthy
so long as I eat more oranges,
and tells me the orange
has seeds and so is perpetual;
and we too will come back

15   like the orange trees.
I ask him what he thinks
about death and he says
he will gladly face it when
it comes but won't jump

20   out in front of a car.
I'd gladly give my life
for this man with a sixth
grade education, whose kindness
and patience are true . . .

Still Life with Oranges and Lemons in a Wan-Li Porcelain Dish, Jacob van Hulsdonck.
Oil on panel, private collection.

▲ Critical Viewing: Effect The artist painted these oranges in a highly
realistic style. Which senses do you think he wanted to appeal to?

In Other Words
Simple Plain, Ordinary
scholars smart people who have a lot
  of education
is perpetual will go on forever because
  it produces new fruits

25 The truth of it is, he's the scholar,
   and when the bitter-hard reality
   comes at me like a punishing
   evil stranger, I can always
   remember that here was a man
30 who was a worker and provider,
   who learned the simple facts
   in life and lived by them,
   who held no pretense.
   And when he leaves without
35 benefit of fanfare or applause
   I shall have learned what little
   there is about greatness.

About the Poet

Luis Omar Salinas (1937–2008) is internationally recognized as one of the leading figures in Mexican American poetry. Born near the Texas-Mexico border, Salinas emerged as one of the most important writers in the "Fresno School" of poets in the 1970s and wrote nine books of poetry.

Interact with the Text

2. Imagery
Circle the sensory images on page 294. What do these images make you see, hear, feel, taste, or smell?

_____

_____

_____

_____

_____

_____

3. Form Mental Images
Circle the speaker's description of reality. Explain the description and what it makes you visualize.

_____

_____

_____

_____

_____

_____

_____

4. Imagery
Underline words and phrases that describe the father. How do you "see" him?

_____

_____

_____

_____

Key Vocabulary
provider *n.*, someone who gives necessary things to someone else
pretense *n.*, the act of pretending to do or be something

In Other Words
benefit of fanfare or applause the world celebrating the great things about his life

My Mother Pieced Quilts

by Teresa Palomo Acosta

they were just meant as covers
in winters
as weapons
against pounding january winds

5   but it was just that every morning I awoke
     to these
october ripened canvases
passed my hand across their cloth faces
and began to wonder how you pieced
all these together

10 these strips of gentle communion cotton
     and flannel nightgowns
wedding organdies
dime store velvets

how you shaped patterns square and oblong
     and round
positioned
15 balanced
then cemented them
with your thread
a steel needle
a thimble

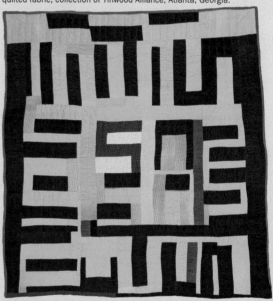

Blocks-and-Strips Quilt, 2003, Mary Lee Bendolph. Corduroy quilted fabric, collection of Tinwood Alliance, Atlanta, Georgia.

▲ **Critical Viewing: Design and Effect** What do the colors and shapes of this quilt make you think of? How do they make you feel?

In Other Words
Pieced Planned, Created
october ripened canvases quilts that we used
   when the weather turned cold
oblong rectangular
a thimble and other sewing tools

20   how the thread darted in and out

      galloping along the frayed edges, tucking them in

      as you did us at night

      oh how you stretched and turned and re-arranged

      your michigan spring faded curtain pieces

25   my father's santa fe work shirt

      the summer denims, the tweeds of fall

      in the evening you sat at your canvas

      —our cracked linoleum floor the drawing board

      me lounging on your arm

30   and you staking out the plan:

      whether to put the lilac purple of easter against the red plaid of winter-going-

         into-spring

      whether to mix a yellow with blue and white and paint the

      corpus christi noon when my father held your hand

      whether to shape a five-point star from the

35   somber black silk you wore to grandmother's funeral

      you were the river current

      carrying the roaring notes

      forming them into pictures of a little boy reclining

      a swallow flying

40   you were the caravan master at the reins

      driving your threaded needle artillery across the mosaic cloth bridges

      delivering yourself in separate testimonies.

      oh mother you plunged me sobbing and laughing

      into our past

In Other Words

frayed old and worn

staking out the plan planning where each
  piece would go

corpus christi noon hot day

river current flowing stream

reclining relaxing

caravan master at the reins one in control

needle artillery weapons

mosaic cloth bridges combinations of cloth

testimonies stories

5. Form Mental Images

Circle the words and phrases on page 296 that show what the quilts look like. Picture in your mind what the speaker describes. Explain how visualizing this helps you understand how the speaker feels about her mother's quilts.

_____

_____

_____

_____

_____

_____

6. Imagery

Underline a phrase that tells how the mother takes control of the quilts. What does this imagery help you "see"?

_____

_____

_____

_____

_____

_____

_____

_____

_____

_____

_____

7. Interpret

Highlight the words and phrases that describe how the speaker feels about the quilts. How do you think the speaker's feelings about the quilts reflect her feelings about her mother?

_____

_____

_____

_____

_____

_____

_____

_____

45   into the river crossing at five
     into the spinach fields
     into the plainview cotton rows
     into tuberculosis wards
     into braids and muslin dresses
50   sewn hard and taut to withstand the
        thrashings of twenty-five years

     stretched out they lay
     armed/ready/shouting/celebrating

     knotted with love
     the quilts sing on

About the Poet

Teresa Palomo Acosta (1949– grew up in the cotton country of Central Texas. She has published three books of poetry and co-authored _Las Tejanas: 300 Years of History_, about the contributions Mexican American women have made to American life.

In Other Words
plainview wide
tuberculosis wards hospital areas
taut to withstand the thrashing strong
   to survive the hard daily use

Selection Review Family Bonds

A. Choose one of the poems. List an example of each type of imagery.

   1. Sensory Image:

   _____

   _____

   2. Literal Image:

   _____

   _____

   3. Figurative Image:

   _____

   _____

B. Answer the questions.

   1. Choose one of the images you listed above. What picture does it create in your mind? Explain what you visualize.

   _____

   _____

WRITING: Write About Literature

A. Plan your writing. List the characteristics of the parents in each of the three selections.

A Raisin in the Sun	My Father Is a Simple Man	My Mother Pieced Quilts

B. Write a comparison paragraph. Describe how the parents in the three selections are similar. Use the examples from your chart to support your comparison.

_____

_____

_____

_____

_____

_____

_____

_____

_____

_____

_____

_____

LITERARY ANALYSIS: Analyze and Compare Poetry

Poetry often uses carefully controlled language, figures of speech, and imagery to appeal to a reader's senses, emotions, and imagination. Poetic elements include the speaker, sound devices, imagery, punctuation and line breaks.

A. Reread the poem "Rosa" below. Underline examples of imagery and sound devices that the author uses to appeal to the reader's senses, emotions, or imagination.

> **Rosa**
> How she sat there,
> the time right inside a place
> so wrong it was ready.
> That trim name with
> its dream of a bench
> to rest on. Her sensible coat.
> Doing nothing was the doing:
> the clean flame of her gaze
> carved by a camera flash.
> How she stood up
> when they bent down to retrieve
> her purse. That courtesy.

B. Consider the poetic elements from "Rosa," and write them in the chart.

Speaker	
Sound Devices (rhyme, rhythm, repetition)	
Imagery	
Punctuation and line breaks	

C. Describe your favorite poem or a poem that has had a positive or negative impact on you. Describe the speaker, sound devices, and imagery.

_____

_____

VOCABULARY STUDY: Interpret Figurative Language

You can sometimes use context clues to help you understand the meaning of **figurative language**.

A. Read the lines from "A Raisin in the Sun." Write what you think the underlined words or phrases mean. Then write the context clues that helped you figure out the meaning.

Sentence	What It Means	Context Clues
WALTER. I'll do whatever it takes to <u>put some pearls around my wife's neck</u>! (p. 630)		
WALTER. And we decided to move into our house. Because my father, he earned it for us <u>brick by brick</u>. (p. 631)		

B. Read each phrase from "My Mother Pieced Quilts." Write the meaning and identify the context clue or clues that helped you find the meaning.

1. "they were just meant as covers / in winters / as weapons / against pounding january winds" (lines 1–4)

    <u>This explains that the quilts were made for warmth. The words <u>winters</u> and <u>winds</u> tell me that the quilts were</u>

    <u>intended to protect against cold weather.</u>

2. "galloping along the frayed edges, tucking them in / as you did us at night" (lines 21–22)

    _____

    _____

3. "you were the caravan master at the reins / driving your threaded needle artillery across the mosaic cloth bridges" (lines 40–41)

    _____

    _____

C. Write a sentence about a summer day using figurative language.

_____

_____

_____

Prepare to Read

▷ **Pass It On**
▷ **If There Be Pain**
▷ **Sonnet 30**

Key Vocabulary

A. How well do you know these words? Circle a rating for each word. Check your understanding of each word by circling the correct synonym. Then complete the sentences. If you are unsure of a word's meaning, refer to the Vocabulary Glossary, page 878, in your student text.

Rating Scale	
1	I have never seen this word before.
2	I am not sure of the word's meaning.
3	I know this word and can teach the word's meaning to someone else.

Key Word	Check Your Understanding	Deepen Your Understanding
❶ conquer (**kon**-kur) *verb* **Rating:** 1 2 3	To **conquer** is to _____. retreat defeat	If I wanted to help my friend conquer a bad habit, I would _____ _____ _____ _____ .
❷ devotion (di-**vō**-shun) *noun* **Rating:** 1 2 3	If you show **devotion**, you show _____. dedication faithlessness	The person I feel the most devotion toward is _____ _____ _____ _____ _____ .
❸ grief (grēf) *noun* **Rating:** 1 2 3	When people feel **grief**, they feel _____. joy sorrow	People experience grief after _____ _____ _____ _____ _____ .
❹ issue (**i**-shoo) *noun* **Rating:** 1 2 3	An **issue** is a _____ that matters to people. statement topic	An issue I am interested in understanding better is _____ _____ _____ _____ _____ .

Key Word	Check Your Understanding	Deepen Your Understanding
5 **refuge** (**re**-fyūj) *noun* **Rating:** 1 2 3	A **refuge** is a place of _____. **shelter** **danger**	One place I could go if I needed a refuge is _____ _____ _____ _____ _____ .
6 **restore** (ri-**stor**) *verb* **Rating:** 1 2 3	To **restore** is to _____. **mend** **destroy**	An example of something people like to restore is_____ _____ _____ _____ _____ .
7 **subside** (sub-**sīd**) *verb* **Rating:** 1 2 3	To **subside** is to _____. **rise** **lessen**	You might make someone's anger subside by _____ _____ _____ _____ _____ .
8 **territory** (**ter**-u-tor-ē) *noun* **Rating:** 1 2 3	When a nation owns **territory**, it owns _____. **buildings** **land**	In my community, I do not go into territory that _____ _____ _____ _____ _____ .

B. Use one of the Key Vocabulary words to write about a time you showed loyalty to a friend.

_____

_____

_____

Before Reading Pass It On

LITERARY ANALYSIS: Analyze Elements of Drama: Characterization

Playwrights create **characterization in drama** using different techniques.
Dialogue shows characters' thoughts and can give background information.
Stage directions tell how characters speak and act.

A. Read the passage below. Pay attention to dialogue and stage directions.
Complete the chart.

Look Into the Text

JUDGE. Where's Echo?

TAILLIGHT. As if you didn't know.

WHISPER. He's at the courthouse.

DOC. [*sarcastically*] "Somebody" filed an assault charge.

JUDGE. [*looking upset*] Oh, I, I, mean, Dawn just said she told the
police what happened to Gram. She didn't tell me . . . I mean,
with everything that happened, I didn't really think about . . .

    [DOC, WHISPER, *and* TAILLIGHT *look at each other and shake
    their heads.*]

DOC. We have to go.

    [DOC, WHISPER, *and* TAILLIGHT *leave.*]

JUDGE. [*speaking to himself*] I have to go, too.

Character	Dialogue	Stage Directions
Judge	"She didn't tell me . . . I mean with everything that happened,"	
Doc		

B. What do the dialogue and stage directions tell you about the characters?

_____

_____

FOCUS STRATEGY: Visualize

How to IDENTIFY EMOTIONAL RESPONSES

1. **Find details** that help you visualize the scene, characters, and events.

2. **Relate details** to your own life. Imagine how you would feel if you experienced those events.

3. **Record your emotional responses** to describe your thoughts about what you read.

A. Read the passage. Use the strategies above to identify emotional responses as you read. Then answer the questions below.

Look Into the Text

WHISPER. I'm sorry, bro'. If I hadn't brought Tiger around, this never would've happened. I just don't want you to go away again.

ECHO. Nah, forget it. It was their fault. [*under his breath*] And mine.

TAILLIGHT. Don't you take the blame for this.

ECHO. [*not happy that Taillight has heard his mumbled comment*] I'm not taking the blame for this. I'm just saying, if I had stayed cool—

TAILLIGHT. [*upset*] Stayed cool? You showed force, man, you showed strength.

---

1. How do you visualize this scene? Describe the picture that you "see" in your mind.

   _____

   _____

   _____

2. How would you feel if you were Echo?

   _____

   _____

B. Return to the passage above and circle the details that helped you visualize the characters and their actions.

EQ **What Holds Us Together? What Keeps Us Apart?**
Explore how friends show loyalty.

A. In "Pass It On," you found out how loyalties and rivalries affect relationships. Complete the Character Description Chart, using information you learned from dialogue and stage directions.

Character Description Chart

Character	What He Says and Does	What This Shows About Him
Doc	Wonders about Martin Luther King, Jr. "I Have a Dream" speech	
Echo		
Judge		

B. Use the information in the chart to answer the questions.

1. Why do you think Echo leaves the bus to help Gram? What do his actions tell you about his character?

_____

_____

2. What issues keep the Hatchets and the Tigers apart? Use **issues** in your answer.

_____

_____

3. What does Judge mean when he tells Echo to "stay strong"?

_____

_____

Standing Together

On the surface, Tupac Amaru Shakur and William Shakespeare don't have much in common. After all, the two men lived centuries apart, in very different worlds. But below the surface, there may be more similarities than you think. Both Shakur and Shakespeare were writers who used poetry as a way to express their ideas about the important **issues** of their times. And both men wrote with passion about friendship, devotion, and loyalty— things that we still care about today.

Key Vocabulary
- **devotion** *n.*, love and dedication you feel toward someone or something
- **issue** *n.*, an important topic or idea that people are concerned about

Interact with the Text

1. Interpret
Underline examples of how Tupac Shakur and William Shakespeare were similar. Why is this information important?

_____

_____

_____

_____

_____

_____

_____

_____

2. Form and Style

Identify the rhyme scheme of lines 6–9. How do you know?

_____

_____

_____

_____

_____

_____

_____

_____

3. Emotional Responses

What do you visualize and feel when you read lines 5–9? How does your emotional response help you understand the poem?

_____

_____

_____

_____

_____

_____

_____

_____

_____

_____

If There Be Pain...

song lyrics by Tupac Shakur
as performed by Providence
and RasDaveed El Harar

Providence:

If there be pain
All you have to do is call on me
If there be pain
All you have to do is call on me

Together (Providence and RasDaveed El Harar):

5 To be with you
And before you hang up the phone
You will no longer be alone
Together we can never fall
Because our love will conquer all

Key Vocabulary

conquer *v.*, to defeat or beat a person or thing

Providence:

10 If there be pain
Reach out for a helping hand
If there be pain
And I shall hold you wherever I am . . .

Together:

Wherever I am
15 Every breath I breathe will be into you
For without you here my joy is through
My life was lived through falling rain
So call on me if there be pain

RasDaveed El Harar:

(chanting)

Providence:

Every breath I breathe will be into you
20 For without you here my joy is through
My life was lived through falling rain
So call on me . . .

Together:

If there be pain

In Other Words
(chanting) (adds more lyrics of his own)

4. Interpret
Summarize lines 10–13.
How does the speaker
show devotion to a friend?
Use **devotion** in your
response.

5. Emotional Responses
Choose a line that you
relate to. Based on your
experience, explain your
emotional response.

6. Form and Style
A sonnet is a tightly controlled form of poetry. Describe the form and style.

_____

_____

_____

_____

_____

_____

_____

_____

_____

7. Emotional Responses
Write the speaker's main point in your own words. Describe your response and how it helps you understand the poem.

_____

_____

_____

_____

_____

_____

_____

_____

_____

_____

Sonnet 30

by William Shakespeare

When to the sessions of sweet silent thought
I summon up remembrance of things past,
I sigh the lack of many a thing I sought,
And with old woes new wail my dear time's waste:
5   Then can I drown an eye, unused to flow,
For precious friends hid in death's dateless night,
And weep afresh love's long since cancell'd woe,
And moan the expense of many a vanish'd sight:
Then can I grieve at grievances foregone,
10   And heavily from woe to woe tell o'er
The sad account of fore-bemoaned moan,
Which I new pay as if not paid before.
But if the while I think on thee, dear friend,
All losses are restor'd and sorrows end.

Key Vocabulary
grief _n._, sorrow and sadness
● **restore** _v._, to return something to
   the way it was before

Sonnet 30

A Modern Paraphrase

When in moments of quiet thoughtfulness

I think about the past,

I regret that I did not achieve all that I wanted,

And it saddens me to think of the years that I wasted:

5   Then I cry, though I am not one who cries often,

For my good friends who have died,

And I cry again over heartbreaks that ended long ago,

And mourn the loss of many things that I have seen and loved:

Then I grieve again over past troubles,

10 And sadly I remind myself, one regret after another,

Of all the sorrows and disappointments in my life,

And they hurt me more than ever before.

But if I think of you at this time, dear friend,

I regain all that I have lost and my sadness ends.

Interact with the Text

8. Interpret

Reread "Sonnet 30" on page 310. How did the modern paraphrase help you understand the original poem?

_____

_____

_____

_____

In Other Words

achieve do, accomplish
mourn am saddened by, grieve
disappointments failures, frustrations

Selection Review Standing Together

A. Describe what you visualized as you read each selection.

1. "If There Be Pain" _____

_____

_____

2. "Sonnet 30" _____

_____

_____

3. "Sonnet 30: A Modern Paraphrase" _____

_____

_____

B. Write about an experience that one of the selections made you remember. List the emotions you felt in the T Chart.

T Chart

I Remember	I Feel

C. Answer the questions.

1. How does the rhymed couplet at the end of Shakespeare's "Sonnet 30" help you understand the sonnet's message?

_____

_____

2. What message about friendship do Shakur and Shakespeare share?

_____

_____

Reflect and Assess

WRITING: Write About Literature

A. Shakur wrote: "Together we can never Fall / because our love will conquer all." Plan your writing. In the chart below, list examples from each selection that support this theme.

Pass It On	If There Be Pain	Sonnet 30

B. Use the examples you listed to write a paragraph describing how this theme applies to each of the selections. Then add your opinion about this idea of friendship.

_____

_____

_____

_____

_____

_____

_____

_____

_____

LITERARY ANALYSIS: Literary Criticism

Literary criticism is the evaluation, analysis, description, or interpretation of literary works. A literary criticism usually follows one of these approaches:

- **Biographical:** based on how the author's life affects the work
- **Aesthetic:** focused on what makes a work appealing to the reader
- **Historical:** based on research of a specific time period and how it influenced the work

A. Read the examples in the chart. Then write which approach the critic used.

Example of Literary Criticism	Critic's Approach
Even people who do not normally read science fiction will be engaged by the lovable characters and exquisite detail.	
My research shows that the portrayal of the old man in the novel is actually a commentary on industrialization in 1899.	
It is evident that the author called on memories of his troubled youth when he wrote this story.	

B. Read the description of "Pass It On" from a critic. Then answer the questions.

> "Pass It On" provides a true account of the urban environment in the early eighties and the deep consequences of business and political practices of the time. Impressively, the human spirit emerges from the blight of this practice, producing a significant literary achievement.

1. Which type of approach is this? How do you know?

_____

2. Do you agree with the critic's claim? Why or why not?

_____

C. Write your own brief aesthetic literary criticism of "Pass It On."

_____

_____

VOCABULARY STUDY: Denotation and Connotation

Denotation is the exact meaning, or definition, of a word. **Connotation** is a meaning or feeling that is commonly added or attached to the word.

A. Read the words and their denotations in the chart below. Write a negative or positive connotation for each.

Word	Denotation	Connotation
alone	by yourself	
darkness	the absence of light	
private	confidential or personal	
tricky	clever or smart	

B. Read the following paragraph. Rewrite the paragraph using words with negative connotations for each of the underlined words and phrases

> My dog, Skippy, is wild. He nips the neighbors a lot. When he drinks his water out of his bowl, he makes a puddle. He gets angry when we try to take his food away. He does not like to be brushed.

_____

_____

_____

_____

_____

_____

C. Study the difference between the paragraphs. Why would a writer use words or phrases with negative connotations?

_____

_____

_____

_____

_____

Prepare to Read

▷ **Voices of America**
▷ **Human Family**

Key Vocabulary

A. How well do you know these words? Circle a rating for each word. Check your understanding by marking an *X* next to the correct definition. Then provide an example. If you are unsure of a word's meaning, refer to the Vocabulary Glossary, page 878, in your student text.

Rating Scale	
1	I have never seen this word before.
2	I am not sure of the word's meaning.
3	I know this word and can teach the word's meaning to someone else.

Key Word	Check Your Understanding	Deepen Your Understanding
1 alien (ā-lē-un) *noun* **Rating:** 1 2 3	☐ a native ☐ a foreigner	Example: _____ _____ _____ _____
2 ashamed (u-**shāmd**) *adjective* **Rating:** 1 2 3	☐ embarrassed ☐ proud	Example: _____ _____ _____ _____
3 feature (**fē**-chur) *noun* **Rating:** 1 2 3	☐ a facial part ☐ a body type	Example: _____ _____ _____ _____
4 interpret (in-**ter**-prut) *verb* **Rating:** 1 2 3	☐ to change something ☐ to translate something	Example: _____ _____ _____ _____

Key Word	Check Your Understanding	Deepen Your Understanding
5 major (**mā**-jur) *adjective* **Rating:** 1　2　3	☐ great importance ☐ little importance	Example: _____ _____ _____ _____ _____
6 melodious (me-**lō**-dē-us) *adjective* **Rating:** 1　2　3	☐ pleasant-sounding ☐ harsh-sounding	Example: _____ _____ _____ _____ _____
7 minor (**mī**-nur) *adjective* **Rating:** 1　2　3	☐ large ☐ small	Example: _____ _____ _____ _____ _____
8 variety (vu-**rī**-u-tē) *noun* **Rating:** 1　2　3	☐ uniformity ☐ diversity	Example: _____ _____ _____ _____ _____

B. Use one of the Key Vocabulary words to write about what being part of a community means to you.

_____
_____
_____

Before Reading Voices of America

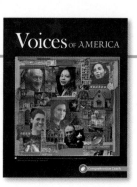

LITERARY ANALYSIS: Analyze Figurative Language

Poets use **figurative language** to create images and appeal to a reader's senses and emotions. They use **metaphors** to compare two different things and **personification** to give human qualities to animals, objects, or ideas.

A. Read the excerpts from the poems below. Look for examples of figurative language. Then write the poet's meaning in the chart.

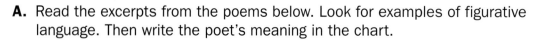

Look Into the Text

I hear America singing, the varied
    carols I hear,
Those of mechanics, each one
singing his as it should be
    blithe and strong,
The carpenter singing his as he
    measures his plank or beam,
The mason singing his as he
    makes ready for work, or leaves
    off work, . . .
           —Walt Whitman

I, too, sing America.
I am the darker brother.
They send me to eat in the kitchen
When company comes,
But I laugh,
And eat well,
And grow strong. . . .
           —Langston Hughes

Figurative Language	Poet's Meaning
"I hear America singing, the varied carols I hear"	
"They send me to eat in the kitchen."	
"I am the darker brother."	

B. Answer the question about the poems.

How do Whitman and Hughes use metaphors and personification to describe America?

_____

_____

_____

FOCUS STRATEGY: Visualize

How to IDENTIFY SENSORY IMAGES

Focus Strategy

1. Read Look for details and descriptions that appeal to your senses.

2. Reflect Think about what sense the image appeals to.

3. Respond Describe how the image makes you feel or what it makes you think.

A. Read the excerpt from the poem. Use the strategies above to identify sensory images. Complete the chart and answer the questions below.

Look Into the Text

> . . . American but hyphenated,
> viewed by Anglos as perhaps exotic,
> perhaps inferior, definitely different,
> viewed by Mexicans as alien,
> (their eyes say, "You may speak
> Spanish but you're not like me") . . .
> —Pat Mora

Read	Reflect	Respond
"viewed by Anglos as perhaps exotic, / perhaps inferior,"		
"(their eyes say, 'You may speak / Spanish but you're not like me')"		

1. Which senses do the images appeal to?

_____

_____

2. How do these sensory images help you understand the speaker's feelings?

_____

_____

Selection Review Voices of America

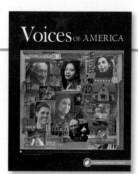

 What Holds Us Together? What Keeps Us Apart?
Discover what it means to belong to a community.

A. In "Voices of America," you read about how some people feel connected
to a community and how others feel separated. Complete the web with
lines from the poems that show how people can feel like aliens
in America.

Details Web

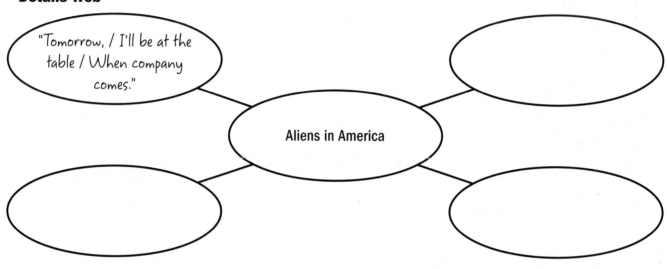

"Tomorrow, / I'll be at the table / When company comes."

Aliens in America

B. Use the information in the web to answer the questions.

1. What causes the speakers in the poems to feel like aliens in America?
   How do the images help you understand their experience?

   _____

   _____

   _____

2. How does this collection of poems show the variety of cultures in
   America? Use **variety** in your answer.

   _____

   _____

   _____

3. Which poem do you think best expresses what being part of a
   community should be? Explain.

   _____

   _____

   _____

Connect Across Texts

The poems in "Voices of America" describe what it means to belong to a country. As you read this poem by Maya Angelou, think about what it means to belong to the "Human Family."

HUMAN FAMILY
BY MAYA ANGELOU

All Human Beings are Born Free and Equal in Dignity and Rights, 1998, Ron Waddams. Acrylic on board, private collection, The Bridgeman Art Library.

▲ **Critical Viewing: Effect** Study the effect of the curved arms in this painting. How does it show the relationship among the people?

Interact with the Text

1. Interpret
Why do you think the artist chose to paint this family in this way?

_____

_____

_____

_____

_____

_____

_____

_____

2. Use Sensory Images

Underline the phrases that explain the **variety** of skin tones in the human family. How do these images help you understand the poem?

_____

_____

_____

_____

_____

_____

_____

_____

_____

3. Rhythm and Rhyme

Circle the words that rhyme in lines 13–16. How do these words affect the rhythm of the poem?

_____

_____

_____

_____

_____

_____

_____

_____

_____

_____

_____

_____

I note the obvious differences
in the human family.
Some of us are serious,
some thrive on comedy.

5   Some declare their lives are lived
as true profundity,
and others claim they really live
the real reality.

The variety of our skin tones
10 can confuse, bemuse, delight,
brown and pink and beige and purple,
tan and blue and white.

I've sailed upon the seven seas
and stopped in every land,
15 I've seen the wonders of the world,
not yet one common man.

Key Vocabulary
variety *n.*, mix of different things

In Other Words
declare insist, say
as true profundity in a great, meaningful way
bemuse confuse, puzzle
one common man a person who is
totally ordinary

I know ten thousand women
called Jane and Mary Jane,
but I've not seen any two
20 who really were the same.

Mirror twins are different
although their features jibe,
and lovers think quite different thoughts
while lying side by side.

25 We love and lose in China,
we weep on England's moors,
and laugh and moan in Guinea,
and thrive on Spanish shores.

We seek success in Finland,
30 are born and die in Maine.
In minor ways we differ,
in major we're the same.

Key Vocabulary
- **minor** *adj.*, small or unimportant
- **major** *adj.*, great in size or importance

In Other Words
jibe match, go together
moors open, empty land

6. Rhythm and Rhyme

Underline the words that change the rhythm of the poem. What is the effect of this change?

_____

_____

_____

_____

_____

_____

I note the obvious differences
between each sort and type,
35 but we are more alike, my friends,
than we are unalike.

We are more alike, my friends,
than we are unalike.

We are more alike, my friends,
40 than we are unalike.

Selection Review Human Family

A. Complete the chart with words and phrases from the poem that appealed to your senses. Describe what you visualize using as many senses as you can.

You Notice	You Visualize

B. Answer the questions.

1. How did recognizing rhyme and rhythm help you as you read the poem? What does the rhythm of this poem remind you of?

_____

_____

2. Why does Angelou believe that we are more alike than different?

_____

_____

Reflect and Assess

WRITING: Write About Literature

A. Plan your writing. List examples from each poem that describe what it means to be an American.

Voices of America	Human Family

B. Which poem speaks most directly to you about what it means to be an American? Write a paragraph explaining your choice. Include specific examples from the poem to support your opinion.

_____

_____

_____

_____

_____

_____

_____

_____

_____

Integrate the Language Arts

LITERARY ANALYSIS: Allusions

An **allusion** is a reference to a well-known person, place, event, artwork, or work of literature. Understanding what a writer is alluding to can help you understand his or her meaning.

A. Read each example of allusion. Then write the meaning of the allusion.

Allusions	Meaning
Sometimes my brother thinks it's funny to sneak up behind me and scream. I get so scared. His new nickname should be Stephen King!	
I'll know who took the last cookie by the beating of your tell-tale heart.	
Chris didn't like to spend money. He was no Scrooge, but he seldom purchased anything except the bare necessities.	

B. Answer the questions.

1. Why do you think the title of Hughes' poem is "I, Too"? What is it alluding to?

_____

_____

2. What is the message of "I, Too"?

_____

_____

3. How does the allusion help you understand the message of "I, Too"?

_____

_____

C. Write a short paragraph about a community. Include at least one allusion in your paragraph.

_____

_____

_____

VOCABULARY STUDY: Interpret Figurative Language

Figurative language is language not meant to be taken literally. Instead it goes beyond its direct, word-for-word meaning to express ideas in imaginative ways.

A. Complete the chart by explaining the meaning of this figurative language from "I Hear America Singing" (page 682) and "I, Too" (page 684).

Figurative Language	Meaning
"I hear America singing."	
"I, too, sing America."	
"They send me to eat in the kitchen When company comes."	
"Tomorrow I'll be at the table When company comes."	

B. Complete the chart by explaining the meaning of figurative language from "Where Is My Country?" (pages 686–687) and "Legal Alien" (pages 688–689).

Lines with Figurative Language	Meaning
"Tucked between boundaries striated between dark dance floors and whispering lanterns"	
"a handy token sliding back and forth between the fringes of both worlds"	

Read for Understanding

1. Genre What kind of text is this selection? How do you know?

2. Topic Write a topic sentence to tell what the text is mostly about.

Reread and Summarize

3. Key Ideas Circle words or phrases that best express the key ideas in each section.

- Section 1: lines 1–27
- Section 2: lines 28–45

4. Summary Use your topic sentence and notes to summarize the text.

Mending Wall

BY ROBERT FROST

Something there is that doesn't love a wall,
That sends the frozen-ground-swell under it,
And spills the upper boulders in the sun;
And makes gaps even two can pass abreast.
5 The work of hunters is another thing:
I have come after them and made repair
Where they have left not one stone on a stone,
But they would have the rabbit out of hiding,
To please the yelping dogs. The gaps I mean,
10 No one has seen them made or heard them made,
But at spring mending-time we find them there.
I let my neighbor know beyond the hill;
And on a day we meet to walk the line
And set the wall between us once again.

In Other Words

Something there is There is something
gaps spaces so
abreast side by side

15 We keep the wall between us as we go.
   To each the boulders that have fallen to each.
   And some are loaves and some so nearly balls
   We have to use a spell to make them balance:
   'Stay where you are until our backs are turned!'
20 We wear our fingers rough with handling them.
   Oh, just another kind of outdoor game,
   One on a side. It comes to little more:
   There where it is we do not need the wall:
   He is all pine and I am apple orchard.
25 My apple trees will never get across
   And eat the cones under his pines, I tell him.
   He only says, 'Good fences make good neighbors.'
   Spring is the mischief in me, and I wonder
   If I could put a notion in his head:
30 '*Why* do they make good neighbors? Isn't it
   Where there are cows? But here there are no cows.
   Before I built a wall I'd ask to know
   What I was walling in or walling out,
   And to whom I was like to give offense.
35 Something there is that doesn't love a wall,
   That wants it down.' I could say 'Elves' to him,
   But it's not elves exactly, and I'd rather
   He said it for himself. I see him there
   Bringing a stone grasped firmly by the top
40 In each hand, like an old-stone savage armed.
   He moves in darkness as it seems to me,
   Not of woods only and the shade of trees.
   He will not go behind his father's saying,
   And he likes having thought of it so well
45 He says again, 'Good fences make good neighbors.'

Stonewall with pines, Vermont, John Churchman.

In Other Words

There where it is In fact
is all pine has all pine trees
a notion an idea

5. Compare Representations
What is the poet's message about the wall in lines 23–36? Underline details the poet uses to express this message.

What message does the photo convey about the wall?

What details support the photographer's message?

6. Compare Representations
Circle two other details in the poem that suggest ideas and feelings about walls and neighbors. How do the ideas and feelings expressed in the poem contrast with those expressed in the photo?

CLOSE READING Mending Wall

Discuss

7. **Synthesize** With the class, discuss ways that poets and photographers use details to suggest ideas and feelings.

	Techniques for Suggesting Ideas and Feelings	Details
Poem		
Photographs		

Compare the ideas and feelings expressed in "Mending Wall" and the photograph. Give specific details from "Mending Wall" and the photo to support your comparison.

_____

_____

_____

8. **Write** Use your notes from question 7 to write a paragraph that explains how poems and photographs use details to suggest ideas and feelings. If you need more space, continue your writing on another piece of paper.

_____

_____

_____

_____

_____

_____

_____

_____

Connect with the EQ — What Holds Us Together? What Keeps Us Apart?

Consider what makes good neighbors.

9. **Viewpoint** According to the poem, what holds people together? What things can keep them apart? Use specific evidence from the poem to support your response.

_____

_____

_____

_____

_____

_____

_____

_____

_____

10. **Theme** According to the speaker's neighbor, "Good fences make good neighbors." Do the poem's details support this worldview? Write a paragraph to explain your opinion, including evidence from the text to explain your ideas.

_____

_____

_____

_____

_____

_____

_____

_____

Key Vocabulary Review

A. Use these words to complete the paragraph.

bond	invest	refuge	territory
devotion	major	successful	variety

It was a big, _____ decision when I joined a club during high school. The group met
(1)

twice a month to build a _____ for injured animals. It was encouraging to see that we
(2)

all had great _____ to the cause. In no time, the club felt like a second family. Our
(3)

_____ continued after the school year ended, so we decided to _____ money
(4)   (5)

in a _____ that will be the perfect site for a _____ of birds to make their
(6)   (7)

homes. I know our project will be _____ because anything is possible if you work together.
(8)

B. Use your own words to write what each Key Vocabulary word means.
Then write a synonym for each word.

Key Word	My Definition	Synonym
1. alien		
2. ashamed		
3. grief		
4. integrity		
5. loyalty		
6. melodious		
7. minor		
8. subside		

Unit 7 Key Vocabulary

alien	conquer	• integrity	loyalty	pretense	subside
ashamed	• devotion	• interpret	• major	provider	successful
• bond	• feature	• invest	melodious	refuge	territory
• collapse	grief	• issue	• minor	• restore	variety

• **Academic Vocabulary**

C. Answer the questions using complete sentences.

1. How can you **conquer** your fears?

   _____

   _____

2. Describe an **issue** that affects your life.

   _____

   _____

3. Which **feature** of your face is your favorite?

   _____

   _____

4. How could someone **restore** a friendship?

   _____

   _____

5. Describe what a good **provider** does for his or her family.

   _____

   _____

6. Why might someone **collapse**?

   _____

   _____

7. Why would it be useful to be able to **interpret** another language?

   _____

   _____

8. Why might someone put on a **pretense**?

   _____

   _____

Acknowledgments

Teresa Palomo Acosta: "My Mother Pieced Quilts" by Teresa Palomo Acosta from *Festival de Flor y Canto*. Copyright © by Teresa Paloma Acosta. Used by permission of the author.

Alfred Publishing Co., Inc.: "I Am Somebody" words and music by Joseph Saddler, Nathaniel Glover, and Larry Dukes. Copyright © 1987 by WB Music Corp., E/A Music, Inc. and Grandmaster Flash Publishing, Inc. All rights administered by WB Music Corp. All rights reserved. Used by permission of Alfred Publishing Co., Inc.

Annick Press: "Ad Power" from *Made You Look* by Shari Graydon. Copyright © 2003 by Shari Graydon. Published by Annick Press. Reprinted with permission.

Susan Bergholz Literary Services: "A Smart Cookie" from *The House on Mango Street* by Sandra Cisneros. Copyright © 1984 by Sandra Cisneros. Published by Vintage Books, a division of Random House, Inc., New York, and in hardcover by Alfred A. Knopf in 1994. Reprinted by permission of Susan Bergholz Literary Services, New York. All rights reserved.

"My Father Is a Simple Man" by Luis Omar Salinas from *The Sadness of Days*. Copyright © 1987. Reprinted by permission of Susan Bergholz Literary Services, New York. All rights reserved

Center for Media Literacy: "A Long Way to Go: Minorities and the Media" by Carlos Cortes, from *Media 7 Values*, Issue 38, Winter, 1987. Copyright © 1987 by the Center for Media Literacy, www.medialit.org. Used by permission.

Curtis Brown: "The Baby-Sitter" by Jane Yolen from *Things That Go Bump in the Night*. Copyright © 1989 by Jane Yolen, published by HarperCollins. Reprinted by permission of Curtis Brown, Ltd.

Excerpt from *The Creativity Crisis* by Po Bronson and Ashley Merryman. Copyright © 2010 by Po Bronson and Ashley Merryman. Used by permission of Curtis Brown, Ltd.

Eric Feil: "The World Is in Their Hands" by Eric Feil from Inspire Your World. Used by permission of the author.

HarperCollins: "Curtis G. Aikens Sr." by Dan Rather from *The American Dream*. Copyright © 2001 by Dan Rather. Reprinted by permission of HarperCollins Publishers.

Joel Hoffmam: "Puddle" by Arthur Porges from *Alfred Hitchcock's Mystery Magazine*. Copyright © 1972 by Arthur Porges. Reprinted by permission of Joel Hoffman.

Learning Seed: "How to Detect Bias in the News" by Jeffrey Schank/Learning Seed. Reprinted by permission of Learning Seed LLC.

Life: "In the Heart of a Hero" by Johnny Dwyer from *Life*, November 2005. Copyright © 2005 by Life Inc. Reprinted with permission. All rights reserved.

Lowenstein-Yost Associates: "Beware: Do Not Read This Poem" from *Ishmael Reed: New and Collected Poems, 1964–2006*. Copyright © 1988 by Ishmael Reed. Permission granted by Lowenstein-Yost Associates, Inc.

McClatchy-Tribune Information Services: "Miami Pilot Dubbed 'Emerging Explorer' by National Geographic" from the *Miami Herald*, June 5, 2012, Copyright © 2012 the McClatchy Company. Used by permission of The McClatchy Company.

Hal Leonard: "If There Be Pain" by Tupac Shakur. Copyright © 2000 Microhits Music Corp. Reprinted by permission of Hal Leonard.

National Geographic Society: "Was There a Real King Arthur?" by Robert Steward from *Mysteries of History*. Copyright © 2003 by the National Geographic Society. Reprinted with permission of the National Geographic Society.

Harold Ober Associates: "Thank You, M'am" by Langston Hughes from *The Short Stories of Langston Hughes*. Copyright © 1996 by Langston Hughes. By permission of Harold Ober Associates.

Pearson Education, Inc.: "The Tell-Tale Heart" from *Great American Short Stories* retold by Emily Hutchinson. Copyright © 1994 by Pearson Education, Inc., publishing as AGS Globe. Used by permission.

Penguin Group (USA) Inc.: "Euphoria" by Lauren Brown. Copyright © 2000 by 17th Street Productions. by permission of Viking Penguin, A Division of Penguin Young Readers Group, A Member of Penguin Group (USA) Inc., 345 Hudson Street, New York, NY 10014. All rights reserved.

Excerpt from *The Grapes of Wrath* by John Steinbeck. Copyright © 1939, renewed 1967 by John Steinbeck. Used by permission of Viking Penguin, a division of Penguin Group (USA) Inc.

"The Sword in the Stone," from *King Arthur and the Legends of Camelot* by Molly Perham. Copyright © 1993 by Molly Perham. Used by permission of Viking Penguin, A Division of Penguin Young Readers Group, A Member of Penguin Group (USA) Inc., 345 Hudson Street, New York, NY 10014. All rights reserved.

Philadelphia Inquirer: "The Fast and the Fuel Efficient" by Akweli Parker from the *Philadelphia Inquirer*, April 16, 2006. Copyright © 2006 by the Philadelphia Inquirer. Reprinted with permission of the Philadelphia Inquirer, all rights reserved.

Public Broadcasting Service: "What Is News?" from Greater Washington Educational Telecommunications Association, source: pbs.org.

Random House: "The Good Samaritan" from *Finding Our Way* by René Saldaña, Jr. Copyright © 2003 by René Saldaña Jr. Used by permission of Random House Children's Books, a division of Random House, Inc.

"A Message for Black Teenagers" from *Magic Johnson: My Life* by Earvin "Magic" Johnson. Copyright © 1992 by June Bug Enterprises. Used by permission of Random House, Inc.

Excerpt from *A Raisin in the Sun* by Lorraine Hansberry. Copyright © 1958 by Robert Nemiroff, as an unpublished work. Copyright © 1959, 1966, 1984 by Robert Nemiroff. Copyright renewed 1986, 1987 by Robert Nemiroff. Caution: Professionals and amateurs are hereby warned that A Raisin in the Sun, being fully protected under the Copyright Laws of the United States of America, the British Empire, including the Dominion of Canada, and all other countries of the Universal Copyright and Berne Conventions, is subject to royalty. All rights, including professional, amateur, motion picture, recitation, lecturing, public reading, radio and television broadcasting, and the rights of translation into foreign languages, are strictly reserved. Particular emphasis is laid on the question of readings, permission for which must be secured in writing. All inquiries should be addressed to the William Morris Agency, 1350 Avenue of the Americas, New York, NY 10019, authorized agents for the Estate of Lorraine Hansberry and for Robert Nemiroff, Executor. Used by permission of Random House, Inc.

"What's Wrong with Advertising" from *Ogilvy on Advertising* by David Ogilvy. Copyright ©1985 by David Ogilvy. Reprinted by permission of Carlton Publishing Group. Used by permission of Random House, Inc.

"The Woman in the Snow" from *The Dark Thirty* by Patricia C. McKissack. Copyright © 1992 by Patricia C. McKissack. Used by permission of Alfred A. Knopf, an imprint of Random House Children's Books, a division of Random House, Inc. Used by permission of Random House, Inc.

Scholastic: "A Job for Valentín" from *An Island Like You* by Judith Ortiz Cofer. Copyright © 1995 by Judith Ortiz Cofer. Reprinted by permission of Scholastic Inc.

"A Raisin in the Sun" by Lorraine Hansberry, adapted by Rachel Waugh, *Scholastic Scope*, September 20, 2004. Reprinted by permission of Scholastic Inc.

Simon & Schuster: "The Fashion Show" adapted from *The Other Side of the Sky* by Farah Ahmedi with Tamim Ansary. Text © 2005 Nestegg Productions LLC. Used with the permission of Simon Spotlight Entertainment, an imprint of Simon & Schuster Children's Publishing Division.

Efrem Smith: "Hip-Hop as Culture" by Reverend Efrem Smith. Reprinted by permission of the author.

Nancy Stauffer Associates: "Superman and Me" by Sherman Alexie from *The Most Wonderful Books: Writers on Discovering the Pleasures of Reading*, edited by Michael Dorris and Emilie Buchwald. Copyright © 1997 by Sherman Alexie. All rights reserved. Reprinted by permission.

Richard Thompson: "Teens Open Doors" by Richard Thompson from the *Boston Globe*, June 29, 2006. Copyright © 2006 by Richard Thompson. Reprinted by permission of the author.

Time: "The Hidden Secrets of the Creative Mind" by Francine Russo from *Time*, January 16, 2006. Copyright © 2006 by Time Inc. Reprinted by permission.

"Rosa Parks" by Rita Dove from "Time's 100 Most Important People of the Century" from *Time*, June 14, 1999. Copyright © 1999 Time Inc. Reprinted by permission.

Tribune Media Services: "Is Google Making Us Stupid?" by Nicholas Carr from *The Atlantic*, July 1, 2008. Copyright © 2008 by The Atlantic Media Co. Used by permission of Tribune Media Services. Reprinted by permission.

WGBH/Boston: "Juvenile Justice" from Frontline/WGBH Educational Foundation. Copyright © 2005 WGBH/Boston. Used by permission.

What Kids Can Do: "Creativity at Work" by Abe Louise Young, from the website "What Kids Can Do." Reprinted by permission of What Kids Can Do, Inc.

Nellie Wong: "Where Is My Country?" by Nellie Wong from *Chinese American Poetry: An Anthology*, edited by L. Ling-Chi Wang and Henry Yiheng Zhao. Copyright © 1987 by Nellie Wong. Reprinted by permission of the author.